UNVEILING THE SECRET OF BLOODLINE CLEANSING

Breaking Bondages And Receiving The
Full Victory Jesus Paid For Us To Receive

Djordje Djordjic

Copyright

Copyright © 2024 Djordje Djordjic

No part of this book may be reproduced, reprinted, stored in a retrieval system, transmitted in any form or means, including electronic, mechanical, photocopying, recording, or otherwise, without express permission of the publisher.

Hardcover ISBN: 9798865617273
Softcover ISBN: 9798865616825
Kindle ASIN: B0CLXZ1YFK
Google eBook ID: BXNB7USYPCN
Imprint: Independently Published
Book Version: 1.0.7

Printed in the United States of America. All rights reserved.

Bible In Basic English
Scripture quotations marked "BBE" are taken from the Holy Bible, Bible In Basic English Version (Public Domain).
https://www.o-bible.com/bbe.html

Berean Standard Bible
The Holy Bible, Berean Standard Bible, "BSB" is produced in cooperation with Bible Hub, Discovery Bible, OpenBible.com, and the Berean Bible Translation Committee (Public Domain).
https://www.berean.bible

World English Bible
Scripture quotations marked "WEB" are taken from the Holy Bible, World English Bible Version (Public Domain).
https://worldenglish.bible

Literal Standard Version
Scripture quotations marked "LSV" are taken from the Holy Bible, Literal Standard Version (LSV) (Covenant Press 2020).
https://www.lsvbible.com

American Standard Version
Scripture quotations marked "ASV" are taken from the American Standard Version Bible (Public Domain).

New King James Version
Scripture taken from the New King James Version. Copyright © 1982 by Thomas Nelson, Inc. All rights reserved.

King James Version
Scripture quotations marked "KJV" are taken from the Holy Bible, King James Version (Public Domain).

Disclaimer

Let me begin by saying that I have no personal animosity toward anyone who may hold different beliefs than I do. I firmly believe that everyone deserves to be treated with fairness, respect, and kindness, as discrimination is both morally and legally wrong. Heaven will undoubtedly be a diverse place, not because of our outward differences, but because of the faith that brings believers together from all walks of life. The thoughts and writings I share reflect my own beliefs, and do not necessarily represent the views of any organization or employer I may be associated with. These works, which have been written through God's grace, are published with the hope that they will bring help and edification to others. My personal beliefs and the creative work I pursue are separate from my professional responsibilities and this and all other publications are protected under the First Amendment, which guarantees the right to express oneself freely, including through writing and other forms of communication. I am grateful for the legal protections in place, which ensure that my right to pursue these personal projects remains secure, as they do not interfere with my duties. My hope is that these freedoms allow me to continue sharing my work without concern for unjust consequences in the workplace.

Preface

You might be wondering why another book? There are many Christian books out there. While this may be true, I believe this one is unique. Up until the past few recent years, there have been some voids in the area of deliverance for believers, and for people around the world seeking freedom. There are books emerging with newer revelations and fresh perspectives that have come out in just the past few years. And I hope this book is an addition to the arsenal of the believer in both deliverance and prayer. Breakthroughs are received *from* the decrees of God, and they are obtained *within* a heavenly courtroom. Much like a military that gets its orders from higher ups then engages in battle, we receive the decree then it to be enforced. As a law cannot be enforced if it doesn't exist, so the battlefield of prayer must have heaven's backing and support if breakthrough and victory is to be achieved on a massive scale. Many people have viewed deliverance from an old lens which has worked here and there, but it has lacked consistency. And if you want to know a thing or two about God, He's pretty consistent, which tells me there's a better way to look at deliverance because His Hand is in it. Ultimately the victory is through and by the power of God, but the spiritual enemy has evolved and so should our tactics as well. The answers of yesterday may not be adequate for the problems of tomorrow, which is one reason this book is now before your eyes or being played within your ears. I want to encourage you to pay close attention as you read or listen, and ask Holy Spirit to expand on the knowledge and revelation already contained within this book for you, and may the ceiling of this book and its revelations be the floor which you start your deeper spiritual journey on. With that being said, let us continue. Many have resisted and fought the enemy without seeing total freedom, and I don't believe that's God's will for any believer.

Romans 8:37 BSB

"No, in all these things we are more than
conquerors through Him who loved us."

I don't know about you, but more than conquerors doesn't sound like *hold on until Jesus comes back, fight the good fight of faith brother, hang in there, you'll make it.* More than conquerors sounds like to me, walking with the Lord, and walking on the devil. We're walking with Jesus, and last time I checked, Satan got kicked out of Heaven, and Jesus took the keys from him when He descended into Hades:

Revelation 1:17-20 BSB

"When I saw Him, I fell at His feet like a dead man. But He placed His right hand on me and said, "Do not be afraid. I am the First and the Last, the Living One. I was dead, and behold, now I am alive forever and ever! And I hold the keys of Death and of Hades. Therefore write down the things you have seen, and the things that are, and the things that will happen after this. This is the mystery of the seven stars you saw in My right hand and of the seven golden lampstands: The seven stars are the angels of the seven churches, and the seven lampstands are the seven churches."

This book is for those in need of breakthrough and freedom, and for those who have cried out for years for God to deliver them but haven't seemed to have received that powerful breakthrough yet. This is for the ones who have cried in silence and heartache wondering when it's going to stop. This is for the ones that felt forgotten, ashamed, and pummeled by spiritual attacks, this is for those who have been living in fear, this is for the ones that have felt like modern day Jobs. Today is the day that it starts to change. Declare over yourself that today is the day that you start walking in overcoming faith, love, joy, peace, righteousness, and tranquility, in Jesus name.

Job 23:1-7 BSB

"Then Job answered: "Even today my complaint is bitter. His hand is heavy despite my groaning. If only I knew where to find Him, so that I could go to His seat. *I would plead my case before Him* and fill my mouth with arguments. I would learn how He would answer, and consider what He would say. Would He contend with me in His great power? No, He would certainly take note of me. Then an upright man could reason with Him, and I would be delivered forever from my Judge."

So, if you have come across this book, chances are you were either:

      A. Curious about the topic of bloodline cleansing

      B. Are in current need of a breakthrough

      C. Holy Spirit led you here

      D. You heard of the book by another person or source

      E. Or you're one of those rare few that has given the LORD their yes, surrendered to the call of ministry upon your life and the LORD, with or without you knowing it, led you to this book.

And if you've found yourself in a position of a season of spiritual warfare, or an intense spiritual attack, regardless of how it sounds you are actually in the optimal situation for spiritual growth and strengthening, even if it's painful. Think of hardships as an incubator for growth. If you feel like you're fighting for the sanity of your mind, you are in a time of spiritual strengthening. You have been given the opportunity to show the LORD and the enemy that through Christ you can do all things. You really think that you have been going through hell on earth by accident?

Job 1:6-8 BSB

"One day the sons of God came to present themselves before the LORD, and Satan also came with them. "Where have you come from?" said the LORD to Satan. "From roaming through the earth," he replied, "and walking back and forth in it." Then the LORD said to Satan, "Have you considered My servant Job? For there is no one on earth like him, a man who is blameless and upright, who fears God and shuns evil."

It doesn't matter how intense the spiritual battle may be, you are in a position to overcome, trust me I've experienced it in a way that I don't think many have. If you've been praying: "God, have your way in me. I surrender to Your will and call for my life. Do whatever you have to do to get me there." Maybe that was one of the reasons you started threatening the kingdom of darkness because You started surrendering. Remember those prayers? And maybe you didn't say that word for word, but you started pursuing Jesus in a greater way, and you've hit a point in your walk with the Lord where you're in a fight. In this time you are now called to take up your shield of faith, helmet of salvation, breastplate of righteousness, the shoes of the gospel of peace, and the Sword of the Spirit which is the word of God. God didn't give us His armor and the Sword of the Spirit for no reason. It's through that battle that you come out stronger in your faith after you overcome it. And I'm not writing this as someone who doesn't understand. Trust me, for those who have contemplated taking the early way out because of a spiritual attack, you're not the only one. You are called to be more than a conqueror through Christ who loves you. You can't quit because your life is too valuable, and think of all the people that your destiny is connected to. Think about your family and the ones who need you most. Regardless of what the case may be, the prayers in this book will be helpful tools to shut ungodly generational doors and receive deliverance and freedom. Deliverance can go two ways. Most people think of internal deliverance, but it can also be external freedom from spiritual oppression. Oppression is external, while possession is internal, there's a difference. When God delivered the children of Israel out of Egypt, He delivered them from oppression. Egypt was a picture of the world, sin, idolatry, abortion, and bondage. Moses and God even referenced Egypt as the *iron furnace*:

Deuteronomy 4:20 BSB

> "Yet the LORD has taken you and brought you out of the iron furnace, out of Egypt, to be the people of His inheritance, as you are today."

Jeremiah 11:4 ASV

> "which I commanded your fathers in the day that I brought them forth out of the land of Egypt, out of the iron furnace, saying, Obey my voice, and do them, according to all which I command you: so shall ye be my people, and I will be your God;"

Iron can be symbolic of *strongholds,* and a furnace can be symbolic of a spiritual *trial.* It's the very thing that the LORD showed to Abraham in one of his encounters with him. The LORD said Abraham's seed would serve under the yoke of bondage four-hundred years in a land that was not their own.

Genesis 15:13-16 BSB

> "Then the LORD said to Abram, "Know for certain that your descendants will be strangers in a land that is not their own, and they will be enslaved and mistreated for four hundred years. But I will judge the nation they serve as slaves, and afterward they will depart with many possessions. You, however, will go to your fathers in peace and be buried at a ripe old age. In the fourth generation your descendants will return here, for the iniquity of the Amorites is not yet complete."

Introduction

You may notice as you read this book that there are lots of Scriptures in it. This is intentional because whenever a revelation is taught it is supposed to fit flush with the Scriptures. It's questionable if it doesn't. Part one of this book contains a lot of good and revelatory teachings that all believers would benefit from, and the second section of this book contains prayers for those who are looking for deliverance. These prayers do not have to be prayed, but they are there for those seeking freedom from specific things they've been trying to overcome. Not every prayer is meant for everybody, and some topics are personal. So, I'm just letting everyone know ahead of time so that when they get to the end of the first section, they've been made aware of what the second section is about. Some Scripture quotes use older versions of the Bible not because I prefer those versions, but it's simply due to copyright laws, that's all. I also want to make clear that this book is not meant to make anyone focused on sin, but rather to help people receive freedom. We acknowledge, confess, ask for forgiveness, receive and walk in the Lord's forgiveness. Ignoring a problem is not the solution, and the quicker a spiritual problem is addressed the better. If you've been feeling accusations against you, been met with trial after trial, spiritual opposition after spiritual opposition, I'm here to tell you: *You don't have to endure the storm, you can change it!* There is hope! Our God is the God of the breakthrough! [1]Sometimes the breakthrough is in the confession and testimony of our own lips. When the apostle Paul was departing to Jerusalem, he spoke to a number of the disciples and said to them before his departure:

Acts 20:20 BSB

"I did not shrink back from declaring anything that was helpful to you as I taught you publicly and from house to house,"

May this book be a source of freedom for the body of Christ and beyond all over the world. A healthy perspective to have is to keep our eyes fixed on the goodness of our God and the mercy of our Savior. May our hearts be aware of the gift of His Presence. Every born again believer currently walking with Jesus is a citizen of Heaven, a saint and a child of God maturing into sonship. You are the head and not the tail, you are above and not beneath, no weapon formed against you shall prosper, every tongue that rises up against you in judgment shall be condemned, you are a Blood bought child of God, you are more than a conqueror through Him who loves you, and you can do all things through Christ who strengthens you, in Jesus name! Our God is so much bigger than the enemy, and never should be, as the People of God focus on the problem more than Jesus our Messiah. He has conquered death, defeated hell, plundered the grave, and redeemed a people for Himself to call His Own while handing us the baton of *The Great Commission* in Mark 16. May this book serve its purpose and bring multifaceted freedom into the lives of the readers and far beyond, and may this book be like the arrows that the king of Israel struck the ground with leading to victories but in a much greater measure:

2 Kings 13:17-19 BSB

"Open the east window," said Elisha. So he opened it and Elisha said, "Shoot!" So he shot. And Elisha declared: "This is the LORD's arrow of victory, the arrow of victory over Aram, for you shall strike the Arameans in Aphek until you have put an end to them." Then Elisha said, "Take the arrows!" So he took them, and Elisha said to the king of Israel, "Strike the ground!" So he struck the ground three times and stopped.

But the man of God was angry with him and said, "You should have struck the ground five or six times. Then you would have struck down Aram until you had put an end to it. But now you will strike down Aram only three times."

Isaiah 61:1-11 BSB

"The Spirit of the LORD GOD is on Me, because the LORD has anointed Me to preach good news to the poor. He has sent Me to bind up the brokenhearted, to proclaim liberty to the captives and freedom to the prisoners, to proclaim the year of the LORD's favor and the day of our God's vengeance, to comfort all who mourn, to console the mourners in Zion— to give them a crown of beauty for ashes, the oil of joy for mourning, and a garment of praise for a spirit of despair. So they will be called oaks of righteousness, the planting of the LORD, that He may be glorified. They will rebuild the ancient ruins; they will restore the places long devastated; they will renew the ruined cities, the desolations of many generations. Strangers will stand and feed your flocks, and foreigners will be your plowmen and vinedressers. But you will be called the priests of the LORD; they will speak of you as ministers of our God; you will feed on the wealth of nations, and you will boast in their riches. Instead of shame, My people will have a double portion, and instead of humiliation, they will rejoice in their share; and so they will inherit a double portion in their land, and everlasting joy will be theirs. For I, the LORD, love justice; I hate robbery and iniquity; in My faithfulness I will give them their recompense and make an everlasting covenant with them. Their descendants will be known among the nations, and their offspring among the peoples. All who see them will acknowledge that they are a people the LORD has blessed. I will rejoice greatly in the LORD, my soul will exult in my God; for He has clothed me with garments of salvation and wrapped me in a robe of righteousness, as a bridegroom wears a priestly headdress, as a bride adorns herself with her jewels. For as the earth brings forth its growth, and as a garden enables seed to spring up, so the LORD GOD will cause righteousness and praise to spring up before all the nations."

Author's Foreword

If you're in need of a breakthrough, you are in the right place. I want to make it clear that in order to pray these prayers and for them to carry weight, you must be saved. I'm talking about a genuine born-again Holy Spirit-filled experience and a life living under the Lordship of Christ:

John 3:5-7 BSB

"Jesus answered, "Truly, truly, I tell you, no one can enter the kingdom of God unless he is born of water and the Spirit. Flesh is born of flesh, but spirit is born of the Spirit. Do not be amazed that I said, 'You must be born again.'"

If you're reading this and don't currently know the Lord Jesus as your personal Lord and Savior, I want to let you know that the LORD loves you. The Lord Jesus came and paid a high price for you to be His, and you have a destiny upon your life. It's up to you to say yes and receive the best that God has for you. If you want to give God your yes at this moment, then I invite you to read the Scriptures below and then pray the following prayer out loud while meaning it from your heart as you pray them before the LORD:

Scripture For Salvation

Romans 10:8-13 BSB

"But what does it say? "The word is near you; it is in your mouth and in your heart," that is, the word of faith we are proclaiming: that if you confess with your mouth, "Jesus is LORD," and believe in your heart that God raised Him from the dead, you will be saved. For with your heart you believe and are justified, and with your mouth you confess and are saved. It is just as the Scripture says: "Anyone who believes in Him will never be put to shame." For there is no difference between Jew and Greek: The same LORD is LORD of all, and gives richly to all who call on Him, for, "Everyone who calls on the name of the LORD will be saved."

Prayer of Salvation

"Lord Jesus, I believe in my heart and confess with my mouth that you are LORD and Savior. I choose this day whom I will serve, and I choose to serve You. Please forgive me of my sins, transgressions, iniquities, and any generational iniquities that were in my family lineage. I ask You, Lord Jesus, to bring freedom to me in every area of life. I also ask You to empower me to walk in Holiness, Purity, Power, Surrender, and Obedience to You. To be a carrier of the Fire and Glory of God burning inside of me, and radiating through me all the days of this life that You have bestowed upon me. May I carry the Fire of God on the altar of my heart, and may it continually burn with fervent passion for you. I accept You as my LORD and Savior. I believe You died on the cross on my behalf and I dedicate my life to You Lord Jesus, the Son of God, and to the Kingdom Purposes of God. Help me to fulfill the God-given Prophetic Destiny that the Heavenly Father and the Counsel of God established for me before I was born into the Earth. Lord Jesus, I receive you as my LORD and Savior today. I ask you to set me free in this very moment and as I pray these prayers, in Jesus Name. Amen."

Prayer of Rededication For Those Who Knew The LORD But Drifted Away

"Lord Jesus, forgive me for distancing myself from you in times past. I now choose to rededicate and recommit my life to you. I ask You Lord Jesus to free me from any strongholds of sins and iniquity, forgive me of my sins and transgressions and use this life for the Expansion of your Kingdom and for your Glory, in Jesus Name, amen!"

Prayer of Surrender

"Lord Jesus, I surrender to the will of the Father for my life. Please separate worldly, negative, and toxic friendships from me. I ask You to handpick good, godly friendships for me that are going to encourage, edify, and strengthen me. Friendships that are necessary for me to fulfill my God-given Destiny, in Jesus name."

Prerequisites

Before starting the prayers section of this book, it would be a good idea to make sure that you have at least an hour of set apart time with the LORD and this book with little to no distractions. Some practical things you can do to help that are:

I. Turn on Do-Not-Disturb mode on your electronic devices. If you need some assistance on how to do that, just go to your web browser and look up: "How to turn on Do Not Disturb mode on my phone?"

II. If you get reminded of your To-Do List, I encourage you to bring a notebook and a writing utensil during your prayer time so that you can write down your To-Do List as they come to you. Once you've written those things down, just set the notebook aside, so you don't get distracted while communing with the LORD.

III. I would recommend bringing some water with you into your place of prayer.

IV. Try planning the general bloodline cleansing prayer part of this book during a time of day or night when you will have at least an hour of uninterrupted time.

You may read the teaching section whenever you'd like, however, I would recommend praying the bloodline cleansing prayers during a time with little to zero distraction. If you're a mom and have children to attend to I would recommend praying the bloodline cleansing prayers at a time during the night when the kids are in bed. And you can slip away into your secret place, outside on the porch or even in your vehicle if you don't want to wake anybody up. Whatever works best for you to have some uninterrupted time, feel free to do that, it's no problem.

Disclaimer

I want to issue a brief disclaimer here in this book, specifically for those who have come to faith in Christ and have had a traumatic past that God is now helping that person heal from. There are certain chapters or words that may be triggering to some. There is a chance that God brought you to this book, or even brought this book to you in some cases, for your healing. I want us as believers to understand that there are people who went through very traumatic experiences that they have carried from childhood, in some cases, to adulthood. Of course not everyone can relate to that, but for those who were around people who abused their authority need healing and I hope this book is a source of healing to those who read its contents. As believers, we are called to focus on the goodness of God and never should we focus on evil more than good. But there are those who need to confront what they have experienced in order to overcome it, and they don't have to do it alone, there is hope. Just like Daniel's three friends, they didn't stand in that fire alone, but they came out in better condition than when they first went in. They went in bound but came out free, they went in with fear and came out with confidence and unshakable faith!

Joshua 1:9 BSB

"Have I not commanded you to be strong and courageous? Do not be afraid; do not be discouraged, for the LORD your God is with you wherever you go."

Psalms 23:3 BSB

"He restores my soul; He guides me in the paths of righteousness for the sake of His name."

Exodus 15:26 BSB

"…For I am the LORD who heals you."

Psalms 147:3 BSB

"He heals the brokenhearted and binds up their wounds."

CHAPTER 1: CONFRONTING FEAR

Not everyone is going to experience this, but for those that might, if at any time before or during the prayer sections of this book if you start to hear voices in your head or threats, that's a sign you're about to hit something in the spirit. So if you feel fear before or during these prayers, just know:

2 Timothy 1:7 LSV

"for God did not give us a spirit of fear, but of power, and of love, and of a sound mind;"

James 2:19 BBE

"You have the belief that God is one, and you do well: the evil spirits have the same belief, shaking with fear."

If you at any time during reading this book or praying the prayers you experience or hear voices saying things along the lines of:

1. "If you pray these prayers, then ____ will happen."
2. "Don't you dare pray those prayers."
3. "If you pray these prayers, I'll ____."
4. "If you read this book, I'll ____."

These are just some examples of intimidation, so remember this my dear reader, within these prayers you are *not* going to be *on* a battlefield but rather presenting your case *in* a courtroom. You do not have to fight your battles alone for even a second:

> Deuteronomy 3:22 BSB
>
> "Do not be afraid of them, for the LORD your God Himself will fight for you."

If you've ever had fear hold you back from going to church, I want to encourage you that you should never let that keep you from going to church. Fear is not the believers' portion. In an earthly court case, if either the defendant or the prosecutor don't show up to the court, the case likely ends in a default judgment and results in an automatic loss for the person that never showed up. On top of that, it's difficult to render verdicts in a court case where no testimony or evidence gets brought to the court! Now parallel that in the spiritual realm. How many people have lost court cases because they never showed up in prayer to testify? The kingdom of darkness has for hundreds of years afflicted, harassed, destroyed, caused identity issues, broken marriages, broken homes, crises, wars, tempted God and even accused His people. To say that the LORD doesn't keep a detailed record of all the pain and destruction that the enemy has caused, I believe would be inaccurate. How else would He judge the fallen angels and the enemy on the last day, and why would the word mention that books were opened on judgment day? The enemy has accused God's people long enough, and it's time that the people of God take the fight to him in the courts and receive the full victory that Jesus paid for on our behalf. You might be wondering: *that sounds great, but what are we going to use*? The Blood of the Lamb and the word of our testimony.

> Revelation 12:11 KJV
>
> "And they overcame him by the blood of the Lamb, and by the word of their testimony; and they loved not their lives unto the death."[2]

The English word *overcame* in this verse is translated from the Koine Greek word **nikaō** which means: *"Subdue, (literally or figuratively) conquer, overcome, prevail, get the victory."* The English word used here in this verse as testimony is the Greek word **marturia** which means: *"Evidence given (judicially or generally): record, report, testimony, witness."* Kind of reminds you of the English word martyr, doesn't it? So let's take the words and put them together to give us a greater understanding as to what the God's Word is truly saying here in Revelation:

<u>Revelation 12:11</u>

"And they <u>nikaō</u>, (got the victory, subdued, conquered, prevailed, overcame) him by the blood of the Lamb and by the word of their <u>marturia</u>: (record, testimony, witness, judicial evidence given;) and loved not their lives unto the death."

The widow in Luke 18 understood something. Instead of trying to resist and fight her adversary that was giving her trouble, she went to the judge of the presiding city that was under his jurisdiction to deal with her adversary. Earthly authorities have jurisdictions, and outside those jurisdictions they can only do so much or are not allowed to do anything at all. The major difference between the LORD and earthly authorities is that His jurisdiction spreads across the whole Earth because the Earth is the LORD's and the fullness thereof. If you have ever known somebody that was stalked, threatened or harassed, they either responded one of two ways:

    I. They tried to resist this person by themselves,

or,

    II. They went to a judge, presented evidence against the person harassing them, and secured an order of protection against the person.

With the second option, the responsibility that was upon the person to try to resist, protect, and defend yourself now just became a matter of the court and its officers to uphold the verdict should it ever be violated. You can get a lot more breakthrough and protection going to a judge rather than trying to fight your own battles all the time. *What was once a struggle on the battlefield turns into a swift victory in the courtroom.* If you're wondering why I'm talking about court, it's because this is going somewhere:

> Isaiah 33:22 BSB
>
> "For the LORD is our Judge, the LORD is our lawgiver, the LORD is our King. It is He who will save us."

God is our Lawgiver and Judge, and we can enter His Presence in the realm of the Spirit, present our cases with wisdom and sensitivity in partnership with the Holy Spirit and secure verdicts from God's Throne. Then it becomes a matter of His court and His angelic officers to uphold, protect, monitor and defend His righteous verdict on our behalf. Imagine God writing on a heavenly piece of paper and giving it to a specific angel and commanding that angel to enforce and protect the person that verdict pertains to. We must not forget that we are valuable to the LORD because He has given us a destiny to accomplish here on earth before time runs out-and-out. Our destinies are tied into other people's salvation. Not only that, but we also have the privilege of partnering with the Holy Spirit to fulfill what is already written in Heaven about us! [4]

> 2 Timothy 1:9 BSB
>
> "He has saved us and called us to a holy calling, not because of our works, but by His own purpose and by the grace He granted us in Christ Jesus before time began."

> Psalms 139:16 BSB

> "Your eyes saw my unformed body; all my days
> were written in Your book and ordained for
> me before one of them came to be."

God is in Heaven, and He is also on earth with us through His Spirit living within us. Heaven is God's domain and the earth is the children of man's that was bestowed upon mankind for a period of time. Even though Heaven belongs to the LORD just as the earth does, God has given the earth to the children of men for a period of time that He has established and ordained. You can say that He *leased* it to the children of man:

Psalms 115:16 BBE

> "The heavens are the LORD's; but the earth
> he has given to the children of men."

Now, of course, the LORD knows the exact day that the lease will expire. But we will know when it expires as well, when we see our King coming with the clouds and His army to establish His reign upon the Earth. And while we are upon this earth, we have the privilege to seek the LORD for the manifestation of His will for our lives and walk it out with Holy Spirit's help. Not to mention receiving eternal rewards for doing so! This is one of the reasons why Holy Spirit is called the Helper, because He helps us fulfill our destinies through the LORD's Power:

John 15:26 BBE

> "When the Helper comes, whom I will send to you from
> the Father even the Spirit of true knowledge who comes
> from the Father—he will give witness about me;"

Zechariah 4:6 BSB

> "So he said to me, "This is the word of the LORD
> to Zerubbabel: Not by might nor by power, but
> by My Spirit, says the LORD of Hosts.""

And we must not forget that Heaven measures success

differently than men. Success is not about finances or sheer numbers in God's Eyes, but *success in the Kingdom is measured by obedience.*[6] We just might be surprised when we get home to Heaven on who is occupying the most exalted places. It just might be the faceless, the unknown names, unknown intercessors, faithful praying mothers and those who gave it all for Jesus without being recognized on Earth for it, but don't think that Heaven doesn't recognize it:

Matthew 19:30 ASV

"But many shall be last that are first; and first that are last."

Speaking of God's will, someone might ask: *"How can we know God's will?"* Well, how do you know what your spouse wants for dinner? *You simply ask them.* God has written His will for us in the Bible, but He also gave us the ability to ask Him for ourselves. Sometimes all the answers we need are in the word for certain questions like: *Is God okay with sexual immorality?*

1 Thessalonians 4:3-7 BSB

"For it is God's will that you should be holy: You must abstain from sexual immorality; each of you must know how to control his own body in holiness and honor, not in lustful passion like the Gentiles who do not know God; and no one should ever violate or exploit his brother in this regard, because the LORD will avenge all such acts, as we have already told you and solemnly warned you. For God has not called us to impurity, but to holiness."

As of 2022 there are an estimated 7.98 billion people on the earth. With that being said, could you imagine if God had to repeat Himself 7.98 billion times to 7.98 billion people about simple and small matters concerning His will? With matters such as: *"LORD, is it your will for me to go to church?"* Hebrews is pretty clear on that answer being a resounding yes:

Hebrews 10:25 BSB

"Let us not neglect meeting together, as some have made a habit, but let us encourage one another, and all the more as you see the Day approaching"

God had His Word and His will written in a Book for us to learn, read, hear and *do* what His Word declares:

James 1:22 BSB

"Be doers of the word, and not hearers only. Otherwise, you are deceiving yourselves."

God's Word *is* His permission. Every good thing in the Word is for us today. This includes all the miracles, signs, wonders, casting out devils, laying hands on the sick and then recovering, the baptism of the Holy Spirit and this includes the Courts of Heaven. For the Bible has plainly declared that our God is the same yesterday, today, and forever. He is the LORD. He does not change:

Malachi 3:6 BSB

"Because I, the LORD, do not change, you descendants of Jacob have not been destroyed."

Hebrews 13:8 BSB

"Jesus Christ is the same yesterday and today and forever."

Biblical Evidence For A Celestial Court

Daniel 7:10 BSB

"A river of fire was flowing, coming out from His presence. Thousands upon thousands attended Him, and myriads upon myriads stood before Him. The court was convened, and the books were opened."

Hebrews 4:16 KJV

"Let us therefore come boldly unto the throne of grace, that we may obtain mercy, and find grace to help in time of need."

I believe it's the LORD's good pleasure to show mercy to man and condemn the enemy on behalf of the pain and hurt that he has caused to the very people that God cares, loves and died for. As I've heard said before by a man of God, He is both the Mercy Seat and the Righteous Judge:

Ephesians 6:12 LSV

> "because our wrestling is not with flesh and blood, but with the principalities, with the authorities, with the world-rulers of the darkness of this age, with the spiritual forces of evil in the heavenly places;"

So if you're feeling fear before or during these prayers, rest assured that it's probably not you, and it might be an indicator to prosecute the spirit of fear. However, please do not skip the teaching part of this book before going into these prayers. *It's time for the prosecutor and accuser to become the prosecuted!*

CHAPTER 2: THE UNIVERSAL LAW OF SOWING AND REAPING

And The Importance And Value of Repentance

Galatians 6:7 BSB

"Do not be deceived: God is not to be mocked. Whatever a man sows, he will reap in return."

The law of sowing and reaping is all around us in the natural. Farmers and anyone who has ever planted fruit or vegetable seeds in the ground understands this law well. Whatever you sow into the ground is what will come up. For example, an apple seed will produce an apple tree yielding apples, an orange seed will produce an orange tree yielding oranges etc. This expands beyond the natural and expands into the supernatural as well, and more so in certain instances. This is one of the reasons that it is important to repent and break agreement. For any time a person was accusing, judging, criticizing, condemning, guilt-tripping or letting someone have a piece of their mind because of something wrong that they did. For two reasons mainly, reason one being our words are seed. This is what Jesus was teaching in the *parable of the sower*:

Luke 8:11 ASV

"Now the parable is this: The seed is the word of God."

Sowing good seeds in life benefits you and others as well. Dealing and repenting for any bad seeds sown is a safe thing to do. The second reason is that when we present our cases before the LORD, how can we ask for forgiveness for something if we have been guilty of committing the same thing? Isn't this exactly what the Lord Jesus and the apostle Paul said?

Matthew 7:1-2 KJV

"Judge not, that ye be not judged. For with what judgment ye judge, ye shall be judged: and with what measure ye mete, it shall be measured to you again."

Mark 11:24-26 KJV

"Therefore I say unto you, What things soever ye desire, when ye pray, believe that ye receive them, and ye shall have them. And when ye stand praying, forgive, if ye have ought against any: that your Father also which is in heaven may forgive you your trespasses. But if ye do not forgive, neither will your Father which is in heaven forgive your trespasses."

Romans 2:1 BSB

"You, therefore, have no excuse, you who pass judgment on another. For on whatever grounds you judge the other, you are condemning yourself, because you who pass judgment do the same things."[7]

It's time that we as the People of God bring an end to hypocritical judgment, bitterness, criticism, and condemnation against others and for us to really learn how to embrace walking in 1 Corinthians 13 love. After all, they will know us not by our theology degree, but by our love:

John 13:35 BSB

"By this everyone will know that you are My disciples, if you love one another."

1 Corinthians 13:4-7 BSB

"Love is patient, love is kind. It does not envy, it does not boast, it is not proud. It is not rude, it is not self-seeking, it is not easily angered, it keeps no account of wrongs. Love takes no pleasure in evil, but rejoices in the truth. It bears all things, believes all things, hopes all things, endures all things."[8]

CHAPTER 3: JUDGE, ADVOCATE, ADVERSARY

Earthly courts have a judge, jury, defense attorney, defendant and the prosecuting attorney, likewise the heavenly courts have those as well. A lot of people haven't understood that Satan is a prosecutor in the heavenly courts, the enemy is still serving a purpose as a prosecuting officer in the heavenly realms. The day will come when the LORD will execute judgment against him and his fallen angels for good, but for now we can present our cases and receive verdicts and acquittals in our favor. The enemy doesn't have much time left, and he knows it, the expected reaction is that he is trying to do as much damage as possible in the time that's left. But unfortunately for him, revelations like these are being taught and shared that are going to empower believers to defend themselves spiritually and even go on the offensive. This book is a tool in the arsenal of a believer. Spiritual revelation is powerful enough to not only protect you spiritually, but also protect your soul and physical body as well:

The Judge of Righteousness

2 Timothy 4:8 KJV

"Henceforth there is laid up for me a crown of righteousness, which the LORD, the righteous judge, shall give me at that day: and not to me only, but unto all them also that love his appearing."

Hebrews 12:23 KJV

"to the general assembly and church of the firstborn, which are written in heaven, and to God the Judge of all, and to the spirits of just men made perfect,"

Jesus Our Advocate

1 John 2:1-2 BSB

"My little children, I am writing these things to you so that you will not sin. But if anyone does sin, we have an advocate[9] before the Father—Jesus Christ, the Righteous One. He Himself is the atoning sacrifice for our sins, and not only for ours but also for the sins of the whole world."

Strong's Definition

"An intercessor, consoler: - advocate, comforter."

The Lord Jesus

John 8:2-12 KJV

"And early in the morning he came again into the temple, and all the people came unto him; and he sat down, and taught them."

Scribes And Pharisees

"And the scribes and Pharisees brought unto him a woman taken in adultery; and when they had set her in the midst, they say unto him, Master, this woman was taken in adultery, in the very act. Now Moses in the law commanded us, that such should be stoned: but what sayest thou? This they said, tempting him, that they might have to accuse him."

Can you imagine the humiliation that woman felt being dragged out of bed with the guy she was cheating on her husband with? In the very act by a group of religious men into a public crowd early in the morning? Having her personal life broadcast before the multitude that were there, oh and not to mention the Son of God! How many of those people were her neighbors? What about the guilt, shame and condemnation that she was feeling? She was probably feeling terrible about herself for what she did, and I would go on to ask what led her to do that? Maybe her husband at the time wasn't giving her the affection she was longing for, possibly ignored or abused her, and she was looking for a means of escape, someone to notice her perhaps? According to the *Torah,* she was to be stoned, and legally it would have been acceptable to do so. The Pharisees and religious leaders had the legal right and the stones firmly gripped in their hands, ready to mercilessly pillage this poor woman. Did you notice how the Pharisees came and used the written Word of God to tempt the Living Word of God, Jesus? What they did was considered lawful under the Old Testament Law. They didn't bring a false accusation. They brought someone who genuinely broke the Law and actually wanted to stone a woman just to tempt Jesus and defile His reputation by men steeped in religious pride and a puffed up ego. There were not many ways around this situation due to the fact that their accusations were literally founded upon the written Word of God. She was clearly guilty. No way of denying that. On one hand, Jesus could have rebutted the religious leaders and said that she was not to be stoned, but then they would've made the argument that He was contradicting Torah and would've probably labeled Him a blasphemer. Possibly would've even tried stoning Him. If He couldn't find a Scriptural way out to save her from her punishment, then He would've carried the reputation of the Rabbi that watched a woman get mercilessly stoned in His Presence without saving her. Had the Lord Jesus said anything else, that woman's future would've had a very different outcome that day. But let's take a look at the rest of this Scripture. Notice what our

Advocate, Champion, Compassionate King and LORD did for this woman:

The Lord Jesus

"But Jesus stooped down, and with his finger wrote on the ground, as though he heard them not. So when they continued asking him, he lifted up himself, and said unto them, He that is without sin among you, let him first cast a stone at her. And again he stooped down, and wrote on the ground."

Scribes And Pharisees

"And they which heard it, being convicted by their own conscience, went out one by one, beginning at the eldest, even unto the last: and Jesus was left alone, and the woman standing in the midst."

The Lord Jesus

"When Jesus had lifted up himself, and saw none but the woman, he said unto her, Woman, where are those thine accusers? hath no man condemned thee?"

The Woman

"She said, No man, LORD."

The Lord Jesus

"And Jesus said unto her, Neither do I condemn thee: go, and sin no more. Then spake Jesus again unto them, saying, I am the light of the world: he that followeth me shall not walk in darkness, but shall have the light of life."

The Lord Jesus Advocated for this woman and saved her, even though the Scriptures called for a justified death on her part. Jesus didn't contradict the Scriptures He Advocated on her behalf and the foreseeable outcome changed. Do you know what that's called? You might have guessed it—*breakthrough*. Can you see the Heart of God, the Heart of our Savior, and the compassionate Wisdom of the Holy Spirit that saved this woman's life? If we breeze through the Scriptures like it's a college textbook to try to intellectually memorize rather than allowing the Word to penetrate our hearts, so much can be missed. That was one of the major differences between the Pharisees and those who were teachable and hungry for God. The Pharisees had big heads and small hearts, while a number of Jesus' first century followers had some knowledge of the Scriptures and big hearts and those were the guys that changed the world through Holy Spirit's power (except the apostle Paul, he had both knowledge and his heart grew once he got saved). When we meditate and apply our hearts to the Scriptures we can get prophetic *rhēma* words, heavenly wisdom, revelatory insights, revelations and heavenly answers to earthly problems as well as questions that have plagued humanity.

Accuser of The Brethren

Revelation 12:10 KJV

"And I heard a loud voice saying in heaven, Now is come salvation, and strength, and the kingdom of our God, and the power of his Christ: for the accuser of our brethren is cast down, which accused them before our God day and night."

Accuser

Greek: κατηγορέω[10]

Strong's Concordance Definition

"From G2725; to be a plaintiff that is to charge with some offense: - accuse object."

The Greek word *katēgoreō* is used twenty-four times in the New Testament. One for each hour in the day because Scripture says that he accuses day and night as we just read. If you're a minister, you've felt a looming sense of accusation and tongues that have risen against you because of previous mistakes. May the prayers contained within this book bring relief to you and shut down the work of the enemy:

Luke 12:58 BSB

"Make every effort to reconcile with your adversary while you are on your way to the magistrate. Otherwise, he may drag you off to the judge, and the judge may hand you over to the officer, and the officer may throw you into prison."

1 Peter 5:8 BSB

"Be sober-minded and alert. Your adversary the devil prowls around like a roaring lion, seeking someone to devour."

Adversary

Greek: ἀντίδικος[11]

Strong's Concordance

"...an opponent (in a lawsuit); specifically Satan (as the arch enemy): - adversary."

Revelation 12:9 BSB

"And the great dragon was hurled down—that ancient serpent called the devil and Satan, the deceiver of the whole world. He was hurled to the earth, and his angels with him."

We can see from the Testimony of Scripture that the enemy is an accuser, adversary, and a plaintiff in a court of law based upon the Greek words used to describe the nature of his character. Doesn't that sound like a prosecuting attorney to you?

CHAPTER 4: LAYING A BIBLICAL FOUNDATION FOR BLOODLINE CLEANSING

If you've ever heard someone say that the term *bloodline* is not found in the Bible, this statement would be true had it not been for Ezekiel 19:10 in the New King James Version. Let's take a look:

> Ezekiel 19:10 NKJV
>
> "'Your mother was like a vine in your bloodline, Planted by the waters, Fruitful and full of branches Because of many waters."

> Joel 3:21 LSV
>
> "And I have declared their blood innocent, That I did not declare innocent, And YHWH is dwelling in Zion!"

The Hebrew word used here for bloodline is דאם (*dâm*) which literally means *blood*. Please note that the only version that I know of that uses the term *bloodline* is the NKJV, while the KJV uses the word *blood*. Either way, bloodline *is* found within the Bible and if you've never heard of the term bloodline, you're not alone. But I'm not here to focus on that topic too much because I'm going to get into the subject of the *heavenly court* which is also commonly referred to as *the courts of heaven*:

Celestial Courtroom

Daniel 7:9-10 BSB

"As I continued to watch, thrones were set in place, and the Ancient of Days took His seat. His clothing was white as snow, and the hair of His head was like pure wool. His throne was flaming with fire, and its wheels were all ablaze. A river of fire was flowing, coming out from His presence. Thousands upon thousands attended Him, and myriads upon myriads stood before Him. The court was convened, and the books were opened."

Isaiah 43:25-27 WEB

"I, even I, am he who blots out your transgressions for my own sake; and I will not remember your sins. Put me in remembrance. Let us plead together. Declare your case, that you may be justified. Your first father sinned, and your teachers have transgressed against me."

The LORD brought up the sins of Adam to the nation of Israel thousands of years after Adam committed the act. He brought up the bloodline. If there's anyone who is skeptical of repenting for past generations' sins, take a look at this:

Exodus 34:6-7 BSB

"Then the LORD passed in front of Moses and called out: "The LORD, the LORD God, is compassionate and gracious, slow to anger, abounding in loving devotion and faithfulness, maintaining loving devotion to a thousand generations, forgiving iniquity, transgression, and sin. Yet He will by no means leave the guilty unpunished; He will visit the iniquity of the fathers on their children and grandchildren to the third and fourth generations."

Job 13:18 BSB

"Behold, now that I have prepared my case,
I know that I will be vindicated."

Hebrew Word For Case

Hebrew: מִשְׁפָּט[12]

Transliteration: mishpât

<u>Strong's Definition</u>

"From שָׁפַט H8199; properly a verdict (favorable or unfavorable) pronounced judicially, especially a sentence or formal decree (human or (particularly) divine law, individual or collectively)…"

Synonym For 'Vindication': Acquittal

<u>Acquittal</u>[13]

1. A legal decision that someone is not guilty with which they have been charged, or the formal dismissal of a charge by some other legal process.

3. Payment of a debt or other obligation; reparations, amends.

4. The act of releasing someone from debt or other obligation; acquittance.

5. Avoidance of danger; deliverance.

<u>Vindicate</u>[14]

1. To clear of an accusation, suspicion, or criticism.

2. To justify by providing evidence.

3. To maintain or defend (a cause) against opposition.

4. To provide justification for.

5. To lay claim to; to assert a right to; to claim.

6. To liberate; to set free; to deliver.

After looking at the Scriptural evidence, you cannot tell me that I'm making this up, I want to show you this so that you can receive greater freedom. We are still in the teaching part of this book, and we'll get to the prayer section of this book soon, but this is laying the foundations, so let's continue.

CHAPTER 5: GOD'S LAW OF CONFESSION

Leviticus 5:5-6 BSB

"If someone incurs guilt in one of these ways, he must confess the sin he has committed, and he must bring his guilt offering to the LORD for the sin he has committed: a female lamb or goat from the flock as a sin offering. And the priest will make atonement for him concerning his sin."

The LORD set a standard for *atonement* in Leviticus 5. Let's take a look at a couple of Scriptures and see if you can spot the *four key ingredients*:

Biblical Steps To Forgiveness With God

#1:

Realizing A Trespass Has Been Committed

John 16:7-8 BSB

"But I tell you the truth, it is for your benefit that I am going away. Unless I go away, the Advocate will not come to you; but if I go, I will send Him to you. And when He comes, He will convict the world in regard to sin and righteousness and judgment:"

#2:

Confessing The Trespass

1 John 1:9 ASV

"If we confess our sins, he is faithful and righteous to forgive us our sins, and to cleanse us from all unrighteousness."

Conviction and confession go hand in hand. If you've ever experienced the conviction of the Holy Spirit, you know that when He brings something to the light, His heart is usually for you to confess what happened was wrong. And sometimes even apologize in order to make things right. Other times it might just be for you to make it right with the LORD.

#3:

Providing The Atoning Sacrifice

1 John 2:1-2 BSB

"My little children, I am writing these things to you so that you will not sin. But if anyone does sin, we have an advocate before the Father—Jesus Christ, the Righteous One. He Himself is the atoning sacrifice for our sins, and not only for ours but also for the sins of the whole world."

Atonement

Hebrew: כָּפַר[15]

Transliteration: kâphar

Strong's Definition

"A primitive root; to cover (specifically with bitumen); figuratively to expiate or condone, to placate or cancel: - appease, make (an) atonement, cleanse, disannul, forgive, be merciful, pacify, pardon, to pitch, purge (away), put off, (make) reconcile (-liation)."

#4:

A Priest To Officiate The Atoning Sacrifice

Leviticus 16:15-16 BSB

"Aaron shall then slaughter the goat for the sin offering for the people and bring its blood behind the veil, and with its blood he must do as he did with the bull's blood: He is to sprinkle it against the mercy seat and in front of it. So he shall make atonement for the Most Holy Place because of the impurities and rebellious acts of the Israelites in regard to all their sins. He is to do the same for the Tent of Meeting which abides among them, because it is surrounded by their impurities."

Leviticus 16:30 KJV

"…for on that day shall the priest make an atonement for you, to cleanse you, that ye may be clean from all your sins before the LORD."

After reading that, someone may say: *Yeah, but that was the Old Covenant*. Remember that we just looked at 1 John 1:9 earlier which clearly shows that God's forgiveness is a *conditional* promise stated that *if* we confess He *is* faithful and just to forgive us. In both the Old and New Covenant, the forerunner to forgiveness was confession. Just like no one is automatically saved, they have to accept Jesus as their LORD and Savior. And likewise we believe with our heart and confess with our mouths unto salvation:

Romans 10:9-11 BSB

"That if you confess with your mouth, "Jesus is LORD," and believe in your heart that God raised Him from the dead, you will be saved. For with your heart you believe and are justified, and with your mouth you confess and are saved. It is just as the Scripture says: "Anyone who believes in Him will never be put to shame."

Conviction, confession, and forgiveness go hand in hand. The teaching that repentance is only a one time thing and that it's not necessary to do anymore is not Biblical. It's an ungodly doctrine that seeks to keep people bound because how can you live a victorious Christian life in Jesus without a willingness to repent? Isn't this exactly what the Lord Jesus taught in the Gospel of Luke?

The Key To Justification: A Humble And Contrite Heart

Luke 18:9-14 BSB

"To some who trusted in their own righteousness and viewed others with contempt, He also told this parable: "Two men went up to the temple to pray. One was a Pharisee and the other a tax collector. The Pharisee stood by himself and prayed, 'God, I thank You that I am not like the other men—swindlers, evildoers, adulterers—or even like this tax collector. I fast twice a week and pay tithes of all that I acquire.' But the tax collector stood at a distance, unwilling even to lift up his eyes to heaven. Instead, he beat his breast and said, 'God, have mercy on me, a sinner!' I tell you, this man, rather than the Pharisee, went home justified. For everyone who exalts himself will be humbled, but the one who humbles himself will be exalted."

We can see the importance of repentance and humility, and although we are not under the law, we can see shadows of the good things to come in it. We are also going to be looking at how Jesus is described in the book of Hebrews, briefly:

Colossians 2:16-18 BSB

"Therefore let no one judge you by what you eat or drink, or with regard to a feast, a New Moon, or a Sabbath. These are a shadow of the things to come, but the body that casts it belongs to Christ. Do not let anyone who delights in false humility and the worship of angels disqualify you with speculation about what he has seen. Such a person is puffed up without basis by his unspiritual mind."

Hebrews 10:1 BSB

"For the law is only a shadow of the good things to come, not the realities themselves. It can never, by the same sacrifices offered year after year, make perfect those who draw near to worship."

Apostle And High Priest of Our Confession

Hebrews 3:1-4 BSB

"Therefore, holy brothers, who share in the heavenly calling, set your focus on Jesus, the apostle and high priest whom we confess. He was faithful to the One who appointed Him, just as Moses was faithful in all God's house. For Jesus has been counted worthy of greater glory than Moses, just as the builder of a house has greater honor than the house itself. And every house is built by someone, but God is the builder of everything."

Hebrews 6:16-20 BSB

"Men swear by someone greater than themselves, and their oath serves as a confirmation to end all argument. So when God wanted to make the unchanging nature of His purpose very clear to the heirs of the promise, He guaranteed it with an oath. Thus by two unchangeable things in which it is impossible for God to lie, we who have fled to take hold of the hope set before us may be strongly encouraged. We have this hope as an anchor for the soul, firm and secure. It enters the inner sanctuary behind the curtain, where Jesus our forerunner has entered on our behalf. He has become a high priest forever in the order of Melchizedek."

Matthew 16:13-18 BSB

"When Jesus came to the region of Caesarea Philippi, He questioned His disciples: "Who do people say the Son of Man is?" They replied, "Some say John the Baptist; others say Elijah; and still others, Jeremiah or one of the prophets." "But what about you?" Jesus asked. "Who do you say I am?" Simon Peter answered, "You are the Christ, the Son of the living God." Jesus replied, "Blessed are you, Simon son of Jonah! For this was not revealed to you by flesh and blood, but by My Father in heaven. And I tell you that you are Peter, and on this rock I will build My church, and the gates of Hades will not prevail against it."

While Jesus was on the earth He functioned in an apostolic mantle carrying a mandate to build His Church. Jesus was our Apostle, Prophet, Pastor (Shepherd), Evangelist, and Teacher (Rabbi). He functioned in the active fivefold ministry while He was on the earth at His First Coming. Jesus pioneered the fivefold ministry by setting an example for us, and on the night of His betrayal there was a transition from His Apostleship and into the Lamb of God slain before the foundations of the world. After He resurrected from the realm of the dead, He taught His disciples (He functioned as Rabbi). Just before He ascended into Heaven, He handed the Baton of the Faith to His disciples, giving them a mandate which we now call the Great Commission:

Mark 16:15-18 BSB

"And He said to them, "Go into all the world and preach the gospel to every creature. Whoever believes and is baptized will be saved, but whoever does not believe will be condemned. And these signs will accompany those who believe: In My name they will drive out demons; they will speak in new tongues; they will pick up snakes with their hands, and if they drink any deadly poison, it will not harm them; they will lay their hands on the sick, and they will be made well."

While Jesus is now in Heaven, He is actively functioning as Heaven's High Priest, the Mediator of the New Covenant, and our Heavenly Advocate:

Hebrews 4:14-16 BSB

"Therefore, since we have a great high priest who has passed through the heavens, Jesus the Son of God, let us hold firmly to what we profess. For we do not have a high priest who is unable to sympathize with our weaknesses, but we have one who was tempted in every way that we are, yet was without sin. Let us then approach the throne of grace with confidence, so that we may receive mercy and find grace to help us in our time of need."

Hebrews 8:6 BSB

"Now, however, Jesus has received a much more excellent ministry, just as the covenant He mediates is better and is founded on better promises."

Hebrews 12:24 BSB

"to Jesus the mediator of a new covenant, and to the sprinkled blood that speaks a better word than the blood of Abel."

1 John 2:1 BSB

"My little children, I am writing these things to you so that you will not sin. But if anyone does sin, we have an advocate before the Father—Jesus Christ, the Righteous One."

When Jesus comes back, He will come back as King. There will be a new Heavens and new Earth, and He will deliver the Kingdom to God the Father. And we will rule and reign with Him, where the Tabernacle of God will be with men. But before Jesus comes as King He had to become our sacrifice, and He is also our High Priest. He is ready to apply His Blood, as long as we simply confess and say, "LORD I did it, I'm sorry. Please forgive me."

CHAPTER 6: PETER'S TRIAL

Peter the apostle experienced accusations in the heavenly realms firsthand. I believe the adversary built a case against Peter, and Peter's words gave the adversary legal grounds to test him because he said that he wouldn't deny Jesus. Peter opened himself up to one of the greatest tests of his life because of what he *said* in self-confidence. If it was said with confidence in God, it might have been different. That opened the door for a test to see whether Peter would live up to the standard of his word that proceeded out of his heart and mouth. It's godly wisdom to choose our words carefully.

Luke 22:31-32 ASV

"Simon, Simon, behold, Satan *asked* to have you, that he might sift you as wheat: but I made supplication for thee, that thy faith fail not; and do thou, when once thou hast turned again, establish thy brethren."

(Author's emphasis added)

Do you know what the Greek word used for *asked* means? Get ready for this:

Asked

Greek: ἐξαιτέομαι [16]

Transliteration: exaiteomai

Strong's Definition

"To demand (for trial): - desire."

The first time I read Strong's definition for that word, my jaw dropped. And according to three separate Bible study applications that I checked, it's the *only time* in the entire New Testament that the Greek word *exaiteomai* is used. And out of curiosity I went to look at some synonyms for the word *demand* and came to find out, one of the synonyms for demand is *subpoena*. To put it this way, in the spiritual realm the enemy demanded (*subpoenaed*) Simon in order to sift him:

Sift [17]

Greek: σινιάζω[18]

Sift [19]

1. To examine (something) carefully.

2. To scrutinize (someone or something) carefully to find the truth.

3. To carefully go through a set of objects, or a collection of information, in order to find something.

Notice how Jesus called Peter by Simon and not by his new name? Why? Because the enemy can't accuse you with your future, he can only accuse based on the past and sometimes the present things unrepented of. The only ammunition the enemy has in the spirit is what's given to him. In the letter to the Roman church, the Holy Spirit and the apostle Paul listed a number of things that *cannot* separate us from the love of God:

Romans 8:38-39 BSB

"For I am convinced that neither death nor life, neither angels nor principalities, neither the present nor the future, nor any powers, neither height nor depth, nor anything else in all creation, will be able to separate us from the love of God that is in Christ Jesus our LORD."[20]

Do you know what isn't on that list? It's the past. Things present and things to come are in there, however the past isn't. Why? Because a past not covered in the Blood of Jesus is one of the things that can try to bring guilt, shame, condemnation and that can separate someone from receiving God's love. But it can't separate Christ's Love from the person. It can only separate someone from receiving the Love of Christ. This is especially true in secret times with the LORD when He is trying to show His love for somebody and their response is: "But LORD, you don't know what I've done." However, they fail to realize that once something is repented of and covered in Jesus' Blood, He chooses to forgive *and* forget it because justice was already served:

Isaiah 43:25 BSB

"I, yes I, am He who blots out your transgressions for My own sake and remembers your sins no more."

The church would greatly benefit from choosing to forgive and forget rather than rehearsing on how someone hurt them. One of the reasons the LORD shed His Blood was to cleanse us from our past. If I recall correctly, I heard a pastor by the name of Dan Mohler actually point that out in a sermon. He preached about how the past isn't mentioned in the list of things that can not separate us from the love of God. I believe the reason that the enemy demanded for Simon's trial was because he was threatened by the man that the Lord Jesus prophesied he would become. Simon wasn't a threat to the kingdom of darkness, however, Peter was:

Matthew 16:13-19 BSB

When Jesus came to the region of Caesarea Philippi, He questioned His disciples: "Who do people say the Son of Man is?" They replied, "Some say John the Baptist; others say Elijah; and still others, Jeremiah or one of the prophets." "But what about you?" Jesus asked. "Who do you say I am?" Simon Peter answered, "You are the Christ, the Son of the living God." Jesus replied, "Blessed are you, Simon son of Jonah! For this was not revealed to you by flesh and blood, but by My Father in heaven. And I tell you that you are Peter, and on this rock I will build My church, and the gates of Hades will not prevail against it. I will give you the keys of the kingdom of heaven. Whatever you bind on earth will be bound in heaven, and whatever you loose on earth will be loosed in heaven."

Peter finally started getting it. He was zealous, hungry and started receiving revelation on who Jesus was and at the same time the Lord Jesus started revealing to Simon more of who Peter was. The enemy started taking notice, and he began examining legal grounds. He accused Simon before God the Father, the Righteous Judge, to try to disqualify him from the apostolic mandate and mantle he was destined to faithfully steward for the LORD and His Kingdom. The adversary didn't come to the Lord Jesus to request a sifting, he came to the Father to request it. Either the Father or Holy Spirit revealed to Jesus the activity going on in the Celestial Courts concerning Peter's destiny so that Jesus could intercede effectively on Peter's behalf. I think the devil demanded a trial to sift him or try to take him out prematurely because he foresaw that Peter was going to become a big problem for him. It's no secret that the wicked do not want the righteous to be in positions of power, and that's exactly what Jesus was preparing Peter for. *Peter was an apostle in the making,* and the devil tried to terminate the process prematurely by spiritually attacking Peter to prevent him from stepping into the apostleship that he was destined for. He was worried about the calling, anointing and the apostolic potential that Peter carried. So in response he tried to prevent, hinder or at least try to delay Peter from stepping into the apostleship God called him to. Can you imagine the amount of guilt, shame, mental warfare, sorrow, accusation, and condemnation that Peter felt after he denied Jesus? He probably had thoughts running through his mind along the lines of: "See, you don't love Him. When He needed you the most, you turned your back on Him. Shame on you." Not to mention his words echoing through his mind like a broken record: "Even if I have to die with you, I will not deny You." Peter's words invited an undesired test, and it ended up being self-condemning. Every time the rooster crowed in the morning, it probably reminded him of that moment when he said: "I don't know the man!" Every time Peter heard a rooster crow, don't you think he was reminded of denying Jesus? The pain that Peter felt during those days was likely difficult to bear, and I wouldn't be surprised if he contemplated taking his own life. But could you imagine the impact that would've gone down the drain if he did that? Thank God that didn't happen. It was probably a very dark couple of days for Peter before Jesus rose but praise be to the LORD for His atoning sacrifice. Jesus shed His Blood, washed Peter's conscience, forgave him and raised Peter up as the apostolic leader he was created to be. You see, we can learn something so valuable by the way Jesus treated Peter after he denied him. He didn't condemn him nor did He bash him, but rather forgave him and gave him an opportunity to repent and change. He even had breakfast waiting for them after they went fishing one night and caught nothing until Jesus showed up. Sometimes believers have not fully grasped that the men and women that we read about in the Bible were not scripted actors or movie stars. They were real people that shed real tears, real blood and some even actually died for their faith. Peter went through some hell and back, and so did Jesus—quite literally on Jesus' end. But no matter how far Peter went, Jesus never gave up on Him, belittled him, and He didn't let him go. Jesus never walked away from Peter or told him that he was done with him and that he should go find another person to follow. He told Him: "Follow Me." Thank You, Jesus. Jesus wasn't the only One there to help the apostles, the Holy Spirit was too:

John 21:21-22 BSB

"When Peter saw him, he asked, "LORD, what about him?" Jesus answered, "If I want him to remain until I return, what is that to you? You follow Me!"

John 15:26 BSB

"When the Advocate comes, whom I will send to you from the Father—the Spirit of truth who proceeds from the Father—He will testify about Me."

Simon the *disciple* was starting to look more like Peter the *apostle*. He was starting to look more like the One that he beheld—Jesus. He was getting closer to fulfilling his destiny. Does anyone find it a coincidence that the enemy attacked Peter right before he preached a sermon in Acts chapter two that resulted in thousands of souls being saved and added to the church that day? *The enemy came right before the breakthrough.* For a time, Simon became the center of Heaven's attention in the Courts, but that didn't stop him.

Peter 2.0

Acts 5:12-16 BSB

"The apostles performed many signs and wonders among the people, and with one accord the believers gathered together in Solomon's Colonnade. Although the people regarded them highly, no one else dared to join them. Yet more and more believers were brought to the LORD —large numbers of both men and women. As a result, people brought the sick into the streets and laid them on cots and mats, so that at least Peter's shadow might fall on some of them as he passed by. Crowds also gathered from the towns around Jerusalem, bringing the sick and those tormented by unclean spirits, and all of them were healed."

The man that we read about in Acts two was not the same man that we read about in Luke twenty-two. As a matter of fact, the men we read about here were not the same men that were arguing with each other on who was the greatest. The enemy tried to bring a *sifting,* God brought about a *shifting*! This was the real Peter. He was already bold, but this time he was bold for the King. Can you see why the adversary requested a trial and a sifting for Peter? This leads me to the next chapter's topic as to the possible legal precedence as to why Peter's trial happened in the first place.

CHAPTER 7.1: INIQUITY AND THE SUBJECT OF INHERITANCE

I asked Holy Spirit one time: *"What is iniquity?"* And I heard: *"Iniquity is generational."* Which was a very vague statement, but nevertheless I know it's true because God doesn't lie. You yourself might be wondering what is iniquity? If you see a common issue that seems to run in a majority of a particular family, chances are it's iniquity at work.

Genesis 4:13 KJV

"And Cain said unto the LORD, My punishment is greater than I can bear."

Iniquity

Hebrew: עָוֹן[21]

Transliteration: 'âvôn

Pronunciation: aw-vone'

<u>Strong's Definition</u>

"From עָוָה H5753; perversity, that is, (moral) evil: - fault, iniquity, mischief, punishment (of iniquity), sin."

This is the first time that we see the Hebrew word used for *iniquity* in the Scriptures, and it was connected to murder. The word *punishment* there in the King James is the Hebrew word *avon* which means *iniquity*. The word itself quite literally means *perversion*. So in reality, the better translation would be: "*And Cain said to the LORD, my iniquity is greater than I can bear.*" If you've ever met someone who was struggling with homosexuality, and they said they were born that way, there might be some truth to that, but of course there may be other factors as well. I believe homosexuality is classified as iniquity because it's a perversion of the relationship the LORD Himself created and intended for a man and woman to have. Let me be clear that the Bible clearly does not condone homosexuality. I believe its classification is the category of iniquity. There are three types of transgressions mentioned in the Bible:

I. Sin

II. Transgression

III. Iniquity

In descending order, least severe on top and most severe on bottom. A part of the reason that the LGBTQIA+ community has grown is because they have welcomed people struggling with homosexuality more than the church has, and they have found an identity there. The issue there is that their new-found *identity* is sin oriented and sin was never meant to be a part of anybody's identity because it's ultimately found in Jesus. *They found more love and acceptance in the LGBTQIA+ community than they did in the church.* Churches were never meant to bash people over the head with condemnation and preach fire and brimstone all the time. Anyone doing that doesn't know God and neither do they love Him nor people:

1 John 4:16-21 BSB

"And we have come to know and believe the love that God has for us. God is love; whoever abides in love abides in God, and God in him. In this way, love has been perfected among us, so that we may have confidence on the day of judgment; for in this world we are just like Him. There is no fear in love, but perfect love drives out fear, because fear involves punishment. The one who fears has not been perfected in love. We love because He first loved us. If anyone says, "I love God," but hates his brother, he is a liar. For anyone who does not love his brother, whom he has seen, cannot love God, whom he has not seen. And we have this commandment from Him: Whoever loves God must love his brother as well."

This is a message for preachers who condemn and beat people over the head for something that they are struggling with. Please do everyone and yourself a favor by putting the mic down, pause preaching, and learn how to love people. You're misrepresenting the LORD until you learn what it means to serve with the right heart and follow Jesus' example rather than spewing hate. Your message laced with fear won't change anybody, however it may scare people into compliance rather than out of love. Jesus said if we love Him, we will obey Him out of love, not fear:

John 14:15 BSB

"If you love Me, you will keep My commandments."

The devil operates out of fear, not love. I'm not saying the truth shouldn't be preached, however it should be spoken but do it with a heart of compassion and love towards people, not a heart full of hate. I feel like I've spent enough time addressing that, so let's get back to the topic of iniquity in the book of Leviticus:

Leviticus 26:40-46 BSB

"But if they will confess their iniquity and that of their fathers in the unfaithfulness that they practiced against Me, by which they have also walked in hostility toward Me — and I acted with hostility toward them and brought them into the land of their enemies—and if their uncircumcised hearts will be humbled and they will make amends for their iniquity, then I will remember My covenant with Jacob and My covenant with Isaac and My covenant with Abraham, and I will remember the land. For the land will be abandoned by them, and it will enjoy its Sabbaths by lying desolate without them. And they will pay the penalty for their iniquity, because they rejected My ordinances and abhorred My statutes. Yet in spite of this, when they are in the land of their enemies, I will not reject or despise them so as to destroy them and break My covenant with them; for I am the LORD their God. But for their sake I will remember the covenant with their fathers, whom I brought out of the land of Egypt in the sight of the nations, that I might be their God. I am the LORD." These are the statutes, ordinances, and laws that the LORD established between Himself and the Israelites through Moses on Mount Sinai."

Up To The Third And Fourth Generation

Numbers 14:17-21 BSB

"So now I pray, may the power of my LORD be magnified, just as You have declared: 'The LORD is slow to anger and abounding in loving devotion, forgiving iniquity and transgression. Yet He will by no means leave the guilty unpunished; He will visit the iniquity of the fathers upon their children to the third and fourth generation.' Pardon, I pray, the iniquity of this people, in keeping with the greatness of Your loving devotion, just as You have forgiven them ever since they left Egypt." "I have pardoned them as you requested," the LORD replied. "Yet as surely as I live and as surely as the whole earth is filled with the glory of the LORD,"

Iniquity could be visited in the Old Covenant up to the third and the fourth generation. I believe that when iniquity is unconfessed and has an active hold on somebody, there might be a level of ownership or claim that the enemy can legally claim in the spiritual realm over a person or bloodline. This is because of the engagement of their patterns of iniquity. It suddenly makes sense why Jesus said:

> John 8:34 BSB
>
> "Jesus replied, "Truly, truly, I tell you, everyone who sins is a slave to sin.""

Even in the book of Jeremiah the LORD said that the generation that He was talking about turned back to the iniquities of their forefathers and furthermore Scripture indicates that sin and iniquity actually bear judicial testimony before the LORD:

> Jeremiah 11:10 WEB
>
> "They have turned back to the iniquities of their forefathers, who refused to hear my words. They have gone after other gods to serve them. The house of Israel and the house of Judah have broken my covenant which I made with their fathers."

> Isaiah 59:12 BSB
>
> "For our transgressions are multiplied before You, and our sins testify against us. Our transgressions are indeed with us, and we know our iniquities:"

> Jeremiah 14:7 BSB
>
> "Although our iniquities testify against us, O LORD, act for the sake of Your name. Indeed, our rebellions are many; we have sinned against You."

That same Hebrew word translated as *testify* in Jeremiah and in Isaiah is also found within the following Exodus Scripture:

> Exodus 20:16 BSB
>
> "You shall not bear false witness against your neighbor."

The LORD was talking about a testimony someone would give in court. I believe one of the reasons why some Christians have not yet tasted the full victory of the Christian life is that there are things testifying against them in the Courts of Heaven. And through a lack of knowledge on how to address it or that it even exists, it has kept them stuck in the same place spiritually. Some of it not even being their own fault but that of their ancestors. Whoever doesn't show up to court most often loses the case in something called a default judgment:

Hosea 4:6 BSB

"My people are destroyed for lack of knowledge. Because you have rejected knowledge, I will also reject you as My priests. Since you have forgotten the law of your God, I will also forget your children."

When we have knowledge of how things operate, carry revelation as well as the spirit of wisdom, and we know something is within God's will, victory is not just a possibility, it's guaranteed.

Spiritual Inheritance

Hebrews 7:9 BSB

"And so to speak, Levi, who collects the tenth, paid the tenth through Abraham."

Abraham's obedience positively affected his future descendants, in particular his great-grandson Levi, but how was that possible when Levi wasn't born yet? Well, Levi was still in his great-grandfather Abraham and therefore God counted it to him even though it was his great-grandfather who tithed to Melchizedek. When we give tithes and offerings to a priesthood, we are tying ourselves to that priesthood. Where our money goes is significant because one righteous act done by Abraham impacted Levi even though he wasn't born over a hundred years later! To provide an example for everyone to understand this a bit better, imagine our bodies are like batons that track runners race with. At the end of their portion of the race, they pass the baton to their next teammate, who also runs their portion of the race. This continues until everybody on their team has run and the last one crosses the finish line, securing the victory. This is a good physical representation of the spiritual picture of the father and or mother handing the family baton of the ministry, the callings, anointing, gifting and spiritual inheritance to their children, both physical and spiritual. They continue that race and legacy. The seed that our bodies came from once resided within our ancestors, and we were born for such a time as this, and it is likely that one or more answers to the world's problems lies within you. Our bodies are a part of our physical inheritance, but we also carry a spiritual inheritance as well as a *heavenly purpose* attached to us. God has given us an assignment of divine purpose and destiny to accomplish for such a time as this. This is what some would call our book in Heaven.[24] Since our human bodies are the physical inheritance we received from our earthly parents, that begs the question: "Do the actions of our ancestors somehow affect us?" I believe the answer is yes, only until it gets confessed and covered in the Blood of Jesus.

Sarah, Rebekah, Rachel

Does anyone else find it a coincidence that Abraham's wife Sarah was barren and unable to have kids outside the LORD's divine intervention? Even then, when her miracle baby Isaac was born and married Rebekah his wife, she was also unable to conceive a successful pregnancy until the LORD intervened.

> Genesis 30:22-23 BSB
>
> "Then God remembered Rachel. He listened to her and opened her womb, and she conceived and gave birth to

a son. "God has taken away my shame," she said."

And when she *did* successfully conceive, she bore twins and named them Esau and Jacob. And when Jacob eventually married Rachel, she wasn't able to have kids? Rachel did eventually have two kids successfully. But do you see the pattern here? How about when Abraham told a deceptive truth that his wife Sarah was actually his sister in order to not get killed by the Egyptians for the sake of his wife? And then Isaac did the same exact thing later in his life with Rebekah!

Genesis 20:2 ASV

"And Abraham said of Sarah his wife, She is my sister: and Abimelech king of Gerar sent, and took Sarah."

Genesis 26:8-9 BSB

"When Isaac had been there a long time, Abimelech king of the Philistines looked down from the window and was surprised to see Isaac caressing his wife Rebekah. Abimelech sent for Isaac and said, "So she is really your wife! How could you say, 'She is my sister'?" Isaac replied, "Because I thought I might die on account of her."

This is my personal opinion, but what if the adversary sensed the destiny of God in their lives and managed to find a legal footing in Abraham or Sarah's life to resist pregnancies? After all, they would be the carriers of the Seed of the Messiah, why wouldn't the enemy want to delay their pregnancies? You know, Job made a comment that he thought was about God, but he was describing something the enemy was doing:

Job 10:4-6 BSB

"Do You have eyes of flesh? Do You see as man sees? Are Your days like those of a mortal, or Your years like those of a man, that You should seek my iniquity and search out my sin—"

But as usual, the LORD broke through anyway. Won't He do it! We know for certain in Abraham's lineage that his father was a priest of an idol, and with a priesthood comes sacrifice. There had to have been some sort of legal right for Sarah, Rebekah, and Rachel to not be able to bear children until the LORD intervened for them. One possibility is that the enemy saw the potential that they carried to be the baton passers of the lineage of the Messiah and to buy time he legally resisted their pregnancies until the LORD intervened and fulfilled His Word. God means what He says! Inheritance can be a good thing or a bad thing depending on the source. God is the giver of every good and perfect gift, and fathers play a part in giving an inheritance to their kids:

James 1:17 BSB

"Every good and perfect gift is from above, coming down from the Father of the heavenly lights, with whom there is no change or shifting shadow."

Proverbs 19:14 KJV

"House and riches are the inheritance of fathers: and a prudent wife is from the LORD."

Spiritual inheritance is good when it comes from the right source. And just because there's a spiritual inheritance passed onto someone doesn't mean they don't have a part to play in stewarding it.

Proverbs 20:21 BSB

"An inheritance gained quickly will not be blessed in the end."

The moment we get born again, God becomes our Father, and we immediately receive an inheritance from Him as well. Even the apostle Paul told Timothy to fan into flame the gift placed within him. I do believe that certain spiritual inheritances are given to or unlocked in the believer in portions over time as they mature in their faith. But similarly to a physical inheritance, an inheritance you don't know about or don't steward well doesn't end up doing you or others much good if you squander it. God is probably not going to give a born again believer who got saved just three days before a national platform to prophesy on because there is a level of maturity that needs to be developed in them. Although God can do it if He really wanted to, typically that's not the case. It also takes humility, something unfortunately society at large has lost sight of. We can see an example of spiritual inheritance in the life of Philip the evangelist and his four daughters who operated in the gift of prophecy or prophetic offices–God knows:

Philip The Evangelist's Daughters

Acts 21:8-9 BSB

"Leaving the next day, we went on to Caesarea and stayed at the home of Philip the evangelist, who was one of the Seven. He had four unmarried daughters who prophesied."

The fact that *all four* sisters were operating in the gift of prophecy or the offices means that there was a very high probability that a spiritual inheritance was passed down from Philip to his daughters. This is why you can see a family full of pastors if there is a pastoral anointing on their lives, or a family full of evangelists because of an evangelistic anointing on that family. *The law of inheritance* is also one of the reasons you can see the bad side of inheritance, which is something negative that runs in a family like substance abuse, addictions, health stuff etc. It's because of natural and spiritual inheritance that is passed down from the previous generations to the next. The unfulfilled assignments that previous generations were given by God still need to be fulfilled. And the gifts that the LORD gives to us match our destinies and assignments. What previous generations didn't accomplish, the present and future generations will be called to keep building and finish what was started in the LORD's Plan:

The Inherited Faith of Timothy

Spiritual inheritance isn't just from the fathers, but also from the mothers. I don't want mothers to feel left out because I think one of the more underappreciated roles in life is a mother. However, oftentimes, the value of a mother is often realized later in life when the kids grow up and start to realize what it's like to be a parent. As a parent, you've likely made personal sacrifices that have gone unseen in the eyes of your children, but who's to say that God doesn't see them? Hagar was in the desert with her son Ishmael when they ran out of water. He was so thirsty that Hagar believed he was close to the point of death that she cried out to God, and He answered her and provided water for the young lad. Through her encounter with Him, we get this account from Scripture:

Genesis 16:13 BSB

> "So Hagar gave this name to the LORD who had spoken to her: "You are the God who sees me," for she said, "Here I have seen the One who sees me!"

For all the godly mothers out there, whether your children see your sacrifices or not, thank you for being there for them. The role of godly parents is important, and there are things you can impart to your children even from a young age. The apostle Paul gave us some insight into the spiritual inheritance that was passed down to Timothy from his mother:

2 Timothy 1:5-6 BSB

> "I am reminded of your sincere faith, which first dwelt in your grandmother Lois and your mother Eunice, and I am convinced is in you as well. For this reason I remind you to fan into flame the gift of God, which is in you through the laying on of my hands."

Timothy had a praying grandmother and a praying mother. He got the double dose! Paul said that he was persuaded that the faith that was in his grandmother Lois and his mother Eunice was now in Timothy as well. There was a *spiritual inheritance* that was passed down through the generations and family lineage to Timothy. Talk about a gift of faith! Inheritance is a good thing as long as the source of the inheritance is godly.

The Miracle Called Seed

1 Corinthians 15:37-38 BSB

> "And what you sow is not the body that will be, but just a seed, perhaps of wheat or something else. But God gives it a body as He has designed, and to each kind of seed He gives its own body."

Ever heard of the phrase, *the apple didn't fall far from the tree?* Well, this is because an apple seed inherits the genetics of the parent tree that it came from. The seed within the apple is a byproduct of its parent tree. This is why there are different types of apples, because each apple tree's DNA is unique to its own species. Not all apples look or taste the same because they are unique. Our bodies are living seeds that are the byproduct of our mother and father. Our bodies were at one point smaller than a seed that grew, and somewhere along our development the LORD placed our souls and spirits inside our bodies:

Zechariah 12:1 BSB

> "This is the burden of the word of the LORD concerning Israel. Thus declares the LORD, who stretches out the heavens and lays the foundation of the earth, who forms the spirit of man within him:"

We *are* a spirit, we *have* a soul, and we are *in* our human bodies. Before we were born again, we were basically a soul living in and through a body. When we are born again, God's Spirit links with our spirit and our spirit *becomes* saved. As we continue our Christian walk, our soul is in the process of *being* saved and our bodies are *awaiting* the time of redemption when the Lord Jesus comes back for His Bride. The Scripture also advises us to be renewed in the spirit of our mind–the mind being a part of the rational soul:

Ephesians 4:23 KJV

"and be renewed in the spirit of your mind;"

This is the fullness of salvation when our spirit, soul, mind, and body become fully redeemed and glorified. After briefly looking at some research about seeds, I came across a research paper about how viruses and diseases that can be transferred or transmitted through the seed of a plant. I believe curses have a gradual decaying effect on DNA. So, I got curious and did some research on the subject of: *Can genetic mutations be transferred from plant seeds?* I came across an article that said the following: *"Depending on which tissue is involved, the change can be passed onto the next generation through seeds."* The article went further on to talk about genetic mutations in connection to plants, but the point I want to get at is, if this is true concerning plants, how about humans? What if the curse that came upon the ground because of Adam's disobedience in the Garden of Eden actually affected the genetic code of not only plant life but human life and DNA as well? After all, the entire human race was inside of Adam when he was cursed in the form of seed. If you've ever read the Bible in the King James Version and noticed that it says *seed* when talking about descendants, it's because that's what our bodies came from–our bodies are living seeds!

The 1992 Experiment

Back in 1992 there was a scientific experiment done with human DNA that was done by Rollin McCraty, Mike

Atkinson, and Dana Tomasino. After this study they came to the conclusion saying in their paper that they well acknowledged but poorly understood phenomena such as spontaneous remission in cancer, the health rewards of a strong faith and the positive effect of prayer. Now, for those who are interested in researching this further I have left a footnote with the link where you can personally see the study for yourself because the paper is copyrighted material.[25]

The Serpent Deceives Eve

Genesis 3:1-21 BSB

"Now the serpent was more crafty[26] than any beast of the field that the LORD God had made. And he said to the woman, "Did God really say, 'You must not eat from any tree in the garden?'" The woman answered the serpent, "We may eat the fruit of the trees of the garden, but about the fruit of the tree in the middle of the garden, God has said, 'You must not eat of it or touch it, or you will die.'" "You will not surely die," the serpent told her. "For God knows that in the day you eat of it, your eyes will be opened, and you will be like God, knowing good and evil." When the woman saw that the tree was good for food and pleasing to the eyes, and that it was desirable for obtaining wisdom, she took the fruit and ate it. She also gave some to her husband, who was with her, and he ate it. And the eyes of both of them were opened, and they knew that they were naked; so they sewed together fig leaves and made coverings for themselves. Then the man and his wife heard the voice of the LORD God walking in the garden in the breeze of the day, and they hid themselves from the presence of the LORD God among the trees of the garden. But the LORD God called out to the man, "Where are you?" "I heard Your voice in the garden," he replied, "and I was afraid because I was naked; so I hid myself." "Who told you that you were naked?" asked the LORD God. "Have you eaten from the tree, of which I commanded you not to eat?" And the man answered, "The woman whom You gave me, she gave me fruit from the tree, and I ate it." Then the LORD God said to the woman, "What is this you have done?" "The serpent deceived me," she replied, "and I ate."

The Serpent Is Cursed

"So the LORD God said to the serpent: "Because you have done this, cursed are you above all livestock and every beast of the field! On your belly will you go, and dust you will eat, all the days of your life."

The Promised Seed

"And I will put enmity[27] between you and the woman, and between your seed and her seed. He will crush your head, and you will strike his heel."

The Punishment of Mankind

"To the woman He said: "I will sharply increase your pain in childbirth; in pain you will bring forth children. Your desire will be for your husband, and he will rule over you." And to Adam He said: "Because you have listened to the voice of your wife and have eaten from the tree of which I commanded you not to eat, cursed is the ground because of you; through toil you will eat of it all the days of your life. Both thorns and thistles it will yield for you, and you will eat the plants of the field. By the sweat of your brow you will eat your bread, until you return to the ground — because out of it were you taken. For dust you are, and to dust you shall return." And Adam named his wife Eve, because she would be the mother of all the living."

Their First Clothing

"And the LORD God made garments of skin for Adam and his wife, and He clothed them."

The curse on the ground affected the ground as well as the

rest of the animals and plants. To help us understand, we have to go back to when God was creating the world. Adam's body came from the ground, as did all the trees, animals, and plants. This is why the healthy food available comes from the ground because the earth knows how to sustain herself. I believe the curse of death and decay is why we see a gradual decay and composition of fruits if they aren't eaten within a certain time frame after being plucked off of the tree. Or if they naturally fall off the tree and decompose. I'm going to go out on a limb and say that we can probably title the curse that came upon the ground and mankind as: "The curse of death and decay." The curse of genetic decay began to take effect upon the Earth on both man and beast alike, along with the plants and herbs because they all came from the ground and even on Eve because she came from Adam.

Genesis 1:11 BSB

"Then God said, "Let the earth bring forth vegetation: seed-bearing plants and fruit trees, each bearing fruit with seed according to its kind." And it was so."

Genesis 2:7 BSB

"Then the LORD God formed man from the dust of the ground and breathed the breath of life into his nostrils, and the man became a living being."

And as for the tree of knowledge of good and evil, I don't think the problem was as much as that tree being there. Rather, I think the source of the issue was the lustful desire for the fruit of the tree that eventually produces corruption:

2 Peter 1:4 WEB

"by which he has granted to us his precious and exceedingly great promises; that through these you may become partakers of the divine nature, having escaped from the corruption that is in the world by lust."

I don't think Adam and Eve's marriage was ever the same again. I don't think until that point in their marriage they ever got into an argument, but after the fall, love turned into self gratification, beauty turned into bitterness and patience turned into frustration. Eve probably was angry and bitter towards Adam because of what and how things went down, and probably even at herself because of what had happened. Can you imagine the deep regret, sorrow, and shame that Adam must have felt after what happened? And what was it like for God the Father, the Lord Jesus and Holy Spirit to see His perfect creation be subjected to a curse? Could you imagine what it would be like for the LORD to see thousands of years of the hurt, pain and human suffering from hundreds of generations? What do you think that does to His Heart when He sees that? I'm not surprised at all that Lord Jesus came because His Heart was probably ripped open, tested and grieved time and time again by seeing His creation suffer the way it did–the very ones He loves. A hero is someone that risks their lives to save another's and that's exactly who our Jesus is. I declare that the Body and Bride of Christ as well as the world will come into a greater understanding of the Sacrifice and Love of our Lord and Savior Jesus Christ, in Jesus Name, amen.

Romans 6:23 WEB

"For the wages of sin is death, but the free gift of
God is eternal life in Christ Jesus our Lord."

CHAPTER 7.2: WHAT IS AN ALTAR?

Okay, before we go any further, you may have noticed the word *altar*, and you might be wondering *what is an altar?* And that's exactly what I'm going to address in this chapter for us. An altar is a platform of sacrifice. Altars are Biblical, and they are mentioned several times in the Old Testament. We have the Altar of God mentioned, and there are also foreign altars mentioned in the Bible that were erected to forgiven deities and idols. An altar is a spiritual platform of sacrifice for spirits that empower the spirits. Think of altars like a stomach for spirits. Of course, spirits don't physically eat, but they can receive spiritual sacrifices. If your American altar is not in your everyday vocabulary because of the amount of technological advancements and culture, but if you go to Mexico, Africa, and areas with high levels of witchcraft there are altars in those areas. War is actually a form of altar sacrifice to spirits that feed off bloodshed, such as spirits who like to cause wars and conflicts. I believe Europe is a hotspot for principalities thirsty for bloodshed, gods of war, if you want to call it that. Of course, God's Heart is not bloodshed, but unfortunately people who don't know Jesus as their Lord and Savior provoke the world to bloodshed through their ideals and corrupt minds and corrupt hearts. It's really disgusting what some men and women do and think behind closed doors, but when there is war, the spirits that feed off bloodshed are receiving that bloodshed on the ground. The blood spilled on through war and people killing each other.

Abortion is another altar that spirits feed from because of the bloodshed of infants. In the Old Testament, we see an example of Moloch, which was a bull headed Canaanite or deity (some debate exists on the origins of this ungodly idol) who people would sacrifice infants to. The idol means nothing in and of itself, however the spirit behind the idol is a different story. Spirits do not have physical bodies themselves and when someone created a physical image for a spirit to attach itself to, whatever sacrifice made to that physical statue is being given to the spirit behind it. There is one healthy altar on the Earth, and that is Christianity. Every other altar is set up to demons and principalities. This includes Islam, Buddhism, pagan religions etc. As you read, you'll gain a better understanding of altars. After the LORD flooded the earth because of the wickedness and iniquity of man, Noah did something that touched God's Heart. He built an altar to the LORD and sacrificed on it. Building an altar is nothing new within the Word that we see, however it is the very first time that we see the Word *altar* used in the entire Bible. So, what is an altar? *An altar is a place of sacrifice that is directly connected to the spirit that is being sacrificed to on the altar.* "You mean altars can be built to spirits?" Absolutely they can, it's actually what happened in the nation of Israel's history. We can look at the Bible and see that the children of Israel built altars to foreign idols. The LORD called them other lovers. We're going to take a look at Elijah's Mount Carmel encounter that I would like to call *the Mount Carmel experience*, but before we get into that, let's break down the definition of an altar in Hebrew and Koine Greek:

What Is An Altar?

Hebrew: מזבח

Pronunciation: miz-bay'-akh

The Hebrew word altar comes from the Hebrew word *zabach*, meaning to slaughter or sacrifice. The altar was often the meeting place of humanity and God. I say humanity and God because it was typical for creation to initiate the encounter with our Creator–there was almost always some sort of sacrifice brought to the Lord. Whether it was a grain offering, a drink offering, prayer or a sin sacrifice that was offered. However, there is an exception in this when we see The Angel of the Lord interact with Gideon and King Solomon sacrificed a thousand burnt offerings to the Lord after the Lord spoke to him in a dream. Altars were the universal zip code for worship. Altars have a few common aspects, so let's take a look at some of them.

The Four Elements of An Altar

1. Uncut Stone or Earth

Deuteronomy 27:5-8 LSV

> "and built an altar there to your God YHWH, an altar of stones; you do not wave iron over them. You build the altar of your God YHWH with complete stones, and have caused burnt-offerings to ascend on it to your God YHWH, and sacrificed peace-offerings, and eaten there, and rejoiced before your God YHWH, and written on the stones all the words of this law, well engraved."

The Lord permitted two materials to build the altar, which were uncut stones and dirt. These were acceptable before Him as the building material for the altar. Seems kind of odd why God would specifically mention these two, but you'll understand why here in a few minutes. The whole purpose of why God said to not use tools on the stones of the altar was to keep it natural. Symbolizing that man made sacrifices and man made platforms were not sufficient, and only what He directly created and approved could be legitimately used. This is what happened to Cain. Cain presented an offering to the Lord from the ground by the work of his own hands, but Abel presented an offering from His Hand. Did you catch that? God created the animals, but Cain presented an offering grown from the ground that was cursed in Genesis 3. He presented a cursed offering to God. Do you see why God rejected his offering? He wanted to give God a cursed item. Do you want to know the cool thing about the stones that would make up the altar? We are called living stones in the Word!

1 Peter 2:3-5 LSV

"if it so be that you tasted that the LORD is good, to whom coming—a living stone—having indeed been disapproved of by men, but with God—choice and precious, 5 and you yourselves are built up as living stones into a spiritual house, a holy priesthood, to offer up spiritual sacrifices acceptable to God through Jesus Christ."

Someone might say: "Well, that's stone, but what about dirt?" When God created Adam He used the ground to form his body, so man's body was made from the earth, and both dirt and dust come from the earth.

Genesis 2:7 LSV

"And YHWH God forms the man—dust from the ground, and breathes into his nostrils breath of life, and the man becomes a living creature."

2. Wood

Leviticus 1:7 LSV

"and the sons of Aaron the high priest have put fire on the altar, and arranged wood on the fire;"

Another important aspect of an altar is the fuel for the fire, in this case wood. Wood was the fire's fuel. The wood underneath would sustain the fire that consumed the offering. Jesus was hung on two cross-beams that were made out of wood.

3. Sacrifice

Leviticus 1:8 LSV

> "and sons of Aaron, the priests, have arranged the
> pieces, with the head and the fat, on the wood,
> which is on the fire, which is on the altar;"

The sacrifice was offered directly to God. Oftentimes the Levitical priests would sacrifice bulls, rams, goats, and lambs on the altar as prescribed in the law of Moses as well as grain offerings and drink offerings. From Exodus' Passover that required a family to take a lamb for themselves and cover their households with the blood of the lamb for protection while they were in Egypt, to Leviticus. Where God gave more detailed and very specific instructions on how sacrifice was to be done and what animals were and were not acceptable on His altar, one of the acceptable ones being a lamb. As long as that lamb qualified as blemish free and without defect, symbolizing perfection. Do you know what one of the titles that Jesus notoriously holds is? The Lamb of God:

> John 1:29 LSV
>
> "On the next day John sees Jesus coming to
> him and says, "Behold, the Lamb of God, who
> is taking away the sin of the world;"

From the Promise in Genesis 3, the Passover in Exodus, to the law in Leviticus, to Hosea the prophet, to the Gospels all the way to Revelation you see hints to Jesus all throughout the Scriptures. The hints just get more obvious as the Bible progresses until it's blatantly clear that Jesus c can be seen in the Scriptures from beginning, middle and to end. Could that be one of the reasons Jesus said:

> Revelation 1:19 LSV
>
> "Write the things that you have seen, and the things that are,
> and the things that are about to come after these things;"

4. Fire

Leviticus 6:12 KJV

> "And the fire upon the altar shall be burning in it; it shall not be put out: and the priest shall burn wood on it every morning, and lay the burnt offering in order upon it; and he shall burn thereon the fat of the peace offerings."

Last, but by no means least, the fourth critical ingredient of an altar is fire. Fire is symbolic of purification, refining, passion and judgment. When Jesus was on the Cross, He endured God's judgment because He bore our sins in His Body on the tree. He offered Himself as the ultimate offering once and for all, making the world's largest down payment in history that covered the largest spiritual debt that we had. Paying it in full and thereby nullifying death as well as securing our eternity as we work out our salvation as the Bible says:

Malachi 3:3 LSV

> "And He has sat, a refiner and purifier of silver, And He has purified the sons of Levi, And has refined them as gold and as silver, And they have been bringing a present near to YHWH in righteousness."

We have as born again believers a living altar inside of us. We are living, breathing and walking altars for the LORD's Presence through His Spirit residing in us. Jesus made the sacrifice providing enough fuel for the fire for our salvation, but we can also add fuel to the fire by our own worship, prayer, thanksgiving, sacrifices, fasting, prayer, reading God's Word and fellowshipping with other passionate believers. This is why the Lord desires us to be burning for Him. If we couldn't control our temperature in the Spirit, Jesus wouldn't have rebuked Laodicea for being lukewarm!

Revelation 3:14-22 LSV

> "And to the messenger of the assembly of the Laodiceans write: These things says the Amen, the Witness—the Faithful and True—the Chief of the creation of God: I have

known your works, that you are neither cold nor hot; I
wish you were cold or hot. So—because you are lukewarm,
and neither cold nor hot, I am about to vomit you out of
My mouth; because you say—I am rich, and have grown
rich, and have need of nothing, and have not known that
you are the wretched, and miserable, and poor, and blind,
and naked; I counsel you to buy from Me gold fired by fire,
that you may be rich, and white garments that you may
be clothed, and the shame of your nakedness may not be
revealed, and with eye-salve anoint your eyes, that you
may see. As many as I cherish, I convict and discipline; be
zealous, then, and convert; behold, I have stood at the door,
and I knock; if anyone may hear My voice, and may open
the door, I will come in to him, and will dine with him, and
he with Me. He who is overcoming—I will give to him to
sit with Me in My throne, as I also overcame and sat down
with My Father in His throne. He who is having an ear—
let him hear what the Spirit says to the assemblies."

The whole purpose of the Old Testament altar was to meet with God. Just like every other spiritual principle and foreshadow, if the LORD wasn't in it then it was truly pointless–there's a word for that, and it's called man made religion. The altar was one of the places where the priests, prophets, and people came into God's Presence. However, the New Testament reality of born again believers is that the Presence of God has gotten into us and wherever we are we can encounter Him! Wherever we are, there He is. He is with us always!

Matthew 28:20 KJV

"Teaching them to observe all things whatsoever I
have commanded you: and, lo, I am with you alway,
even unto the end of the world. Amen."

The altar has already been built, the sacrifice has already been made, we are the living stones that make up the altar!

We already have the fire living inside of us, all we need to do is just maintain and stoke that fire!

Deuteronomy 4:24 LSV

"for your God YHWH is a consuming fire—a zealous God."

Hebrews 12:29 LSV

"for our God is also a consuming fire."

Elijah's Offering

1 Kings 18:30-40 LSV

"And Elijah says to all the people, "Come near to me"; and all the people come near to him, and he repairs the altar of YHWH that is broken down; and Elijah takes twelve stones, according to the number of the tribes of the sons of Jacob, to whom the word of YHWH was, saying, "Israel is your name"; and he builds an altar with the stones, in the Name of YHWH, and makes a trench, as about the space of two measures of seed, around the altar. And he arranges the wood, and cuts the bullock in pieces, and places it on the wood, and says, "Fill four pitchers of water, and pour them on the burnt-offering, and on the wood"; and he says, "Do it a second time"; and they do it a second time; and he says, "Do it a third time"; and they do it a third time; and the water goes around the altar, and he has also filled the trench with water. And it comes to pass, at the going up of the evening present, that Elijah the prophet comes near and says, "YHWH, God of Abraham, Isaac, and Israel, let it be known today that You are God in Israel, and that I, Your servant, have done the whole of these things by Your word; answer me, O YHWH, answer me, and this people then knows that You are YHWH God; and You have turned their heart backward." And a fire falls from YHWH, and consumes the burnt-offering, and the wood, and the stones, and the dust, and it has licked up the water that is in the trench. And all the people see, and fall on their faces, and say, "YHWH,

He is the God! YHWH, He is the God!" And Elijah says to them, "Catch the prophets of Ba'al; do not let a man escape from them"; and they catch them, and Elijah brings them down to the Brook of Kishon, and slaughters them there."

Did you know that there was a drought in the region during this Biblical passage? How many gallons of water were poured out on that sacrifice not one but multiple times? How many people were thinking: *We could have used that water to feed our flocks and drink for ourselves?* But little did Elijah know that sacrifice would cause a rainstorm that gave them much more water than what they sacrificed.

1 Kings 18:1 LSV

"And the days are many, and the word of YHWH has been to Elijah in the third year, saying, "Go, appear to Ahab, and I give rain on the face of the ground"

Solomon's Sacrifice

Before, God came to Solomon in a dream and asked him: *"What do you want me to do for you?"* Solomon the night before this dream happened sacrificed on the Altar of the LORD.

2 Chronicles 1:6-13 ASV

"And Solomon went up thither to the brazen altar before Jehovah, which was at the tent of meeting, and offered a thousand burnt-offerings upon it. In that night did God appear unto Solomon, and said unto him, Ask what I shall give thee. And Solomon said unto God, Thou hast showed great lovingkindness unto David my father, and hast made me king in his stead. Now, O Jehovah God, let thy promise unto David my father be established; for thou hast made me king over a people like the dust of the earth in multitude. Give me now wisdom and knowledge, that I may go out and come in before this people; for who can judge this thy people, that is so great? And God said to Solomon, Because this was in thy heart, and thou hast not asked riches, wealth, or honor, nor the life of them that hate thee, neither yet hast asked long life; but hast asked wisdom and knowledge for thyself, that thou mayest judge my people, over whom I have made thee king: wisdom and knowledge is granted unto thee; and I will give thee riches, and wealth, and honor, such as none of the kings have had that have been before thee; neither shall there any after thee have the like. So Solomon came from the high place that was at Gibeon, from before the tent of meeting, unto Jerusalem; and he reigned over Israel."

Elijah had the people pour gallons of water on a sacrifice in the midst of a three-year drought. To the rest of the people, it might have seemed like it was a foolish decision because what they saw as a waste of precious water, God saw as a precious offering. God does not see as man sees, but He looks at the heart. His way is higher, and we would benefit greatly to start seeing things the way He sees them. Indeed, what looked like foolishness to man, God saw as an extravagant offering to Him. And let me tell you something, the water that they poured out on the offering was not wasted, because whatever is given to God is never wasted by God. By the hand of man an offering was made, and by the Hand of God a reward was released. They gave to the LORD what they could, and the LORD did what they couldn't—He released the rain!

1 Kings 18:44 KJV

"And it came to pass at the seventh time, that he said, Behold, there ariseth a little cloud out of the sea, like a man's hand. And he said, Go up, say unto Ahab, Prepare thy chariot, and get thee down, that the rain stop thee not."

Why do the Scriptures specifically say that a cloud like a man's hand arose out of the sea? Because by the hand of man a drink offering was poured out to God, and by the Hand of God there was a torrential downpour initiated. You see, whatever you put into God's Hands, you can expect

Him to multiply it. Jesus took five loaves and two fish and used it to successfully provide for thousands of people in the wilderness. You can't tell me that your offerings aren't significant, because if God can take a man's lunch and multiply it to an all-you-can-eat buffet. All limitations are thrown out the window. We serve the God of miracles! All it takes on our end is willingness!

CHAPTER 7.3: BUILDING AN ALTAR

You might be wondering, how do I build an altar, how would I go about doing that, I'm new to this? Well, in the Old Testament, they would physically build altars but that is no longer any form of requirement. Since Jesus's Cross has become the Highest Altar of this Age, and He Himself tends to the Altar as the sole High Priest.

Hebrews 6:19-20 WEB

"This hope we have as an anchor of the soul, a hope both sure and steadfast and entering into that which is within the veil, where as a forerunner Jesus entered for us, having become a high priest forever after the order of Melchizedek."

If you want to strengthen Your relationship with the LORD, number one, we have to understand that He is a person. The whole purpose of an altar was to be a meeting place between two spiritual realms, where the super met the natural, making it a supernatural experience. We now as born again believers have the Holy Spirit living within us, and there is no need for us to build a physical altar anymore, it's all in our hearts. In fact, for someone to build a physical altar to worship God in the New Covenant would be going back to the old way of worship and law, to which Paul the Apostle had this to say about:

Galatians 5:4-6 BSB

"You who are trying to be justified by the law have

been severed from Christ; you have fallen away from grace. But by faith we eagerly await through the Spirit the hope of righteousness. For in Christ Jesus neither circumcision nor uncircumcision has any value. All that matters is faith, expressed through love."

Paul was speaking about the act of circumcision however, this I believe would also apply to Old Testament forms of worship. Remember, we have been set free from the Law of sin and death, and we have been liberated to live by the law of grace and the Spirit of Life:

Romans 8:1-5 BSB

"Therefore, there is now no condemnation for those who are in Christ Jesus. For in Christ Jesus the law of the Spirit of life set you free from the law of sin and death. For what the law was powerless to do in that it was weakened by the flesh, God did by sending His own Son in the likeness of sinful man, as an offering for sin. He thus condemned sin in the flesh, so that the righteous standard of the law might be fulfilled in us, who do not walk according to the flesh but according to the Spirit. Those who live according to the flesh set their minds on the things of the flesh; but those who live according to the Spirit set their minds on the things of the Spirit."

So when I speak about building an altar, I'm in reality talking about strengthening our relationship with the Lord through these things listed below:

1. Faith
2. Love
3. Obedience
4. Worship
5. Surrender

6. Prayer

7. Bible Reading

Hebrews 11:6 BSB

"And without faith it is impossible to please God, because anyone who approaches Him must believe that He exists and that He rewards those who earnestly seek Him."

God spoke to Abraham to sacrifice his son Isaac on a mountain that He would show him when he got there. When he got there, Isaac carried the wood he would be laid on. God wasn't advocating human sacrifice. God, no! But He was giving Abraham a once in a lifetime experience and a way to connect with the LORD when the Father was going to sacrifice Jesus. Jesus was to the Father what Isaac was to Abraham, his only-begotten son through Sarah. God told Abraham that Isaac would be his heir and not Ishmael. We see this in the Scriptures because before Abraham could do it, an Angel of God cried out to him to *wait!* The LORD was giving Abraham an opportunity to connect with the LORD's Heart in a deeper way that I don't think any other person could in the exact same way. Other than a father who lost a son serving in the military. Which isn't the exact same scenario, but probably feels similar to what Abraham was feeling during the hike to the mountain. God was testing Abraham to see if the Promise of God became more important to him rather than the God Who made the Promise to him. A piece of advice, don't let the promises of God that you behold become more significant to you than the God Who made those promises to you. Without Him, we wouldn't even have those promises because the fulfillment comes from Him not ourselves, even though we have an important part to play at various times. And that's how you strengthen the altar of your relationship with God for those who have been walking with the LORD already for some time, and for those new to the Faith, this is how you begin to build it. Remember, it is God who called you, He already knows everything you think He doesn't, and yes He still chose you. Now go kick some devil's hindquarters and walk in the Call of God upon your life! You are not your own, you're His! So the next time something messes with you, just remember they mess with Him. But don't forget to walk in love towards your brothers and sisters in Christ, they are not your enemies, they are your family!

CHAPTER 8: THE MYSTERY OF THE BLOOD

Leviticus 17:11 BSB

"For the life of the flesh is in the blood, and I have given it to you to make atonement for your souls upon the altar; for it is the blood that makes atonement for the soul."

Hebrews 9:22 BSB

"According to the law, in fact, nearly everything must be purified with blood, and without the shedding of blood there is no forgiveness."

There is an association with blood and atonement that's mentioned both in the Old Testament and in the New. I came across a separate online article about two Harvard geneticists who managed to figure out how much data can be stored into a single drop of human blood according to the article, *"...can fit on the tip of your pinky."*[28] That tells me DNA can recognize and reject foreign entities and contains memories. This explains why there are blood types, and why the human body can recognize and reject incorrect blood types as well. The fact that the human body can categorize blood types shows that the human body is actually a living organism that is much more intelligent than people give the body credit for. A single gram of blood can hold seven hundred terabytes of data. As of November 1, 2023, the largest capacity solid state drive in the world can hold one hundred terabytes of data, and that's only fourteen percent of what a single gram of human blood can store. And if you're wondering what one gram looks like, the United States penny weighs about 2.5 grams. I'm inclined to believe that our blood contains records of information and testifies of what went on in previous generations. This might be a new concept for many, but did you know that blood actually has a voice?

> Genesis 4:10 BSB
>
> "What have you done?" replied the LORD. "The voice of your brother's blood cries out to Me from the ground."

Abel's blood was crying out and testifying about his murder and most likely for vengeance against Cain. The Hebrew word used for *cries out* literally means to *shriek*. How many of us reading this book do you think had ancestors who shed blood, including but not limited to war? Do you see why this would make bloodline cleansing vital as we go deeper in our walks with the Lord? When we confess and repent we are dealing with known, unknown and even unresolved issues that might be present in our bloodlines—removing any legal rights of the enemy and through that we revoke access because in the spiritual realm *no legal rights equals no legal fights*. Furthermore, the Word gives us revelation that the Blood of Jesus is *speaking* a better word on our behalf.[30]

> Hebrews 12:24 BSB
>
> "to Jesus the mediator of a new covenant,
> and to the sprinkled blood that speaks a
> better word than the blood of Abel."

The Weapon of Repentance And The Blood of Jesus

One of the greatest weapons that we have in the kingdom of God is our repentance mingled with Jesus' Precious and Holy Blood. Blood is a spiritual currency, and it's the very thing that Jesus shed to purchase our freedom. Sometimes repentance can be greater than the sword, and times even greater than warring in the spirit. Repentance can turn an entire nation around by the power of God. Repentance can turn a marriage that's been on its toes into a loving embrace. Repentance can mend relationships that were strained, restore what was lost, grab the attention of Heaven, and it can heal relationships that were not on speaking terms. Just ask Jacob and Esau:

Genesis 33:3-4 BSB

> "But Jacob himself went on ahead and bowed to the ground seven times as he approached his brother. Esau, however, ran to him and embraced him, threw his arms around his neck, and kissed him. And they both wept."

2 Chronicles 7:14 BSB

> "and if My people who are called by My name humble themselves and pray and seek My face and turn from their wicked ways, then I will hear from heaven, forgive their sin, and heal their land."

Did you notice that the sword wasn't mentioned in the healing of the land? *But what about warring in the spirit?* If God's people focused more on obedience and repentance rather than only warring in the spirit, their blood pressure would decrease, their frustration would go away, their hearts would have more peace. They wouldn't need to strive as much, they would go farther because obedience is greater than sacrifice, and their joy would start to come back. Repentance and obedience brings healing. God was saying to repent and turn to Him wholeheartedly, and He would do the healing. Now I'm not undermining warring in the spirit because sometimes it takes saying enough is enough and standing on God's Word, but *sometimes repentance is the key to our breakthrough.* It's better to lift our hands to Heaven, lay down the pride, turn to the LORD wholeheartedly, receive a verdict and mandate from Heaven and then pick up the sword to enforce Heaven's decrees. You'll get farther doing that rather than blindly swinging your sword hoping to hit something. Repentance and obedience gives God a reason, and legal right to bless somebody. Repentance coupled with obedience is powerful.

CHAPTER 9: ARE CURSES AND BLESSINGS REAL?

If you've ever wondered if curses were real, I'm here to tell you they are. The Bible does indeed mention blessings and curses. Actually, as a matter of fact, the LORD was the one who mentioned them. Everything you read, *other than the Bible*, a good attitude to have is: "Okay that sounds good, but give me Scripture to back up your point." Wisdom, insight, revelation, and prophecy that is extremely unbiblical and contradicts the Word of God, can be ungodly doctrine or heresy. So if you're skeptical about curses and blessings, and you're looking for a Scriptural reference about blessings and curses you are welcome to take a full look at Deuteronomy twenty-eight which, I will only be partially quoting due to the sheer length of the chapter but let's take a look at blessings and curses from a Biblical point of view:

The Blessings of Obedience

Deuteronomy 28:1-14 BSB

"Now if you faithfully obey the voice of the LORD your God and are careful to follow all His commandments I am giving you today, the LORD your God will set you high above all the nations of the earth. And all these blessings will come upon you and overtake you, if you will obey the voice of the LORD your God: You will be blessed in the city and blessed in the country. The fruit of your womb will be blessed, as well as the produce of your land and the offspring of your livestock— the calves of your herds and the lambs of your flocks. Your basket and kneading bowl will be blessed. You will be blessed when you come in and blessed when you go out. The LORD will cause the enemies who rise up against you to be defeated before you. They will march out against you in one direction but flee from you in seven. The LORD will decree a blessing on your barns and on everything to which you put your hand; the LORD your God will bless you in the land He is giving you. The LORD will establish you as His holy people, just as He has sworn to you, if you keep the commandments of the LORD your God and walk in His ways. Then all the peoples of the earth will see that you are called by the name of the LORD, and they will stand in awe of you. The LORD will make you prosper abundantly— in the fruit of your womb, the offspring of your livestock, and the produce of your land—in the land that the LORD swore to your fathers to give you. The LORD will open the heavens, His abundant storehouse, to send rain on your land in season and to bless all the work of your hands. You will lend to many nations, but borrow from none. The LORD will make you the head and not the tail; you will only move upward and never downward, if you hear and carefully follow the commandments of the LORD your God, which I am giving you today. Do not turn aside to the right or to the left from any of the words I command you today, and do not go after other gods to serve them."

Deuteronomy 28:15-68 Contains the Old Testament curses and hardships for disobedience, which you can look up on your own time should you want to. But I will quote a few verses just so you can see that curses are indeed mentioned in the Bible and are most certainly not fake:

Deuteronomy 28:15-16 BSB

"If, however, you do not obey the LORD your God by carefully following all His commandments and statutes I am giving you today, all these curses will come upon you and overtake you: You will be cursed in the city and cursed in the country."

Even the Lord spoke to Adam and Eve in Genesis three and told them that they were under a curse because of what they did. The serpent, woman, and man got three unique curses with varying severities. The serpent got the lengthiest one, Adam getting the second-harshest punishment, and the women getting the shortest punishment. Eve's curse was pain during childbirth, which was not inherited by Adam or any other male in history. The curses outlined in Genesis three were gender-specific. I believe the varying levels of severity for the curses were in proportion to the varying degrees of guilt between the three. Now, as a believer don't freak out because we are not under the curse of the Law because Jesus became the curse for us when He hung on the Cross, which I will get to in a moment. However, as born again believers we should plead the Blood of Jesus over specific things that we are seeking freedom from, which can vary depending on the individual. When we do this, we are actively revoking legal rights that the enemy has had over us individually and at times even over our families. The very rights darkness was standing on become like spiritual sand that can be easily swept away by the water of God's Judgment:

Galatians 3:13-14 BSB

"Christ redeemed us from the curse of the law by becoming a curse for us. For it is written: "Cursed is everyone who is hung on a tree." He redeemed us in order that the blessing promised to Abraham would come to the Gentiles in Christ Jesus, so that by faith we might receive the promise of the Spirit."

God saved Noah, his family and a number of animals in the

Ark through water. The same water that brought salvation to one brought judgment and death to another. The water represented salvation for Noah and his family, but it also represented judgment against the world. The whole history of Noah's Ark is symbolic of water baptism for the believer. As you go into the water, it symbolizes your old self dying and new life upon coming out of the water symbolizing a new beginning just like Noah and his family.[31] When God saves us He typically introduces Himself as our Father, and as we grow in intimacy with Him and get to know Him, and open ourselves up more to Him there is a bond of Friendship that develops between us and the LORD, and as we mature He reveals Himself as the Judge. He is for us, not against us. Jesus shed His Blood, so we could be forgiven and redeemed. We have established from the Scriptures the foundation that the enemy is the adversary and accuser of the brethren. And on the other hand, God the Father, the Lord Jesus and Holy Spirit are fighting for us. If we've learned anything from the LORD, it's that true love fights and sacrifices for those it loves. After all, it's who He is:

1 John 4:8 BSB

"Whoever does not love does not know God, because God is love."

Jesus fasted Heaven for 33 years to purchase our freedom, healing, deliverance, victory, and our destinies back but more importantly our hearts, love, and *loyalty* to Him. If you're struggling with loving the LORD the way you desire to or if you're battling something, just know that Jesus has made The Way out towards freedom. Confession, repentance, His Blood, speaking life over yourself and actively applying the finished work of the cross are a part of the process to freedom. After deliverance and freedom are received, what you speak over yourself is extremely important, which leads me to the next chapter, *taming the tongue.*

CHAPTER 10.1: TAMING THE TONGUE

Proverbs 18:21 BSB

"Life and death are in the power of the tongue,
and those who love it will eat its fruit."

It's important to be mindful of what we are speaking over ourselves and to repent for speaking anything negative against ourselves, others and even the LORD. You can ask the LORD to annul the negative words spoken against you by yourself and others. This may include your family, strangers, authority figures, dad, mom, those in positions of spiritual authority over your life, the criminal justice system, police officers and the list goes on because words have power regardless of who speaks them:

James 3:2-12 BSB

"Not many of you should become teachers, my brothers, because you know that we who teach will be judged more strictly. We all stumble in many ways. If anyone is never at fault in what he says, he is a perfect man, able to control his whole body. When we put bits into the mouths of horses to make them obey us, we can guide the whole animal. Consider ships as well. Although they are so large and are driven by strong winds, they are steered by a very small rudder wherever the pilot is inclined. In the same way, the tongue is a small part of the body, but it boasts of great things. Consider how small a spark sets a great forest ablaze. The tongue also is a fire, a world of wickedness among the parts of the body. It pollutes the whole person, sets the course of his life on fire, and is itself set on fire by hell. All kinds of animals, birds, reptiles, and creatures of the sea are being tamed and have been tamed by man, but no man can tame the tongue. It is a restless evil, full of deadly poison. With the tongue we bless our LORD and Father, and with it we curse men, who have been made in God's likeness. Out of the same mouth come blessing and cursing. My brothers, this should not be! Can both fresh water and salt water flow from the same spring? My brothers, can a fig tree grow olives, or a grapevine bear figs? Neither can a salt spring produce fresh water."

Matthew 12:34-37 BSB

"You brood of vipers, how can you who are evil say anything good? For out of the overflow of the heart, the mouth speaks. The good man brings good things out of his good store of treasure, and the evil man brings evil things out of his evil store of treasure. But I tell you that men will give an account on the day of judgment for every careless word they have spoken. For by your words you will be acquitted, and by your words you will be condemned."

Matthew 15:10-11 BSB

"Jesus called the crowd to Him and said, "Listen and understand. A man is not defiled by what enters his mouth, but by what comes out of it."

Avoiding Self Sabotage

Self-sabotage is something that can easily be avoided. Self sabotage is defined as: "A deliberate action aimed at weakening someone (or something, a nation, etc.) or preventing them from being successful, through subversion, obstruction, disruption, and/or destruction." [32] Self sabotage can happen when someone speaks negatively about themselves or others out of emotion rather than the unction of God's Spirit because there is power in the tongue. If you're having a hard time with speaking life over yourself, your circumstances or even other people, just ask the LORD to heal your heart and help you speak life over yourself, your destiny and others:

Job 22:28 WEB

"You shall also decree a thing, and it shall be established to you. Light shall shine on your ways."

Psalms 141:3 BBE

"O LORD, keep a watch over my mouth; keep the door of my lips."

It's one thing for someone to speak negatively against you, but it's a totally different thing for you to speak negatively against yourself. For example, if someone's in court and a prosecuting attorney is accusing a defendant, it carries more weight if the defendant says it from their own mouth that they were guilty. When it comes to the LORD, it's much better to confess the guilt of committing something because Jesus' Blood can be received as immediate payment upon confession. We can ask Jesus for His Blood to speak and testify a better word on our behalf before the Courts of Heaven to silence the accusations of the enemy. And we can also ask the Father for a verdict of mercy, freedom, breakthrough, and a personal protection order that restrains the enemy both in the present and in the future. When we agree with the LORD, things start to shift.

CHAPTER 10.2: THE DYNAMICS OF PRAYER

Matthew 21:22 BSB

"If you believe, you will receive whatever you ask for in prayer."

Many people pray, but how many know the dynamics of prayer and how prayer works? If you've ever thought to yourself, *how does prayer work? How does saying words result in me being forgiven? How do my words have enough power and influence to cause change?* Well, in this chapter, I'm going to answer those questions by giving us some Biblical insight into how prayer works because words have power behind them.

The Power of Words

Proverbs 18:21 BSB

"Life and death are in the power of the tongue, and those who love it will eat its fruit."

The Power of Testimony

When someone is in a courtroom, their verbal testimony carries weight and causes progress in the courtroom. This is an excellent example of the power of our words. As a matter of fact, Jesus said that our words would be taken into account:

> Matthew 12:36-37 BSB
>
> "But I tell you that men will give an account on the day of judgment for every careless word they have spoken. For by your words you will be acquitted, and by your words you will be condemned."

Jesus is our High Priest, and as High Priest when we pray it enables Him to proceed with His priestly duties on our behalf because God relies on consent to move in our lives without any restriction on the Earth. Of course God intervenes, but oftentimes when He intervenes in a person's life He places that person on a believers' heart to pray for them just before He intervenes, and sometimes it's to pray for specific things as well. If you've ever had somebody on your heart strongly, and you just felt the urge to pray for them, I want to encourage you not to ignore that. Just pray for them, speak the Scriptures over them, pray for their safety, and speak life over them. While doing this, just listen to Holy Spirit and ask Him specifically to lead you in what you should pray for them.

Words Are The Catalyst To The Application of The Blood of Jesus

When we pray, we release testimony in the spirit. A part of the reason that prayer works is that when God created the world, He spoke it into existence. The LORD created man in His Image, so a measure of the power of His spoken word was also given to mankind. So when men and women of God speak, changes initiate. That's a major reason to be mindful of what we speak over ourselves and even others as well.[1] I'm preaching to myself as I'm typing this out, too. When we pray prayers of repentance in accordance to God's Word, the reason God is able to forgive us is because of the down payment Jesus made by shedding His Blood:

> Leviticus 17:11 BSB

> "For the life of the flesh is in the blood, and I have given it to you to make atonement for your souls upon the altar; for it is the blood that makes atonement for the soul."

So when we pray for forgiveness, and we confess with our mouths, we are invoking Jesus to apply His Blood as the payment for sin, transgression, and iniquity. That's why the Father can forgive us, it's not because we just said some words, but it's because we provided our testimony through confession and Jesus' Blood silenced the accusations by paying the ransom for us.

1 John 1:9 BSB

> "If we confess our sins, He is faithful and just to forgive us our sins and to cleanse us from all unrighteousness."

Revelation 12:11 BSB

> "They have conquered him by the blood of the Lamb and by the word of their testimony. And they did not love their lives so as to shy away from death."

And if necessary, the angels of heaven can be sent to enforce protection or a verdict from the throne on our behalf whether that be to protect, defend, uphold, help, minster, or deliver:

Psalms 103:20 BSB

> "Bless the LORD, all His angels mighty in strength who carry out His word, who hearken to the voice of His command."

Think of your words as a seed. If those words are in alignment with God's Word and His Will, then the LORD causes that seed to sprout and grow into something beautiful and full of life. At the same time, if the seed that you've spoken of is in alignment with death, loss, and destruction, then guess who wants to water that seed and cause it to grow? That's right, the enemy does. So it's important what we're speaking not only about ourselves, but others as well.

CHAPTER 10.3: ANSWERING THE MYSTERY OF SOVEREIGNTY

Many people believe that God is sovereign over everything. They will say that God is covering and anyone that says otherwise is a heretic or is preaching false doctrine. I'm going to show you how this statement does not stand the test of Scripture. In Genesis Moses gives us an account through defying revelation on how the Lord created the heavens in the Earth, everything that is within them and also how he created man and woman on the Earth. I created Adam and Eve before he actually made them. He said, let us make man in our image according to our likeness and a few words later he said, let them have dominion over the Earth over the fish of the sea over the birds of the air. In Scripture, we can clearly see Jesus talking about that God is Spirit, and those that worship Him must worship in Spirit and in Truth. Since God is Spirit, who did He mean by let them have dominion, and who was He speaking to? Well, we know in Scripture that the angels were present during the time of creation because the book of Job talks about how they rejoiced when the Earth was created.

Job 38:4-7 BSB

> "Where were you when I laid the foundations of the earth? Tell Me, if you have understanding. Who fixed its measurements? Surely you know! Or who stretched a measuring line across it? On what were its foundations set, or who laid its cornerstone, while the morning stars sang together and all the sons of God shouted for joy?"

One possible answer is that when the Lord was creating heaven and earth, He was speaking into the world, but also to the angels. Which would explain why He would clarify let them have dominion over the Earth over the fish of the sea over the birds of the air, the cattle over the livestock thing that creeps upon the Earth. He was excluding spirits and even Himself to a degree when He said that, which is a part of the reason, I believe, God searches for vessels and willing people to use, but so does the devil. God honors His own Word once He speaks it, even if it places a limitation on Him:

> Genesis 1:26 KJV
>
> "And God said, Let us make man in our image, after our likeness: and let them have dominion over the fish of the sea, and over the fowl of the air, and over the cattle, and over all the earth, and over every creeping thing that creepeth upon the earth."

So if God obeys His own Word, who are we not to? The Hebrew word used there that is translated as dominion in the King James Version is a Hebrew word called *radah*, it was translated as *dominion*, *reign*, and *rule* in the Old Testament. Now, some people might say that their Bibles say "Sovereign Lord," but that word *radah* is not used in the New Testament, and it's not used to describe God as Sovereign Lord in the Old either. As a matter of fact, Jesus even said that it is not the will of our Heavenly Father that one of these little ones should perish:

> Matthew 18:14 BSB

> "In the same way, your Father in heaven is not willing that any of these little ones should perish."

Are little kids perishing? Have little kids died of cancer? Have people died before their time? Have little kids been kidnapped and abducted? Unfortunately yes, they have. Is that pleasing to the Lord? *Absolutely not!*

Matthew 18:6-7 BSB

> "But if anyone causes one of these little ones who believe in Me to stumble, it would be better for him to have a large millstone hung around his neck and to be drowned in the depths of the sea. Woe to the world for the causes of sin. These stumbling blocks must come, but woe to the man through whom they come!"

For those that subscribe to the theology that God is Sovereign, why in the world does Scripture admonish us to fight the good fight of the faith in 1 Timothy if that was the case? And why in the world in Nehemiah are we admonished to fight for our families if God is totally Sovereign?

1 Timothy 6:12 BSB

> "Fight the good fight of the faith. Take hold of the eternal life to which you were called when you made the good confession before many witnesses."

Nehemiah 4:14 BSB

> "After I had made an inspection, I stood up and said to the nobles, the officials, and the rest of the people, "Do not be afraid of them. Remember the Lord, who is great and awesome, and fight for your brothers, your sons and your daughters, your wives and your homes."

God is absolutely, one hundred percent sovereign in Heaven, and He is absolutely able and powerful to intervene upon our requests here on Earth. *However, there is a reason that God gave us the ability to pray, and it is to invite Him to work on our behalf*. If God was Sovereign and in control all the time, why does Scripture admonish us to *pray without ceasing*? And if God is Sovereign, why do people sin and willfully disobey Him? Are you starting to realize how elementary and foolish, "God is in control," is beginning to sound?

1 Thessalonians 5:17 BSB

"Pray without ceasing."

It is often through prayer that God intervenes. The ideology that God is sovereign and in control all the time is a mindset that the devil loves to use to attempt to disarm God's people of a fighting spirit. God didn't create us to be a passive spiritual punching bag! My Bible says that we are more than conquerors through Him who loved us and through Christ we can do all things through Him who strengthens us. My Bible says fight the good fight of the faith. My Bible says, do not grow weary in well doing, for in due season we shall reap a harvest *if* we don't give up. The key word there is *if*. My Bible says that no weapon formed against us will prosper, and every tongue that rises up against us shall be condemned. It doesn't say that no weapon will be formed, it says that those that *are* formed *won't prosper*. We have to understand that the *Earth is not a playground, it's a battleground.* The sooner we start treating it as such is when we'll see greater victories and destinies fulfilled. Why do you think we have a shield of faith, a helmet of salvation, the breastplate of righteousness, the Sword of the Spirit, and the sandals of the Gospel of peace? If God is sovereign and in control, why do we need armor and a spiritual weapon? Even Jesus said to sell your extra cloak and buy a sword:

Luke 22:35-38 BSB

"Then Jesus asked them, "When I sent you out without purse or bag or sandals, did you lack anything?" "Nothing," they answered. "Now, however," He told them, "the one with a purse should take it, and likewise a bag; and the one without a sword should sell his cloak and buy one. For I tell you that this Scripture must be fulfilled in Me: 'And He was numbered with the transgressors.' For what is written about Me is reaching its fulfillment." So they said, "Look, Lord, here are two swords." "That is enough," He answered."

If God is sovereign, why in the world would He have created an angelic army? If God is sovereign, why is there going to be a war in Heaven before He wraps it all up? One of the greatest lies that the devil has slipped into some churches is that God is sovereign, always in control, and there's no need to fight. Calvinism takes the *go* out of the *Gospel*. Another common misconception is: *"If it's God's will, then it'll come to pass. If it's meant to be, it'll be. No need to do anything on our part."* If someone thinks that way, they're lazy and shouldn't expect anything from the LORD:

Proverbs 10:4 WEB

"He becomes poor who works with a lazy hand, but the hand of the diligent brings wealth."

Proverbs 12:24 BSB

"The hand of the diligent will rule, but laziness ends in forced labor."

If you convince an army that they need only to do nothing, then you have established yourself as the dominant fighting force that can easily plunder your opponents. There's a spiritual army that has been working overtime on the earth to steal, kill, destroy, deceive, and much of the church has been so passive about it, as if they don't have assignments to accomplish and carry out. It was not Jesus' will for people that He delivered from demons to be demon possessed by demons. He took no pleasure in the death of Lazarus, how could He? He wept! As for children perishing, we see that some things have happened on Earth outside of God's will, and outside His control because He wasn't invited into the situation, and people partnered with evil spiritual forces to accomplish certain tasks. God has the ability to control everything on Earth that He has been given the authority to. He has the power, we have the authority to allow Him to work in our lives. That's why *walking in God's will is a choice, not a mandate*—it doesn't happen automatically. You have to knowingly choose to be in God's will in order to be in God's will. This means yielding to His leading which requires obedience to do correctly, asking Him to open His doors in His will, and to shut doors that aren't in His will:

Revelation 3:7 BSB

"To the angel of the church in Philadelphia write:
These are the words of the One who is holy and true,
who holds the key of David. What He opens no one
can shut, and what He shuts no one can open."

Peter understood this. He asked Jesus to call Him out on the water. He didn't just step out of the boat before Jesus said to come out, he stepped out of the boat after Jesus told him to come. Furthermore, he identified Jesus, and then he asked Jesus to say the word, and Jesus indeed did. Then, and only then, Peter stepped out of the boat and walked not on the water, but rather on the Word. Peter wasn't walking on the water, he was walking on the word of Jesus through his faith. Even though Jesus' word was invisible. At that moment, Peter was able to physically walk on what Jesus had enabled him to walk on water. It was the Word of Jesus and his faith that kept him afloat. And it was the anchor of fear that sank him when he took his eyes off of the Anchor of his soul. Even in our lives, we can welcome God to walk on the water of our lives through our words, actions, and prayers. Why do you think in the Scriptures it says believe in your heart and confess with your mouth, and you shall be saved?

Romans 10:8-12 BSB

"But what does it say? "The word is near you; it is in your

mouth and in your heart," that is, the word of faith we are proclaiming: that if you confess with your mouth, "Jesus is Lord," and believe in your heart that God raised Him from the dead, you will be saved. For with your heart you believe and are justified, and with your mouth you confess and are saved. It is just as the Scripture says: "Anyone who believes in Him will never be put to shame." For there is no difference between Jew and Greek: The same Lord is Lord of all, and gives richly to all who call on Him,"

James 1:5 BSB

"Now if any of you lacks wisdom, he should ask God, who gives generously to all without finding fault, and it will be given to him."

God gives wisdom to those who ask Him. If God is sovereign, why does the Bible tell us to ask, seek, pray, knock, believe, and be obedient? It's because we have an important part to play! There are three options in life:

1. Do It Your Way.

2. Do It The Devil's Way.

or

3. Do It God's Way.

That's it, there is no in between. Good actions are rewarded, and wickedness is often recompensed. Even in Joshua's day, God set before them to choose between death or life, obedience or disobedience. He clearly outlined the blessings of obedience, and the curses of rebellion. The word literally says, choose this day whom you will serve:

Joshua 24:15 BSB

"But if it is unpleasing in your sight to serve the LORD, then choose for yourselves this day whom you will serve, whether the gods your fathers served beyond the Euphrates, or the gods of the Amorites in whose land you are living.

As for me and my house, we will serve the LORD!"

Psalms 81:13-16 BSB

"If only My people would listen to Me, if Israel would follow My ways, how soon I would subdue their enemies and turn My hand against their foes! Those who hate the LORD would feign obedience, and their doom would last forever. But I would feed you the finest wheat; with honey from the rock I would satisfy you."

Proverbs 8:32-36 BSB

"Now therefore, my sons, listen to me, for blessed are those who keep my ways. Listen to instruction and be wise; do not ignore it. Blessed is the man who listens to me, watching daily at my doors, waiting at the posts of my doorway. For whoever finds me finds life and obtains the favor of the LORD. But he who fails to find me harms himself; all who hate me love death."

We can choose to live on the mountain of obedience, blessings, prosperity, discipline, peace, self-control, love and holiness, or you can choose the other side of the spectrum which I highly wouldn't recommend because it's costly. Not only for you but for your children, trust me, if you've seen kids who are a mess, just look at their parents, you'll likely see where they got it from. , and not all bad kids are a result of parents, but most of the time it's the case with some exceptions. Now, of course, they are actions that can be taken for the greater good of others such as stopping a school or mass shooter, protecting your family, house, kids to give an example. You can't tell me someone walking in rebellion is walking in God's will. Now of course it's not about being perfect, or even a perfect parent, but simply putting in the effort is a huge part. When you try, you're already fifty percent there. Think about it, let's say hypothetically you started a business with the goal of getting your first million. The fact that you started the business means you're already fifty percent done with your goal. The other half is working to acquire the second part of your goal! You can't sit at the table of demons and drink from the cup of the LORD. It's either One or the other, you can only serve One Master—people can't serve both God and the devil or else they will love one and despise the other...

CHAPTER 10.4: ASK IN FAITH AND YOU SHALL RECEIVE

Luke 11:9-10 BSB

"So I tell you: Ask, and it will be given to you; seek, and you will find; knock, and the door will be opened to you. For everyone who asks receives; he who seeks finds; and to him who knocks, the door will be opened."

Faith is the belief that *what* you pray and ask for *will be* granted beyond a shadow of a doubt. Faith does not doubt, faith demonstrates. A genuine and healthy faith produces good works without the person even trying to do it because it will naturally flow from them:

James 2:26 KJV

"For as the body without the spirit is dead, so faith without works is dead also."

It was by faith that Abel offered a better sacrifice than his brother Cain. It was by faith that Enoch was raptured. It was by faith that Noah built the Ark. It was by faith that Abraham obeyed God to move out of his father's house and move into a foreign country to do what God called him to do. It was by faith that Joseph told the Israelites to bring his body up with them when God visited and delivered them from the iron furnace of Egypt. Likewise, it was by faith the walls of Jericho came crashing down. It was by faith that Samuel anointed David as the next king. It was by faith that David took his shot at Goliath with the Stone. It was by faith that men and women of God overcame the world, and it is through faith that we please God, not by works alone:

1 John 5:4 BSB

"because everyone born of God overcomes the world. And this is the victory that has overcome the world: our faith."

Hebrews 11:6 BSB

"And without faith it is impossible to please God, because anyone who approaches Him must believe that He exists and that He rewards those who earnestly seek Him."

So remember, when you ask and pray, even including the prayers contained within this book, *ask in faith.*

CHAPTER 11: KEEPING A CLEAN SLATE BEFORE HEAVEN

When Moses was writing the *Torah* by divine revelation, also known as the *Pentateuch* (the first five books of the Bible), he wasn't present yet at the time of the people that he was writing about, yet he knew all these details, including the meticulous ones. So much so that he even knew what God was thinking:

> Genesis 8:20-22 BSB
>
> "Then Noah built an altar to the LORD. And taking from every kind of clean animal and clean bird, he offered burnt offerings on the altar. When the LORD smelled the pleasing aroma, He said in His heart, "Never again will I curse the ground because of man, even though every inclination of his heart is evil from his youth. And never again will I destroy all living creatures as I have done. As long as the earth endures, seed time and harvest, cold and heat, summer and winter, day and night shall never cease."

How did Moses know what the LORD said in His Heart? It was by *divine revelation and his intimacy* with God that unveiling His Heart to Moses:

> Psalm 25:14 KJV

> "The secret of the LORD is with them that fear him;
> And he will shew them his covenant." [33]

Moses feared the LORD, and he had a covenant with Him. The reason he knew what he did was because God showed him Adam to Noah, Noah to Abraham, Abraham to Joseph and his brothers, from Joseph all the way to their day in the wilderness. Every meticulous detail that he wrote down from Genesis to Deuteronomy came from the memory of God. God keeps an excellent record of events, words, situations, and our obedience. If the LORD took notice of a group of Israelite sons that obeyed their father's instruction, how much more when we obey His?

Jeremiah 35:18-19 BSB

> "Then Jeremiah said to the house of the Rechabites: "This is what the LORD of Hosts, the God of Israel, says: 'Because you have obeyed the command of your forefather Jonadab and have kept all his commandments and have done all that he charged you to do, this is what the LORD of Hosts, the God of Israel, says: Jonadab son of Rechab will never fail to have a man to stand before Me.'"

If you're wondering how the LORD keeps a record of our obedience, I believe I have a partial answer to this question, which leads me into my next chapter, *the Books of Heaven*.

CHAPTER 12: THE BOOKS OF HEAVEN

The Bible mentions several books. Some of them are physical and some spiritual. We access those through divine revelation from the Spirit of God. The Word talks about multiple books that are in Heaven, so let's take a look at some of them:

Physical Books

Book of The Covenant

Exodus 24:7 ASV

"And he took the book of the covenant, and read in the audience of the people: and they said, All that Jehovah hath spoken will we do, and be obedient."

Book of The Wars

Numbers 21:14 ASV

"Wherefore it is said in the book of the Wars of Jehovah, Vaheb in Suphah, And the valleys of the Arnon,"

Book Of The Chronicles

1 Kings 14:19 ASV

"And the rest of the acts of Jeroboam, how he warred, and how he reigned, behold, they are written in the book of the chronicles of the kings of Israel."

Book of The Kings of Israel

1 Chronicles 9:1 ASV

"So all Israel were reckoned by genealogies; and, behold, they are written in the book of the kings of Israel. And Judah was carried away captive to Babylon for their transgression."

Book of The Purchase

Jeremiah 32:12 KJV

"and I gave the evidence of the purchase unto Baruch the son of Neriah, the son of Maaseiah, in the sight of Hanameel mine uncle's son, and in the presence of the witnesses that subscribed the book of the purchase, before all the Jews that sat in the court of the prison."

Heavenly Books

The Book of Life is mentioned an additional seven times in Revelation, along with these Scriptures below:

Book of Life

Psalms 69:28 ASV

"Let them be blotted out of the book of life, And not be written with the righteous."

Philippians 4:3 KJV

"And I intreat thee also, true yokefellow, help those women which laboured with me in the gospel, with Clement also, and with other my fellowlabourers, whose names are in the book of life."

"My Book"

Exodus 32:31-33 KJV

"And Moses returned unto the LORD, and said, Oh, this people have sinned a great sin, and have made them gods of gold. Yet now, if thou wilt forgive their sin–; and if not, blot me, I pray thee, out of thy book which thou hast written. And the LORD said unto Moses, Whosoever hath sinned against me, him will I blot out of my book."

Book of The LORD

Isaiah 34:16 KJV

"Seek ye out of the book of the LORD, and read: no one of these shall fail, none shall want her mate: for my mouth it hath commanded, and his spirit it hath gathered them."

Book of Remembrance

Malachi 3:16 KJV

"Then they that feared the LORD spake often one to another: and the LORD hearkened, and heard it, and a book of remembrance was written before him for them that feared the LORD, and that thought upon his name."

Did you notice what the LORD said in Exodus? He said: *"My Book."* The LORD didn't correct Moses and say that He *didn't* have a book, but rather, He actually confirmed that He *does* have a book. The LORD is the Author and Finisher of our faith. [34] The Word could have said He is the Creator of our faith, but instead the Bible says He is the Author of our faith. Does that put a new perspective on seeing the LORD as the Author of eternal salvation and the Author and Finisher of our faith?

Hebrews 5:9 ASV

"and having been made perfect, he became unto all them that obey him the author of eternal salvation;"

Hebrews 12:2 KJV

"looking unto Jesus the author and finisher of our faith; who for the joy that was set before him endured the cross, despising the shame, and is set down at the right hand of the throne of God."

We even see in the Word that there are multiple books in Heaven. We see this specifically in the book of Daniel and in the book of Revelation:

Daniel 7:9-10 BSB

"As I continued to watch, thrones were set in place, and the Ancient of Days took His seat. His clothing was white as snow, and the hair of His head was like pure wool. His throne was flaming with fire, and its wheels were all ablaze. A river of fire was flowing, coming out from His presence. Thousands upon thousands attended Him, and myriads upon myriads stood before Him. The court was convened, and the books were opened."

Revelation 20:11-12 KJV

"And I saw a great white throne, and him that sat on it, from whose face the earth and the heaven fled away; and there was found no place for them. And I saw the dead, small and great, stand before God; and the books were opened: and another book was opened, which is the book of life: and the dead were judged out of those things which were written in the books, according to their works."

What the prophet Daniel saw in his heavenly vision, John the beloved apostle also saw when he was writing the book of Revelation. As a matter of fact, they both noticed the Throne and then the books, in that specific order. So yes, there are books in Heaven. Some of them are waiting to be written into the earth through the LORD's chosen instruments—His scribes. Are you willing to let the LORD use you to author His story?

CHAPTER 13: NOT UNDER LAW, BUT UNDER GRACE

Now in light of the context of what the LORD said in Exodus 32 that He would blot out those who sinned against Him. I want to address this before I go any further. We as New Testament believers are not under law, but we are under grace. We have to understand this because legalism is ugly.

Romans 6:14 KJV

"For sin shall not have dominion over you: for ye are not under the law, but under grace."

Galatians 4:3-7 KJV

"Even so we, when we were children, were in bondage under the elements of the world: but when the fulness of the time was come, God sent forth his Son, made of a woman, made under the law, to redeem them that were under the law, that we might receive the adoption of sons. And because ye are sons, God hath sent forth the Spirit of his Son into your hearts, crying, Abba, Father. Wherefore thou art no more a servant, but a son; and if a son, then an heir of God through Christ."

Hebrews 7:18-19 KJV

"For there is verily a disannulling of the commandment going before for the weakness and unprofitableness thereof.

For the law made nothing perfect, but the bringing in of a better hope did; by the which we draw nigh unto God."

Disannul [35]

"To annul, do away with; to cancel."

Annul [36]

1. "To formally revoke the validity of."

2. "To dissolve (a marital union) on the grounds that it is not valid."

The Old Testament law is done away with under the New Covenant. It was to serve the purpose of providing a code of conduct for the Israelites until Messiah came and fulfilled the requirements of the Law. Once Jesus came and fulfilled the Law, it was formally revoked. Now that we've established that Scripturally, let's continue with the teaching.

CHAPTER 14: UNLOCKING THE MYSTERY OF UNANSWERED PRAYER

If you've been a Christian for any length of time, you might have witnessed someone praying for the sick to see a miraculous healing. Number one, thank the LORD for men and women of God who are willing to step out in faith and pray for the miraculous, that in and of itself is a step of faith. But I want to address something that I believe will be an answer to some questions people have had in past cases where people were standing in faith, praying for a miracle. Maybe they didn't quite see the miraculously healing or breakthrough they wanted. I want to start off by saying the prayer of faith indeed works. Doubting and questioning are not meant to be in the picture. I believe that some past: "Unanswered prayers," were actually prayers that the LORD desired to answer, but legally couldn't do so in certain instances without violating His Word or a spiritual law. Now this may be an entirely new concept for some but if you just went: "Huh, what do you mean? I thought God was all powerful?" He is! But He is also Righteous and Just, and He cannot violate spiritual laws. This can be one of the reasons why someone can pray for someone and there is an immediate answer, and pray the same thing over someone else and experience resistance. I believe that the Body of Christ has had lots of zeal, but inadequate knowledge and wisdom on how to aim that zeal accurately. This is where wisdom and revelation come into play. I love what the ASV says in the Word concerning Apollos:

Acts 18:26 ASV

> "and he began to speak boldly in the synagogue. But when Priscilla and Aquila heard him, they took him unto them, and expounded unto him the way of God more accurately."

Aquila and Priscilla saw the potential and grace of God that Apollos carried, and it was evident in his zeal. So they took the time to invest in him by explaining the Way of God more accurately to him. Sometimes it's not about how *hard* someone prays, sometimes it's about *how* they pray:

Ecclesiastes 10:10 ASV

> "If the iron be blunt, and one do not whet the edge, then must he put to more strength: but wisdom is profitable to direct." [37]

Things happen when we pray–period. Prayer is often the *forerunner* for a move of God. But while we're praying it's useful to have revelation, wisdom, understanding, and knowledge because it makes our prayers more effective and spot on. I like to call this the four levels of understanding. The Word marries the Spirit of wisdom and revelation together in Ephesians. You'll see people at all kinds of levels in life concerning how much of the four levels of understanding they carry. The revelation, wisdom, understanding, and knowledge that they carry is a direct indicator of their level of devotion, hunger, and commitment to God. People with lots of the four levels of understanding live, think, walk, speak, act and pray differently.

The Four Levels of Understanding

1. <u>Revelation</u>
2. <u>Wisdom</u>
3. <u>Understanding</u>
4. <u>Knowledge</u>

Ephesians 1:17 ASV

"that the God of our Lord Jesus Christ, the Father of glory, may give unto you a spirit of wisdom and revelation in the knowledge of him;"

When you know *how* things work, you gain understanding. When you gain understanding, you gain wisdom. When you gain wisdom along with godly character, God can pour out revelation because He knows you won't abuse it, but you'll use it properly for His Glory and His Kingdom. Giving revelation to someone with evil motives is not on God's agenda because they will hurt others by having it. This is why God builds our character so that *when* He gives us revelation, He can trust us to use it in a way that pleases and honors Him instead of grieving Him. The apostle Paul was originally called by his birth name—Saul. Saul wasn't getting the revelations he was getting until He had a revelation of Who Jesus really was. Saul thought Jesus was a sect leader, Paul knew He was the Son of God. The first revelation Paul got was that Jesus was the Messiah. Only after that, Holy Spirit began to unpack spiritual mysteries to Paul. Isn't it like that for all of us who are saved? The first revelation we ever received was the Person of Jesus and our need for a Savior, then the Holy Spirit started building upon that foundational revelation of Jesus as Messiah because He is the Rock and firm foundation. God can give us much required revelation, wisdom, understanding, and knowledge to help us navigate prayer more effectively and see breakthroughs more consistently and faster. There have been times when God has desired to answer certain prayers. But a part of the reason that some prayers didn't seem to be answered I believe is because of outstanding legal issues in the spirit that were not dealt with prior to praying. Of course there are other factors, one being that people praying, are called to pray in faith rather than fear:

James 5:15 BSB

"And the prayer offered in faith will restore the one who is sick. The Lord will raise him up. If he has sinned, he will be forgiven."

There should be absolutely zero fear in the prayers of a Christian because the worst that can happen is an early homecoming to be with the Lord and for someone to grieve over that. That means that there should be absolutely zero fear in the prayers of a Christian because the worst that can happen is an early homecoming to be with the Lord. For someone to grieve over that means that they are grieving not for the person, but because of selfish reasons as to how the temporary loss will affect them emotionally. They are grieving not for the person, but because of selfish reasons as to how the temporary loss will alter them emotionally. I'm not being harsh, I'm just being honest. Let's say, for example, someone was on their sickbed and a group from a church came in to pray for healing. They saw a miraculous breakthrough and full recovery after the prayer, and they went and prayed again for someone else without seeing the immediate breakthrough. Sometimes the reason others have seen immediate breakthroughs and other times felt resistance is not because of a lack of faith. But rather, it could have possibly been legal rights in the spirit that have not yet been addressed and or dealt with properly. If a person that had ancestors in secret societies received prayer, the secret society that their ancestors were involved in made them swear an oath. If they left or disclosed secret information, their future descendants would be cursed with a health issue. The ancestor agreed and swore a vow and curse that included future descendants of their family line. As this ancestor went deeper into the secret society they realized that it was not what they thought it was and left, and upon leaving they started experiencing health issues with varying severity. In order to see the person get healed instead of rebuking the sickness, that should be addressed in a session in the Courts of Heaven with prayers of repentance. Renouncement of sins, transgressions, iniquities, curses, oaths, vows, and covenants and agreements made within the secret society that this person's ancestors were involved in to break these curses. Why would Jesus absorb a curse if there wasn't a reason to?

Galatians 3:13-14 BSB

"Christ redeemed us from the curse of the law by becoming a curse for us. For it is written: "Cursed is everyone who is hung on a tree." He redeemed us in order that the blessing promised to Abraham would come to the Gentiles in Christ Jesus, so that by faith we might receive the promise of the Spirit."

After that, then you pray for the person and see miraculous healing and breakthrough because there aren't any legal mountains in the way. With no legal rights, the enemy can't hold on anymore. If you've ever known anyone who was in a legal battle such as a custody case between children, those legal battles can be a mountain. The people who came to pray for this person have a couple of options and Jesus said if we in faith tell a mountain to move it will obey us:

Mark 11:23 BSB

"Truly I tell you that if anyone says to this mountain, 'Be lifted up and thrown into the sea,' and has no doubt in his heart but believes that it will happen, it will be done for him."

1. Pray Casually.

2. Pray Fervently With Misdirected Zeal.

3. Pray With Discernment And Listen To What Holy Spirit Reveals.

Isaiah 11:2 BSB

The Spirit of the LORD will rest on Him— the Spirit of wisdom and understanding, the Spirit of counsel and strength, the Spirit of knowledge and fear of the LORD.

Ephesians 1:17 BSB

"that the God of our Lord Jesus Christ, the glorious Father, may give you a spirit of wisdom and revelation in your knowledge of Him."

1 Corinthians 12:4-11 BSB

"There are different gifts, but the same Spirit. There are different ministries, but the same Lord. There are different ways of working, but the same God works all things in all people. Now to each one the manifestation of the Spirit is given for the common good. To one there is given through the Spirit the message of wisdom, to another the message of knowledge by the same Spirit, to another faith by the same Spirit, to another gifts of healing by that one Spirit, to another the working of miracles, to another prophecy, to another distinguishing between spirits, to another speaking in various tongues, and to still another the interpretation of tongues. All these are the work of one and the same Spirit, who apportions them to each one as He determines."

The Menorah

There is one Spirit, but multiple aspects of Who He is. The seven branches of the menorah are symbolic of the sevenfold Spirit of God found in Isaiah 11. He is the Spirit of Revelation!

Numbers 8:2 BSB

"Speak to Aaron and tell him: 'When you set up the seven lamps, they are to light the area in front of the lampstand.'"

1. Spirit of The LORD
2. Spirit of Wisdom
3. Spirit of Understanding
4. Spirit of Counsel
5. Spirit of Strength
6. Spirit of Knowledge
7. Spirit of the Fear of the LORD

Revelation 4:5 KJV

"And out of the throne proceeded lightning and thundering's and voices: and there were seven lamps of fire burning before the throne, which are the seven Spirits of God."

It's much more effective to ask Holy Spirit what the root issue is and proceed in His wisdom on how to deal with it. We will all receive great breakthroughs when The Holy Spirit is leading men and women in prayer, rather than men and women trying to lead Him. After all, Holy Spirit knows a thing or two about intercession:

Romans 8:26-27 BSB

"In the same way, the Spirit helps us in our weakness.

> For we do not know how we ought to pray, but the Spirit Himself intercedes for us with groans too deep for words. And He who searches our hearts knows the mind of the Spirit, because the Spirit intercedes for the saints according to the will of God."

By being led in prayer by the very One that knows the Mind of the Father, how can we not see great breakthroughs?

CHAPTER 15: WISDOM IN PRAYER

Ecclesiastes 9:18 BSB

"Wisdom is better than weapons of war, but
one sinner destroys much good."

In a day and age where weapons are quite common the Word of God tells us that wisdom is better than weapons of war? Did I read that correctly? Yet again, the Scriptures emphasize the value of wisdom even over weapons of warfare. This means that wisdom is the leveraging force between victory and defeat. If you've ever heard the phrase: "Work smarter not harder," it rings true both in the natural and spiritual realm. There is a way to pray strategically and hit the target much more efficiently, and accurately through wisdom and strategy, which is something I believe the modern day western church has lacked, that is at least until now. The Hebrew word for wisdom sakal first appears in Genesis 3, and it means wisdom, and to lead wittingly. Wit is defined as the natural ability to perceive and understand, shrewdness, and sound mental faculties. In the first 0.002523% of the Bible we already see wisdom show up which tells us something. Think of it, let's say you were given a limited page limit to write a letter to someone you've known for a long time but haven't spoken to in a while. Chances are you're going to mention the important details early on in the letter, while covering major details. The fact that out of the Bible's one thousand one-hundred eighty nine chapters, wisdom makes an appearance in chapter three shows us that wisdom is a foundational principle. And in order to build efficiently and correctly God's way, wisdom is not only a recommendation, but it is a necessity.

Matthew 7:24-27 BSB

> "Therefore everyone who hears these words of Mine and acts on them is like a wise man who built his house on the rock. The rain fell, the torrents raged, and the winds blew and beat against that house; yet it did not fall, because its foundation was on the rock. But everyone who hears these words of Mine and does not act on them is like a foolish man who built his house on sand. The rain fell, the torrents raged, and the winds blew and beat against that house, and it fell—and great was its collapse!"

In the Biblical Greek, the two words for wisdom are *sophia* and *phronimos*. They both in their simplest form mean wisdom, but they also mean thoughtful. In order to have powerful prayers, we have to marry wisdom and prayer together while we talk to the Lord. Just like a lawyer articulates their case before the judge and jury in a specific way, we too can present our cases with wisdom, and through the Holy Spirit's leading, which will lead to breakthrough. Too often the church has seen prayer as a battle which indeed there is that aspect to it however, prayer is a legal battle well before it is a spiritual battle. If you secure the legal battle, you've already won the spiritual battle, and that is exactly what I hope to help you accomplish through this book by showing you how to pray strategically to see breakthrough, and those stubborn mountains you've been praying to move. And some of you have prayed for a long time, and I, for one, say it's time for a breakthrough!

CHAPTER 15.1: WHY DO WE PRAY

If you've ever wondered why we even pray, that's a valid question. Why do we pray? Is it to make us feel better? Not really, although prayer does do that. Is it because we're required to? No, but it's necessary to maintain a strong relationship with the Lord. I mean really, why do we pray, why did the Lord give us the ability to speak in the first place? What is the importance of prayer? And why does God look for people to do it? Well to understand this, we have to go back to Genesis chapter one. The most important reason that we pray is to give God the invitation to come do what He wants to do when we pray in accordance to His Word and His will. Let us examine this in further detail:

> Genesis 1:26 BSB
>
> "Then God said, "Let Us make man in Our image, after Our likeness, to rule over the fish of the sea and the birds of the air, over the livestock, and over all the earth itself and every creature that crawls upon it."

Who was God referring to when He said *them*? Why even say *them* in the first place, why not just say let man and woman have dominion? Well, it was because the angels of God were present during creation which, I believe, is why the LORD specified let them have dominion. Because He was excluding Himself and the angels to a degree from meddling in the Earth without the consent of humanity. Why else do you think both the LORD and the devil look for willing vessels to use? It's because it's a spiritual law, which we will get into in more detail a bit later within the book. Don't skip and read ahead, just enjoy the process because the book builds upon itself which, by the way, is a great indicator that it's true. Let's continue by looking at Job thirty-eight t get a better understanding of Creation from Heaven's perspective:

Job 38:4-7 BSB

"Where were you when I laid the foundations of the earth? Tell Me, if you have understanding. Who fixed its measurements? Surely you know! Or who stretched a measuring line across it? On what were its foundations set, or who laid its cornerstone, while the morning stars sang together and all the sons of God shouted for joy?"

We know from the Scriptures that both the LORD and angels are spiritual beings from John 4:24 and Hebrews 1:13-14. So when God gave the dominion mandate to Adam and Eve, He forever etched their role of rulership on this Earth until He returns.

Dominion

Power or the use of power; sovereignty over something; stewardship, supremacy. A kingdom, nation, or other sphere of influence; governed territory.

Much like, the owner of the house entrusts his stewards to rule the house while he's away. It doesn't mean that they own the house, it just means that the owner gave them permission to watch over the home, protect it, defend those within it, and keep it clean until he comes back. Does that sound oddly familiar to anyone?

Luke 19:13 KJV

"And he called his ten servants, and delivered them ten pounds, and said unto them, Occupy till I come."

God gave us as humans dominion, or otherwise commonly

known as rulership, over the Earth to occupy it until He returns. Remember the parable of the virgins? Five were wise and five were foolish, half were wise and half were not ready:

Matthew 25:1-4 BSB

"At that time the kingdom of heaven will be like ten virgins who took their lamps and went out to meet the bridegroom. Five of them were foolish, and five were wise. The foolish ones took their lamps but did not take along any extra oil. But the wise ones took oil in flasks along with their lamps."

In order to better understand who Adam and Eve were, we have to understand better Who the Lord is, are you catching what I'm saying? The LORD had a harsh word between Himself and the priests of Malachi's day in which He calls Himself a Great King, let's take a look:

Malachi 1:14 BSB

"But cursed is the deceiver who has an acceptable male in his flock and vows to give it, but sacrifices a defective animal to the Lord. For I am a great King," says the LORD of Hosts, "and My name is to be feared among the nations."

And in whose image did God create man and woman? That's right, in God's Image He created *them*, both male and female He created *them* as we have read in Genesis 1:26. Which means that a part of our identity in the Lord Jesus are kings, which is exactly what John the Beloved apostle penned in the Book of Revelation:

Revelation 1:6 LSV

"He has also made us kings and priests to His God and Father, to Him—the glory and the power through the ages of the ages! Amen."

Another aspect of Who Jesus is can be found in the Book of Hebrews, which is a fascinating book to read if you're going through it for the first time with little to no background knowledge in Jewish culture. Nevertheless, it gives us insight into the Priesthood of Jesus:

Hebrews 3:1 WEB

"Therefore, holy brothers, partakers of a heavenly calling, consider the Apostle and High Priest of our confession, Jesus;"

Hebrews 6:20 BSB

"where Jesus our forerunner has entered on our behalf. He has become a high priest forever in the order of Melchizedek."

One of the hidden revelations about this is the fact that Jesus descended from the line, also commonly referred to as tribe, of Judah. The fact that Jesus is the Eternal High Priest gives us an idea that He is not the Mediator of the Old Covenant, but of a New and better Covenant. It was enacted not by the blood of animal sacrifices, bulls, or even goats, but that of a Spotless Lamb without blemish. This is because in order to be a Levitical priest, you had to be from the descendants of Levi. Jesus wasn't. He came from the line of Judah, of which the Law of Moses doesn't mention any priests that would have come from the tribe of Judah. However, in an old blessing that Jacob (Israel), spoke to his sons before he passed away we get a peep through the window of prophecy that Jacob spoke to Judah his son before he passed away:

Genesis 49:10-12 BSB

"The scepter will not depart from Judah, nor the staff from between his feet, until Shiloh comes and the allegiance of the nations is his. He ties his donkey to the vine, his colt to the choicest branch. He washes his garments in wine, his robes in the blood of grapes. His eyes are darker than wine, and his teeth are whiter than milk."

Shiloh in this context is a reference to Jesus. All throughout

Scripture, we can see Jesus tied into it. All of this to say, priests pray, kings declare, and prophets prophesy. The role of a priest is to pray, and that is what we are called to do, is to pray. It's the holy trifecta. Since we hold the status and office of priesthood, Jesus being our High Priest, when we pray things start to shift when we pray by faith. When we prophesy through His Spirit's leading, and when we declare with our mouths the *rhema* (spoken) and logos (written) Word of God.

Matthew 6:9 WEB

"... Pray like this..."

And that is why we pray...

CHAPTER 16: THE JOSHUA GENERATION

There was a certain day when I was in a prayer meeting and the LORD started speaking to me. So I wrote down what I was hearing, released it to the body and then later saved it in a digital note. Here is a portion of what the LORD said:

Prophetic Word

"Conquer And Occupy."

"Conquer And Occupy."

"Conquer And Occupy."

"I'm Raising Up A Joshua Generation, That's Not Going To Bow The Knee To Baal, But That Are Going To Kiss The Face Of The God Of Jacob."

After reading that, you might be asking yourself: *"What is the Joshua generation exactly?"* To understand the Joshua Generation, we have to biblically understand an aspect of Joshua in connection to the Tent of Meeting:

Exodus 33:7-11 BSB

"Now Moses used to take the tent and pitch it at a distance outside the camp. He called it the Tent of Meeting, and anyone inquiring of the LORD would go to the Tent of Meeting outside the camp. Then, whenever Moses went out to the tent, all the people would stand at the entrances to their own tents and watch Moses until he entered the tent. As Moses entered the tent, the pillar of cloud would come down and remain at the entrance, and the LORD would speak with Moses. When all the people saw the pillar of cloud standing at the entrance to the tent, they would stand up and worship, each one at the entrance to his own tent. Thus the LORD would speak to Moses face to face, as a man speaks to his friend. Then Moses would return to the camp, but his young assistant Joshua, son of Nun, would not leave the tent."

Understanding The Joshua Generation

Joshua was clearly a young man who loved God's Presence. Why else would he not want to depart from the Tabernacle? *The Joshua Generation is a warring generation.* If you've ever read the book of Joshua, you'll find that out very quickly. Another thing about the Joshua generation is that *they came from a generation of parents who didn't really understand the fullness of what God had for them.* They came from parents that didn't quite understand intimacy with God but understood religion. They didn't understand the intimate heart of a warrior that both Joshua and David had. Joshua had a mentor by the name of Moses, and it was Moses who bore the majority of the responsibilities of leading the people, hearing from the LORD, writing and releasing what he heard the LORD say to the rest of the congregation. That kind of sounds like a pastor if you ask me, but I digress. However, Joshua didn't depart from the Tabernacle of Meeting because of his heart, but also he was destined for another call. This call was not to shepherd the wilderness generation but rather lead them into the promised land and that was going to require another set of skills, a different heart and a warrior spirit. He had a leader who was his mentor and temporary spiritual covering which allowed him to soak in the secret place of God's Presence. I believe in that sacred time that he spent in the Tabernacle with the LORD, that God used the time he spent in His Presence to develop an intimate heart in him. Which also led to a brazen strength that enabled him to become the man God used to bring the children of Israel into the promised land successfully. Joshua was a man who *lingered* in the Presence of the LORD. He wasn't a Levitical priest, so he didn't have duties to attend to within the Tabernacle. Nor was he a part of the division of Levites that set up and tore down the Tabernacle when it was time to move camps. So why was he lingering in the Tabernacle of Meeting? It was because that's where the Presence of God was! When God spoke and said: *"I'm raising up a Joshua Generation,"* what we have to understand is Joshua *lingered* in the Presence of the LORD and God cultivated an intimate heart and a warrior spirit in Joshua in the process.

Generation of Faith

Before Joshua began to lead the children of Israel into the Promised Land, he began doubting if he was even capable of leading such a large congregation of God's people. However, this didn't last long because he went from fear to faith, to the point so much so that he was the only recorded person in Scripture who commanded the sun to stand still in faith and it did. The Joshua generation will be a generation full of biblical faith. There was a day when Joshua and his army were in battle with an enemy, and they were losing sunlight. This would have made it difficult to fight because they didn't have night vision goggles back then, so fighting a physical enemy you can't was not easy. So instead of panicking and begging the LORD to change the circumstance or saying: "Oh no, what are we going to do?" Joshua spoke to the circumstance. We see here the dominion and power exercised by a man of God over creation. And by the way, this was way before Jesus even physically came! How much more now that Jesus has come? Joshua spoke to the situation and commanded it to *shift*!

Sun Stand Still

Joshua 10:12-13 BSB

On the day that the LORD gave the Amorites over to the Israelites, Joshua spoke to the LORD in the presence of Israel: "O sun, stand still over Gibeon, O moon, over the Valley of Aijalon." So the sun stood still and the moon stopped until the nation took vengeance upon its enemies. Is this not written in the Book of Jashar? "So the sun stopped in the middle of the sky and delayed going down about a full day."

The fact that Joshua spoke to the LORD and commanded the sun and the moon to stand still until the purpose of the LORD was accomplished, shows that there was a divine partnership between the LORD and Joshua. Usually it's the other way around. God speaks and then man listens; but in Joshua's case, he spoke and the LORD listened. This is what you can call *influence* in the spirit realm. When you speak, because of your relationship and obedience to God, He chooses to listen and obey what you speak. God is God, and man is man. Let's get that straight. But this goes to show because Joshua honored the LORD, the LORD honored him:

1 Samuel 2:30 KJV

"Wherefore the LORD God of Israel saith, I said indeed that thy house, and the house of thy father, should walk before me for ever: but now the LORD saith, Be it far from me; for them that honour me I will honour, and they that despise me shall be lightly esteemed."

Moses

Moses cried out to the LORD when the Israelites were pinned and Pharaoh's chariots were headed their direction, and they were not happy. Moses turned it to the LORD, and the LORD turned it back to Moses, saying: "Why are you crying out to

Me?" And when Moses did what he could, God did what Moses couldn't in his own strength:

Zechariah 4:6 BSB

"So he said to me, "This is the word of the LORD to Zerubbabel: Not by might nor by power, but by My Spirit, says the LORD of Hosts."

Exodus 14:15 BSB

"Then the LORD said to Moses, "Why are you crying out to Me? Tell the Israelites to go forward."

Exodus 14:21 BSB

"Then Moses stretched out his hand over the sea, and all that night the LORD drove back the sea with a strong east wind that turned it into dry land. So the waters were divided,"

And as for Joshua, do you see the stark contrast and growth that he went through in such a short period of time? Joshua was an intimate warrior filled with Biblical faith who didn't mind lingering in the Presence of the LORD. There was something about Joshua that gave him *favor* with God and I think it was his *lingering*, his *faithful obedience* and his *bold faith*. He didn't come from the best example of obedience and faith, but regardless he learned from the past generations' mistakes, conquered the land and saw great victory where the generation before him saw great defeat. The Joshua generation took the Promised Land. So when the LORD says He's raising up a Joshua generation, look out because *Kingdom Warriors are arising*! It's time to take the land! *Hallelujah*!

CHAPTER 17: FOCUSING ON INTIMACY WITH GOD

April 21, 2022

"Passion Leads To Intimacy. Don't Forsake Intimacy."

This was one of the last things that I heard Him say after He spoke about the Joshua Generation in that Word–that's what He ended with. Why is that? Well, how many know that if you aren't careful you can get so focused on spiritual warfare, that you could neglect worship and intimacy. ***The spiritual warfare mentality and the intimacy of the heart need a proper balance.*** Take David for example, God took him from a humble beginning in the shepherds field to the man placed on the throne of Israel. Something David understood was how to be a mighty warrior on the battlefield, and also be personally intimate with God. He opened his heart up to God, and many times cried out personal secrets to Him. We even see this in the Psalms:

Psalms 27:4 ASV

"One thing have I asked of Jehovah, that will I seek after: That I may dwell in the house of Jehovah all the days of my life, To behold the beauty of Jehovah, And to inquire in his temple."

The same man that we read about slaying enemies on the

battlefield is the same man that we see singing his heart out to God in intimate songs of worship–some of those songs even he himself personally composed. I think God saw a side of David's heart that only the LORD Himself saw. A side of David's heart that he didn't even show to his wives. While I'm on this topic, I'm going to interject and say to every man, this is your confirmation that God's will is for you to have *one wife*. It was the way God intended, and just because some men in the Bible had more than one wife doesn't mean it was God's will for them or even that it was somehow pleasing to Him. Loyalty goes a long way, both for your spouse, and to God. Not to mention, the woman that you marry is pretty important, just ask King Solomon:

1 Kings 11:1-9 BSB

"King Solomon, however, loved many foreign women along with the daughter of Pharaoh—women of Moab, Ammon, Edom, and Sidon, as well as Hittite women. These women were from the nations about which the LORD had told the Israelites, "You must not intermarry with them, for surely they will turn your hearts after their gods." Yet Solomon clung to these women in love. He had seven hundred wives of royal birth and three hundred concubines—and his wives turned his heart away. For when Solomon grew old, his wives turned his heart after other gods, and he was not wholeheartedly devoted to the LORD his God, as his father David had been. Solomon followed Ashtoreth the goddess of the Sidonians and Milcom the abomination of the Ammonites. So Solomon did evil in the sight of the LORD; unlike his father David, he did not follow the LORD completely. At that time on a hill east of Jerusalem, Solomon built a high place for Chemosh the abomination of Moab and for Molech the abomination of the Ammonites. He did the same for all his foreign wives, who burned incense and sacrificed to their gods. Now the LORD grew angry with Solomon, because his heart had turned away from the

LORD, the God of Israel, who had appeared to him twice."

The reason I bring David up is to serve as a reminder to not neglect intimacy. If you've been a Christian for over a few years, you've probably run into someone who has had a very warfare oriented mentality, which is not a bad thing. But if that's the only mentality that they have, they are missing out on the fullness and beauty that intimacy with God has to offer. God gave us two legs for balance, two eyes for depth perception, two ears for proper surround sound hearing and two hands for a reason, but He only gave us one heart. Why? Because our hearts are meant to be wholly His and not shared with idols. God has not called His people to have a divided heart but rather a unified spirit with Him. Do you know what the LORD called idols in the Scriptures multiple times? He called them lovers. *May this serve as a reminder in the midst of the battlefield to not neglect our King.*

CHAPTER 18: DOMINION, A GIFT FROM GOD

God bestowed dominion to Adam and Eve over the earth when He created the earth, and as their heirs, we inherit this as well. We see this establishment of the law of dominion in the very first book of the Bible–Genesis. Unfortunately, many have not understood or known of this law of dominion due to the fact that they haven't explored the truth of God's Word:

Genesis 1:26 KJV

"And God said, Let us make man in our image, after our likeness: and let them have dominion over the fish of the sea, and over the fowl of the air, and over the cattle, and over all the earth, and over every creeping thing that creepeth upon the earth."

What we have to understand is that God is a Spirit. When He said let them have dominion, He spoke and released a universal Law in the spirit realm. Now even He Himself is subject to because God's Word is so powerful that when God speaks, even He obeys His Word:

John 4:24 KJV

"God is a Spirit: and they that worship him must worship him in spirit and in truth."

Houston We Had A Problem

Prior to the fall, Adam had full dominion to take that serpent that was speaking to his wife Eve and hurl that thing into kingdom come. But the problem was Adam felt the enticement and lustful desire for the fruit of the tree and loved his wife more than God and sacrificed his relationship with God over his wife Eve. Adam knew what she did, and he understood the consequences because God told him what would happen, so he ate of the tree also. When he yielded to the voice of his wife and the voice of the serpent, he willingly submitted himself under the serpent's authority. Adam didn't get deceived, Eve did. Adam knew what he was about to do. His thought process would've likely been something along the lines of: "If I eat this I die too, but if I don't eat of this fruit then I live with her." That was likely one of his thoughts during that period, and I think he ate that fruit so he could die with her rather than live without her because God told him plain as day that when he ate of it he would surely die. Look what happened to both of them and not only that but the rest of humanity. It's the real origin of the popular phrase *ride or die*. I believe his love for Eve surpassed his love for God which caused him to elevate her above Him and through him exalting Eve they both were brought low. Imagine what would've happened if they were in agreement and told the serpent no and threw him out of the garden and called upon God and told Him what happened? We'd likely be in paradise on this side of heaven right now! But as most of us know, that's sadly not what happened. The only reason death is even in our vocabulary is because of sin. If sin never got introduced into humanity, we'd be living forever right now. Jesus brought and bought back our redemption. It's exactly what redemption means, to bring back something to its original value. For something to be redeemed, it had to have been in a better condition than when it fell. Through this whole drama in the garden, a big issue was created. First Timothy and the epistle of Romans gives us some insight into dominion and obedience:

1 Timothy 2:14 KJV

"And Adam was not deceived, but the woman being deceived was in the transgression."

Romans 6:12-18 BSB

"Therefore do not let sin reign in your mortal body so that you obey its desires. Do not present the parts of your body to sin as instruments of wickedness, but present yourselves to God as those who have been brought from death to life; and present the parts of your body to Him as instruments of righteousness. For sin shall not be your master, because you are not under law, but under grace. What then? Shall we sin because we are not under law, but under grace? Certainly not! Do you not know that when you offer yourselves as obedient slaves, you are slaves to the one you obey, whether you are slaves to sin leading to death, or to obedience leading to righteousness? But thanks be to God that, though you once were slaves to sin, you wholeheartedly obeyed the form of teaching to which you were committed. You have been set free from sin and have become slaves to righteousness."

Had Adam listened to Eve, if she spoke out of Holy Spirit's wisdom rather than the influence of Satan, things wouldn't have happened the way they did. Unfortunately for Adam, that wasn't the case, and out of his love for Eve, he partook of the forbidden fruit as well, thereby submitting to his enemy. When Adam submitted to Satan, he went from being the superior to being a slave, and that's where the transfer of dominion initially happened. The reason I believe God said let them have dominion (talking about mankind) is because He didn't want other spirits to have dominion on the earth. But the enemy found a loophole by tempting them to submit and obey him to transfer that dominion willingly to the rebellious spirit we call Satan and his rebellious fallen angels. Because of that a massive problem emerged and that is the reason a lot of suffering has taken place in human history because dominion was given to a spirit that hates mankind. It was never God's fault.

Houston We Have The Solution

But this is where it gets good. So good in fact that it's literally called the Good News. God was looking for a man to use to shift the earth. The LORD couldn't find a perfectly submitted man to partner with Him for the transfer of dominion out of the hands of Satan and back into His control—well, that is, at least until Jesus. This is one of the reasons Jesus is called the Second Adam because what the original Adam failed to do the Second Adam accomplished. God was looking for a man to stand in the gap to use, but here was the problem, no one was above the dominion of the enemy. Everyone was under the dominion of sin. Some have thought that Jesus didn't even exist until He was born, but this is most definitely not the case, and we can clearly see this in the Gospel of John. Out of all the gospels, this one really focuses on revealing the divinity of Jesus Christ:

John 1:1-5 BSB

"In the beginning was the Word, and the Word was with God, and the Word was God. He was with God in the beginning. Through Him all things were made, and without Him nothing was made that has been made. In Him was life, and that life was the light of men. The Light shines in the darkness, and the darkness has not overcome it."

John 1:9-14 BSB

"The true Light who gives light to every man was coming into the world. He was in the world, and though the world was made through Him, the world did not recognize Him. He came to His own, and His own did not receive Him. But to all who did receive Him, to those who believed in His name, He gave the right to become children of God—

children born not of blood, nor of the desire or will of man, but born of God. The Word became flesh and made His dwelling among us. We have seen His glory, the glory of the one and only Son from the Father, full of grace and truth."

John 8:51-58 BSB

"Truly, truly, I tell you, if anyone keeps My word, he will never see death." "Now we know that You have a demon!" declared the Jews. "Abraham died, and so did the prophets, yet You say that anyone who keeps Your word will never taste death. Are You greater than our father Abraham? He died, as did the prophets. Who do You claim to be?" Jesus answered, "If I glorify Myself, My glory means nothing. The One who glorifies Me is My Father, of whom you say 'He is our God.' You do not know Him, but I know Him. If I said I did not know Him, I would be a liar like you. But I do know Him, and I keep His word. Your father Abraham rejoiced that he would see My day. He saw it and was glad." Then the Jews said to Him, "You are not yet fifty years old, and You have seen Abraham?" "Truly, truly, I tell you," Jesus declared, "before Abraham was born, I am!"

John 17:1-5 BSB

"When Jesus had spoken these things, He lifted up His eyes to heaven and said, "Father, the hour has come. Glorify Your Son, that Your Son may glorify You. For You granted Him authority over all people, so that He may give eternal life to all those You have given Him. Now this is eternal life, that they may know You, the only true God, and Jesus Christ, whom You have sent. I have glorified You on earth by accomplishing the work You gave Me to do. And now, Father, glorify Me in Your presence with the glory I had with You before the world existed."

Exodus 3:13-14 BSB

"Then Moses asked God, "Suppose I go to the Israelites and

say to them, 'The God of your fathers has sent me to you,' and they ask me, 'What is His name?' What should I tell them?" God said to Moses, "I AM WHO I AM. This is what you are to say to the Israelites: 'I AM has sent me to you.'"

Isaiah 48:12-13 BSB

"Listen to Me, O Jacob, and Israel, whom I have called: I am He; I am the first, and I am the last. Surely My own hand founded the earth, and My right hand spread out the heavens; when I summon them, they stand up together."

Revelation 1:17 BSB

"When I saw Him, I fell at His feet like a dead man. But He placed His right hand on me and said, "Do not be afraid. I am the First and the Last,"

Jesus didn't just come into existence one day, He helped create the world along with the Father and Holy Spirit. Jesus laid aside the Garments of Divinity to take up the garments of a Servant in order to help the Father and Holy Spirit in the redemption of humanity and the redemption of dominion back to a pre-fall state. This is why the Book of Psalms and the Book of Hebrews says:

Psalms 40:6-8 LSV

"Sacrifice and present You have not desired, But a body You have prepared for me, Burnt and sin-offering You have not asked. Then I said, "Behold, I have come, In the roll of the scroll it is written of me, I have delighted to do Your pleasure, my God, And Your law is within my heart."

Hebrews 10:5-7 LSV

"For this reason, coming into the world, He says, "Sacrifice and offering You did not will, and a body You prepared for Me; in burnt-offerings, and concerning sin-offerings, You did not delight. Then I said, Behold, I come (in a volume of the scroll it has been written concerning Me), to do, O God, Your will."

One of the reasons that the Lord Jesus came in a human body can be seen in the book of revelation being dominion related in order to transfer dominion of the earth back to mankind. But the Lord did not stop there, He took back several keys.[38]

> Revelation 1:17-18 BSB
>
> "When I saw Him, I fell at His feet like a dead man. But He placed His right hand on me and said, "Do not be afraid. I am the First and the Last, the Living One. I was dead, and behold, now I am alive forever and ever! And I hold the keys of Death and of Hades."

Jesus reclaimed dominion of not just the Earth, but death and hell itself. This is one of the reasons that Jesus is called the Last Adam in Scripture. And the same One that has the keys to death, hell, and the grave said to you and me:

> Luke 10:19 ASV
>
> "Behold, I have given you authority to tread upon serpents and scorpions, and over all the power of the enemy: and nothing shall in any wise hurt you."

> 1 Corinthians 15:45 BSB
>
> "So it is written: "The first man Adam became a living being;" the last Adam a life-giving spirit."

When we submit to God, we actually inherit and carry a measure of His Authority that He gives to us. It was more than likely that the LORD said this to them towards the second half of His Ministry upon the earth because they needed to go through some character building. Before, they were going to be trusted with great authority and power. Kind of like the time when the sons of thunder asked about calling down fire on a city and Jesus corrected them. Our God's Ministry is Life and Life abundantly:

> John 10:10 BSB

"The thief comes only to steal and kill and destroy. I have come that they may have life, and have it in all its fullness."

I believe a part of treading on serpents and scorpions is being in right standing with God. I haven't met anybody who was actively walking in disobedience and rebellion towards God and was walking in total victory. We can see an example of this with Cain and Abel:

Genesis 4:2-5 KJV

"And she again bare his brother Abel. And Abel was a keeper of sheep, but Cain was a tiller of the ground. And in process of time it came to pass, that Cain brought of the fruit of the ground an offering unto the LORD. And Abel, he also brought of the firstlings of his flock and of the fat thereof. And the LORD had respect unto Abel and to his offering: but unto Cain and to his offering he had not respect. And Cain was very wroth, and his countenance fell."

This is why God spoke to Cain to subdue what lied in wait at the door, but unfortunately many of us know what went down instead:

Genesis 4:6-8 BSB

"Why are you angry," said the LORD to Cain, "and why has your countenance fallen? If you do what is right, will you not be accepted? But if you refuse to do what is right, sin is crouching at your door; it desires you, but you must master it. Then Cain said to his brother Abel, "Let us go out to the field." And while they were in the field, Cain rose up against his brother Abel and killed him."

Almost every person in the army is submitted to a superior officer. Hypothetically, let's say there is a lieutenant in an army and this lieutenant is submitted to the general. The general of the army has a superior officer that he himself is submitted to, and so on and so forth, all the way up the chain of command. So if the lieutenant is challenged by those *under* his authority, it's within his *power* to bring correction because he carries the *authority* granted to him by his superior officer. The authority that the lieutenant carries gives him the right to exercise power *lawfully*. So if the lieutenant were to continually and willfully rebel against his superior officer, how long do you think that he would maintain his position and authority as lieutenant? When the lieutenant is submitted to the authority of his superior officer, he actually carries a measure of the power and authority that his superior officer has granted him because of his rank. This is why the centurion said to the Lord Jesus that he himself was a man also submitted under authority. As a centurion in the military, he realized that authority and power comes from submitting to superior officers. He realized that the authority and power that Jesus carried was because of His submission to His Superior Officer–God the Father:[39]

Matthew 8:9 BSB

"For I myself am a man under authority, with soldiers under me. I tell one to go, and he goes; and another to come, and he comes. I tell my servant to do something, and he does it."

The Master's Example of Submission

Luke 22:39-43 ASV

"And he came out, and went, as his custom was, unto the mount of Olives; and the disciples also followed him. And when he was at the place, he said unto them, Pray that ye enter not into temptation. And he was parted from them about a stone's cast; and he kneeled down and prayed, saying, Father, if thou be willing, remove this cup from me: nevertheless not my will, but thine, be done. And there appeared unto him an angel from heaven, strengthening him."

God the Father is the Superior Officer, the Lord Jesus is the Commander of the Armies of the LORD and the Holy Spirit is also an Officer on Earth. He, along with the angels of Heaven, enforce verdicts from the Throne of God:

Psalms 103:20 BSB

"Bless the LORD, all His angels mighty in strength who carry out His word, who hearken to the voice of His command."

And He has called us ambassadors, His governing Bride upon the earth. And let's just be honest here, if Jesus Himself submitted to the Father, who are we not to? We are His *ekklēsía*.[40] The city of Athens actually had an *ekklēsía* which was a politically governing body of the city. According to the history website, the assembly's meetings were held around forty times a year. Within these meetings, the *ekklēsía* had power to make decisions about war, foreign policy, write laws, revise laws, approve or condemn the conduct of public officials and the power to ostracize a citizen. This caused them to be expelled from the Athenian city-state for ten years. This is much like the United States Congress. An *ekklesía* is a governing assembly of believers that carry a measure of *authority* and *power* from the Kingdom of Heaven that the LORD has given to them because they are One Body with Him. The measure of authority is entirely dependent upon that *ekklesía's* obedience. The greater the obedience, the greater the authority:

Ephesians 5:28-33 KJV

"So ought men to love their wives as their own bodies. He that loveth his wife loveth himself. For no man ever yet hated his own flesh; but nourisheth and cherisheth it, even as the LORD the church: for we are members of his body, of his flesh, and of his bones. For this cause shall a man leave his father and mother, and shall be joined unto his wife, and they two shall be one flesh. This is a great mystery: but

I speak concerning Christ and the church. Nevertheless, let every one of you in particular so love his wife even as himself; and the wife see that she reverence her husband."

Speaking of the Bride, Jesus is currently awaiting the command from the Father:Son, go get Your bride–she's ready." But until that day, Jesus told us to *occupy* till He comes:

Luke 19:13 KJV

"And he called his ten servants, and delivered them ten pounds, and said unto them, Occupy till I come."

We are His governing Bride on earth. Remember, we've already established in Genesis 1:26 that God gave man and woman *dominion*. To add to that, the Lord Jesus gave us the *power and authority* over all the power of the enemy:

Genesis 1:26 ASV

"And God said, Let us make man in our image, after our likeness: and let them have dominion over the fish of the sea, and over the birds of the heavens, and over the cattle, and over all the earth, and over every creeping thing that creepeth upon the earth."

Luke 9:1 ASV

"And he called the twelve together, and gave them power and authority over all demons, and to cure diseases."

Luke 10:19 ASV

"Behold, I have given you authority to tread upon serpents and scorpions, and over all the power of the enemy: and nothing shall in any wise hurt you."

Luke 24:49 BSB

"And behold, I am sending the promise of My Father upon you. But remain in the city until you have been clothed with power from on high."

Dominion [42]

1. Power or the use of power; sovereignty over something.

2. Predominance; ascendancy.

3. A kingdom, nation, or other sphere of influence; governed territory.

Authority [43]

1. Power or right to make or enforce rules or give orders; or a position having such power or right.

2. Persons, regarded collectively, who occupy official positions of power; police or law enforcement.

5. Official permission; authorization to act in some capacity on behalf of a ruling entity.

Power [44]

2. Control or coercion, particularly legal or political (jurisdiction).

So Biblically speaking man and woman have dominion (rulership), born again believers also have *authority* (official permission; authorization to act in some capacity on behalf of a ruling entity) and *power* (control or coercion, particularly legal or political jurisdiction). The church was never meant to be powerless, the church was meant to be powerful!

Restoration Of Power To The Lord's Church

"My Church Will Be Powerful Again, And I Will Show The Enemy That My Church Is A Force To Be Reckoned With Once Again. The Latter Glory Is Going To Be So Much Greater Than The Former Glory, I AM The LORD And There Is No Other, None Other Than Me Can Save. And I Will Show The Principalities And Powers The Manifold Wisdom Of God Through My Church Once Again. I AM. Says The

Lord Jesus, "Shalom My People, Shabbat Shalom." [45]

CHAPTER 19: LAWS GOVERNING THE SPIRIT REALM

We have to understand that there are laws governing the spiritual realm, just like there are laws in the physical. Violating these laws can have consequences. God is the Judge, and a Judge can't administer justice without laws being put in place that grant Him the right to administer justice. The KJV Bible mentions *"the law of"* a total of ninety-three times and *"law of"* a total of one-hundred times. We can see some laws in the spiritual realms listed within the Word, and I'm not going to list all of them, but I'm going to list a few here for us so that we can see some examples:

The Law of Dominion

Genesis 1:26 ASV

"And God said, Let us make man in our image, after our likeness: and let them have dominion over the fish of the sea, and over the birds of the heavens, and over the cattle, and over all the earth, and over every creeping thing that creepeth upon the earth."

The Law of Truth

Malachi 2:6 ASV

"The law of truth was in his mouth, and unrighteousness was not found in his lips: he walked with me in peace and uprightness, and turned many away from iniquity."

The Law of Faith

Romans 3:27 ASV

"Where then is the glorying? It is excluded. By what manner of law? of works? Nay: but by a law of faith."

The Law of God

Psalms 37:31 ASV

"The law of his God is in his heart; None of his steps shall slide."

The Law of Firstfruits

Exodus 23:19 BSB

"Bring the best of the firstfruits of your soil to the house of the Lord your God…"

Romans 7:22 ASV

"For I delight in the law of God after the inward man:"

The Law of The Spirit

Romans 8:1-2 KJV

"There is therefore now no condemnation to them which are in Christ Jesus, who walk not after the flesh, but after the Spirit. For the law of the Spirit of life in Christ Jesus hath made me free from the law of sin and death."

The Law of The Spirit of Life

Romans 8:2 KJV

"For the law of the Spirit of life in Christ Jesus hath made me free from the law of sin and death."

The Law of Sin And Death

Romans 8:1-2 KJV

"There is therefore now no condemnation to them which

are in Christ Jesus, who walk not after the flesh, but after the Spirit. For the law of the Spirit of life in Christ Jesus hath made me free from the law of sin and death."

The Law of Christ

Galatians 6:2 KJV

"Bear ye one another's burdens, and so fulfil the law of Christ."

The Law of Liberty

James 1:25 KJV

"But whoso looketh into the perfect law of liberty, and continueth therein, he being not a forgetful hearer, but a doer of the work, this man shall be blessed in his deed."

James 2:12 KJV

"So speak ye, and so do, as they that shall be judged by the law of liberty."

The Law of Confession

1 John 1:9 BSB

"If we confess our sins, He is faithful and just to forgive us our sins and to cleanse us from all unrighteousness."

CHAPTER 20: THE REVELATION OF THE CROSS

Have you ever wondered why Jesus died the way He did, or even why He died at all? Why on a wooden cross? Why was He held up by nails? If you've ever asked those questions, I want to affirm that they are valid questions, and you don't have to feel guilty for questioning these details. If you've thought to yourself: "I don't get it. I know He loves me, but why did He do it the way He did?" After reading this chapter, you will have a deeper understanding and revelation of the Cross. This revelation and power packed chapter will help answer those questions. And I pray that the Holy Spirit unpacks ever deeper revelation to both you and to me as we read. So without further ado, let's dive right in! Hallelujah!

The Cross | God's Answer To Humanity

One night as I was listening to an audio Bible and following along I came across the parable where Jesus talked about the two sons and in specifically in Luke sixteen verse twenty-three:

Luke 16:23 BSB

> "In Hades, where he was in torment, he looked up and saw Abraham from afar, with Lazarus by his side."

I got curious about one of the words and decided to look

up what the word torment was, and it's the Koine Greek word βάσανος, pronounced *basanos*, and it means torture or torment. I wasn't satisfied with that definition, so I did a bit of research and come to find out there it's also a Hebrew word pronounced the same way and spelled באסן. And take a guess at what it means, it means tree, specifically referring to the Tree of Life. [46]* Again, my jaw dropped when I saw this because it immediately connected that the Tree of Life was Jesus. He endured the βάσανος (torment) of the באסן (the Tree of Life). He endured the torture of the tree of life. Jesus said He is the way, the truth, and the life. When Jesus was crucified on the tree, Life was hanging on those two wooden beams and thereby making it the tree of life. The Greek word *basanos* is used in the New Testament a total of three times, which could symbolize the three days that Jesus' Body was in the tomb or the commonly seen three nails that Jesus took. Some believe it may have been four nails, but three is a common depiction.

Forget The Former Things
Isaiah 46:9-13 KJV

> "Remember the former things of old: for I am God, and there is none else; I am God, and there is none like me, declaring the end from the beginning, and from ancient times the things that are not yet done, saying, My counsel shall stand, and I will do all my pleasure: calling a ravenous bird from the east, the man that executeth my counsel from a far country: yea, I have spoken it, I will also bring it to pass; I have purposed it, I will also do it. Hearken unto me, ye stouthearted, that are far from righteousness: I bring near my righteousness; it shall not be far off, and my salvation shall not tarry: and I will place salvation in Zion for Israel my glory."

The LORD declares the end from the beginning. The Hebrew word for declare in this context is *nagad* which means to

---

* Bashan was known for its presence of strong oak trees — Jesus could've likely suffered on an oak beam(s). Oaks were symbolic of strength!

announce or manifest. A part of how the cross works is due to the fact of God's knowledge and foresight of the beginning, middle and end of time. God saw every transgression people would commit from Adam to the very last person born and this is the reason Jesus was able to place one down payment for the past, present, and the future. If you would like a Biblical example of God seeing the future, when the LORD spoke to Abraham about his future descendants He said that they would serve a foreign nation for 400 years before being delivered:

Genesis 15:12-16 BSB

"As the sun was setting, Abram fell into a deep sleep, and suddenly great terror and darkness overwhelmed him. Then the LORD said to Abram, "Know for certain that your descendants will be strangers in a land that is not their own, and they will be enslaved and mistreated four hundred years. But I will judge the nation they serve as slaves, and afterward they will depart with many possessions. You, however, will go to your fathers in peace and be buried at a ripe old age. In the fourth generation your descendants will return here, for the iniquity of the Amorites is not yet complete."

God foresaw well into the future and had already calculated the debt that was to pay at Calvary. The cross was in reality the most expensive debt cancellation payment ever. The Cross was a spiritual transaction that took place, and this is why there was an immediate resurrection of saints after Jesus gave up His Spirit. The cross was the dowry for His Bride–the church without spot or wrinkle.

The Bride's Dowry And the Bridegroom's Sacrifice

Acts 20:28 WEB

"Take heed, therefore, to yourselves, and to all the flock, in which the Holy Spirit has made you overseers, to shepherd the assembly of the LORD and God which he purchased with his own blood."

Ephesians 5:25-27 WEB

"Husbands, love your wives, even as Christ also loved the assembly, and gave himself up for it; that he might sanctify it, having cleansed it by the washing of water with the word, that he might present the assembly to himself gloriously, not having spot or wrinkle or any such thing; but that it should be holy and without defect."

The Koine Greek word used here as *gave* is παραδίδωμι, pronounced *paradidomi*, and it literally means to surrender or yield up. Exactly how Jesus said in the garden that He could have called for a legion of angels, and they would've come to His rescue, but instead chose to surrender Himself up. In ancient Israel, when a man desired to marry a woman, he would pay a dowry for the bride:

Genesis 34:12 BSB

"Demand a high dowry and an expensive gift, and I will give you whatever you ask. Only give me the girl as my wife!"

The Hebrew word used here for dowry is מֹהַר, pronounced *môhar*, and it means a price for a wife. Notice how the father of what would have been the groom tried negotiating a marriage agreement for his son with Israel, who was the father of Dinah.

The Parallel Between Christ The Bridegroom And The Church

The Lord Jesus paid for His Bride at Calvary. Except it didn't cost Him money, it cost Him His life. Just like when God put Adam into a deep sleep, which was symbolic of death, he took a rib from Adam's side, closed up the flesh, made Eve out of the rib and then presented her to Him. Likewise, this is what happened to Jesus. The only difference was Adam's bride was physical and Jesus' Bride is Spiritual:

The Church Is Born

Jesus was put to death on the Cross and as He slept the sleep of death the church was being born. Another reason the Lord Jesus is called the Last Adam in Scripture is because the Church was birthed out of Him:

1 Corinthians 15:45 KJV

"And so it is written, The first man Adam was made a living soul; the last Adam was made a quickening spirit."

John 19:30-34 ASV

"When Jesus therefore had received the vinegar, he said, It is finished: and he bowed his head, and gave up his spirit. The Jews therefore, because it was the Preparation, that the bodies should not remain on the cross upon the sabbath (for the day of that sabbath was a high day), asked of Pilate that their legs might be broken, and that they might be taken away. The soldiers therefore came, and brake the legs of the first, and of the other that was crucified with him: but when they came to Jesus, and saw that he was dead already, they brake not his legs: howbeit one of the soldiers with a spear pierced his side, and straightway there came out blood and water."

Why does the Word go into detail about blood and water coming out of His lungs? Because blood and water flow during birth.

Understanding The Spiritual Trades of The Cross

On top of being the birthplace of the Church, Jesus's Cross was a trading platform. This is the place where the payment for sin and the payment for the law of sin and death was ultimately made, which was death:

Romans 6:23 WEB

> "For the wages of sin is death, but the free gift of
> God is eternal life in Christ Jesus our Lord."

The beating, scourging, nails and scars that He took were for our healing. Job was absolutely right when he said the LORD gives and takes away—He gives us what's good and takes away from us what's bad! He forgives our sins, takes away diseases and in return gives us everlasting life. God is the giver of every *good* and *perfect* gift!

> Job 1:21 BSB
>
> "saying: "Naked I came from my mother's womb, and naked I will return. The LORD gave, and the LORD has taken away. Blessed be the name of the LORD."
>
> Matthew 7:11 BSB
>
> "So if you who are evil know how to give good gifts to your children, how much more will your Father in heaven give good things to those who ask Him!"
>
> James 1:17 BSB
>
> "Every good and perfect gift is from above, coming down from the Father of the heavenly lights, with whom there is no change or shifting shadow."
>
> Hebrews 7:22 KJV

"By so much was Jesus made a surety of a better testament."

One day I ended up looking a definition for the word *surety* that I came across in the Book of Hebrews and found out that it means:

<u>Surety</u> [48]

3. A promise to pay a sum of money in the event that another person fails to fulfill an obligation.

The Divine Exchange

In other words the debt we owed, Jesus became the surety,

and paid the price on our behalf. It's the equivalent of having a co-signer signing as collateral in the event that you could not pay the debt owed by yourself, and thereby becoming the responsibility of the third party to pay it on your behalf. Jesus is our Heavenly Co-Signer! And I want us to take a look at Isaiah 53:1-5 along with some other Scriptures so that we can really see what exactly Jesus took away from us and paid for us to have:

Isaiah 53:1-5 ASV

"Who hath believed our message? and to whom hath the arm of Jehovah been revealed? For he grew up before him as a tender plant, and as a root out of a dry ground: he hath no form nor comeliness; and when we see him, there is no beauty that we should desire him. He was despised, and rejected of men; a man of sorrows, and acquainted with grief: and as one from whom men hide their face he was despised; and we esteemed him not. Surely he hath borne our griefs, and carried our sorrows; yet we did esteem him stricken, smitten of God, and afflicted. But he was wounded for our transgressions, he was bruised for our iniquities; the chastisement of our peace was upon him; and with his stripes we are healed."

The Spiritual Exchanges of The Cross

1. Jesus Took Our Rejection To Give Us His Acceptance

Isaiah 61:1-3, 6-9 KJV

"He was despised, and rejected of men;"

Ephesians 1:6 KJV

"to the praise of the glory of his grace, wherein he hath made us accepted in the beloved."

2. Jesus Took Away Our Sorrows And Grief To Give Us His Joy

"a man of sorrows, and acquainted with grief:"

Nehemiah 8:10 BSB

"Then Nehemiah told them, "Go and eat what is rich, drink what is sweet, and send out portions to those who have nothing prepared, since today is holy to our Lord. Do not grieve, for the joy of the LORD is your strength."

John 15:11 BSB

"I have told you these things so that My joy may be in you and your joy may be complete."

3. Jesus Took Away Shame To Give Us His Boldness

"And as one from whom men hide their face he was despised; and we esteemed him not."

Proverbs 28:1 BSB

"The wicked flee when no one pursues, but the righteous are as bold as a lion."

4. Jesus Took Away Brokenheartedness To Give Us A Healed Heart

"The Spirit of the LORD GOD is upon me; because the LORD hath anointed me to preach good tidings unto the meek; he hath sent me to bind up the brokenhearted,"

5. Jesus Came To Give Liberty To The Captives And The Opening Of The Prison To Those Who Are Bound

"to proclaim liberty to the captives, and the opening of the prison to them that are bound;"

6. Jesus Came To Proclaim The Acceptable Year Of The LORD

"to proclaim the acceptable year of the LORD,"

7. Jesus Came To Proclaim The Day Of The Vengeance Of Our God

"and the day of vengeance of our God;"

John 16:11 KJV

"...of judgment, because the prince of this world is judged."

8. Jesus Came To Comfort All That Mourn

"to comfort all that mourn; to appoint unto them that mourn in Zion,"

9. Jesus Came To Give Us Beauty For Ashes

"to give unto them beauty for ashes,"

10. Jesus Came To Give Us The Oil Of Joy Instead Of Mourning

"the oil of joy for mourning,"

11. Jesus Came To Give Us The Garment Of Praise For The Spirit Of Heaviness

"the garment of praise for the spirit of heaviness;"

12. Came To Establish Us As Oaks Of Righteousness Planted Of The LORD For His Glory

"that they might be called trees of righteousness, the planting of the LORD, that he might be glorified."

13. Jesus Came To Establish Us As A Royal Priesthood

"But ye shall be named the Priests of the LORD: men shall call you the Ministers of our God: ye shall eat the riches of the Gentiles, and in their glory shall ye boast yourselves."

1 Peter 2:9 KJV

"But ye are a chosen generation, a royal priesthood, an holy nation, a peculiar people; that ye should shew forth the praises of him who hath called you out of darkness into his marvellous light:"

14. Jesus Came To Exchange Shame For A Double Portion

"For your shame ye shall have double;"

15. Jesus Came To Exchange Confusion For Rejoicing And A Sound Mind

"and for confusion they shall rejoice in their portion:"

2 Timothy 1:7 LSV

"for God did not give us a spirit of fear, but of power, and of love, and of a sound mind;"

16. Jesus Came To Give Us Double

"therefore in their land they shall possess the double:"

17. Jesus Came To Give Us Joy

"everlasting joy shall be unto them."

18. Jesus Came To Establish A Covenant Through

His Death Between Us And The Father

Psalm 50:5 KJV

"Gather my saints together unto me; Those that have made a covenant with me by sacrifice."

"For I the LORD love judgment, I hate robbery for burnt offering; and I will direct their work in truth, and I will make an everlasting covenant with them. And their seed shall be known among the Gentiles, and their offspring among the people: all that see them shall acknowledge them,"

19. Jesus Came So That We Could Be Blessed

"...that they are the seed which the LORD hath blessed."

20. Jesus Came So That We Could Be Adopted Into God's Family

John 14:18-20 BSB

"I will not leave you as orphans; I will come to you. In a little while, the world will see Me no more, but you will see Me. Because I live, you also will live. On that day you will know that I am in My Father, and you are in Me, and I am in you. Whoever has My commandments and keeps them is the one who loves Me. The one who loves Me will be loved by My Father, and I will love him and reveal Myself to him."

Galatians 4:6 BSB

"And because you are sons, God sent the Spirit of His Son into our hearts, crying out, "Abba, Father!""

Do you see all the exchanges listed within the Word? And that's not all of them! Every single one of these promises are for every born again believer! All the Promises of God are yes and amen *in* Christ Jesus! This means that every promise that's in His Word is for us. They became our *inheritance* once we get born again–filled with the Holy Spirit. We are the sons and daughters of God, and as sons and daughters we have an inheritance from our Father!

2 Corinthians 1:20 KJV

"For all the promises of God in him are yea, and in him Amen, unto the glory of God by us."

Galatians 3:7 LSV

"know, then, that those of faith—these are sons of Abraham,"[50]

Where Did Jesus Go During Those Three Days?

If you've ever wondered what Jesus did during those three days while His physical body was laying in the tomb. I've got some Scripture to help answer that question:[51]

Zechariah 9:11 WEB

"As for you also, because of the blood of your covenant, I have set free your prisoners from the pit in which is no water."

1 Peter 3:18-19 BSB

"For Christ also suffered for sins once for all, the righteous for the unrighteous, to bring you to God. He was put to death in the body but made alive in the Spirit, in whom He also went and preached to the spirits in prison"

Ephesians 4:8-9 BSB

"This is why it says: "When He ascended on high, He led captives away, and gave gifts to men." What does "He ascended" mean, except that He also descended to the lower parts of the earth?"

Jesus not only tasted death for us all, but He Himself descended into the abyss. How else would He strip the enemy from the keys?

Revelation 1:17-18 KJV

"And when I saw him, I fell at his feet as dead. And he laid his right hand upon me, saying unto me, Fear not; I am the first and the last: I am he that liveth, and was dead; and, behold, I am alive for evermore, Amen; and have the keys of hell and of death."

Jesus has the keys of death and of hell itself and due to this coupled with His payment for sins is the reason that we now as His disciples can also raise the dead through God's power. And guess who He gave the keys to?

Matthew 16:19 BSB

"I will give you the keys of the kingdom of heaven. Whatever you bind on earth will be bound in heaven, and whatever you loose on earth will be loosed in heaven."

Since Jesus has the keys to death and hell itself. Who is to say that we can't ask the Lord to open the gates of hell itself, pull a soul from its grasp and return that soul back into its rightful body to receive salvation? After all, it's God's will that everyone be saved and come into the knowledge of the truth:

1 Timothy 2:3-4 BSB

"This is good and pleasing in the sight of God our Savior, who wants everyone to be saved and to come to the knowledge of the truth."

He tasted the lowest of lows, and He is seated high above in the Heavens, far above all principality and power, and now that He is raised He has ascended to the Father. Jesus was still working even after He tasted physical death for all of us. The

King was on the move!

Ephesians 1:20-23 BSB

"which He exerted in Christ when He raised Him from the dead and seated Him at His right hand in the heavenly realms, far above all rule and authority, power and dominion, and every name that is named, not only in the present age but also in the one to come. And God put everything under His feet and made Him head over everything for the church, which is His body, the fullness of Him who fills all in all."

CHAPTER 21: ENFORCING THE FINISHED WORK OF THE CROSS

Sometimes God's M.O.S. is not what we expect it to be. For example, God's way of rendering judgment against the enemy was the Cross of Jesus—two wooden beams and Jesus crucified on it was the answer which to the unrenewed mind of man doesn't sense but through the eyes of divine revelation makes perfect sense when you understand the Scriptures:

Colossians 2:14-15 ASV

"Having despoiled the principalities and the powers, he made a show of them openly, triumphing over them in it. having blotted out the bond written in ordinances that was against us, which was contrary to us: and he hath taken it out of the way, nailing it to the cross;"

John 16:8-11 ASV

"And he, when he is come, will convict the world in respect of sin, and of righteousness, and of judgment: of sin, because they believe not on me; of righteousness, because I go to the Father, and ye behold me no more; of judgment, because the prince of this world hath been judged."

There was a verdict and possibly even multiple verdicts that God the Father issued because of the Cross of our Messiah. Jesus paid for our healing, deliverance, citizenship, and salvation. So how come we haven't seen everyone saved, healed and delivered yet? Well, the work of the Cross is still unfolding but the reason that there was a lack of manifestation with the Promises of God for some is because they didn't enforce the finished Work of the Cross:

John 19:30 BSB

"When Jesus had received the sour wine, He said, "It is finished." And bowing His head, He yielded up His spirit."

Just like there are earthly laws that declare theft, murder, and hacking, just to name a few, as illegal, there are also spiritual laws that declare things as illegal in the spiritual realm. Some of which we have looked at in the previous chapter. These laws have to be enforced, just like earthly laws have to be enforced. Even though laws can be ratified, passed and enacted if there are no officers of the law to enforce it, people can still get away with breaking the law if there are no law enforcement officers to enforce the verdicts rendered. Just like if a judge agrees to place an order of protection against someone per their request, if there is a lack of police officers to enforce that verdict, that order of protection can still be violated without reprimand. Even though it's illegal to violate that order of protection. In the spirit realm, we have already established that God is the Judge. It's all over the world, from Isaiah 33:22 to Hebrews 12:23. God the Father is the Righteous Judge, the Lord Jesus and Holy Spirit are our Heavenly Advocates. The Holy Spirit is also our Advocate, Comforter, Intercessor, and Enforcement Officer. The difference is that the Father and the Lord Jesus for the most part abide in Heaven now with brief visitation here and there if they chose to, but the Holy Spirit is perpetually with us on this earth. The angels that are still serving the Father in Heaven are also officers of God's Word[52] that get dispatched on certain assignments. Remember, the angels execute His Word and do His Commands. His Word are His verdicts.

Psalms 103:20 BSB

"Bless the LORD, all His angels mighty in strength who carry out His word, who hearken to the voice of His command."

Proverbs 16:10 ASV

"A divine sentence is in the lips of the king; His mouth shall not transgress in judgment."

When there are spiritual verdicts that are rendered in our favor against the enemy, it's very possible that the angels of Heaven help enforce those verdicts. The officers prevent the law from being ignored because they enforce them. Likewise, there are laws that govern the spiritual realm and the officers of this realm are God the Father, the Lord Jesus, Holy Spirit, the angels and get this—know us. This is where the Word of God, prayer and the Courts of Heaven come into play. Judges can't render verdicts while they're on vacation at the watermark with their kids having a good time with family. You have to come before the judge's courtroom to present your case. So if we want to see verdicts rendered, we go to spiritual court because that is where the Judge is! This is one of the reasons that the Word says that we have boldness and confidence to come to The Throne of Grace, not the other way around. Because the Throne doesn't come to us, we come to the Throne:

Hebrews 4:16 KJV

"Let us therefore come boldly unto the throne of grace, that we may obtain mercy, and find grace to help in time of need."

Remember that we have established that Heaven is God's domain. A domain is the realm of authority that someone has, whether that be a kingdom, country, region, or city. A spiritual verdict manifests when we cooperate with the LORD, agree with His verdict and present our cases before Him. The breakthrough comes because you've changed the location where you're praying from. If you can get a hold of that, what the enemy got away with in times past, he won't be able to get away with anymore. *Things will start to shift!*

CHAPTER 22: SHIFTING THE STORM

Mark 4:37-41 KJV

"And he arose, and rebuked the wind, and said unto the sea, Peace, be still. And the wind ceased, and there was a great calm. And he said unto them, Why are ye so fearful? how is it that ye have no faith? And they feared exceedingly, and said one to another, What manner of man is this, that even the wind and the sea obey him?"

Why have believers endured past storms instead of commanding them to shift? I think it's due to a lack of understanding of the LORD's power and authority that was bestowed upon His Bride, as we have discussed in a previous chapter. I personally have endured a storm that I believe could have been much shorter had I known *then* what I know *now*. *Operating in dominion shifts things*, just like operating in the Courts of Heaven shifts things. If the disciplines in the boat weren't able to change the storm, then why did Jesus rebuke them for their lack of faith, unbelief, and their hearts for being full of fear? I don't believe we have to endure demonically engineered storms, but rather we overcome them and tell them to shift! When the children of Israel were complaining in the wilderness that they had no clean water to drink, the LORD came and told Aaron and Moses to speak to the Rock to change the situation:

Numbers 20:7-8 BSB

"And the LORD said to Moses, "Take the staff and assemble the congregation. You and your brother Aaron are to speak to the rock while they watch, and it will pour out its water. You will bring out water from the rock and provide drink for the congregation and their livestock."

All Moses had to do was to: "Speak to the Rock," to see the breakthrough, but instead of speaking to the Roc, he struck it. That Rock was Jesus:

Numbers 20:10-12 BSB

"Then Moses and Aaron gathered the assembly in front of the rock, and Moses said to them, "Listen now, you rebels, must we bring you water out of this rock?" Then Moses raised his hand and struck the rock twice with his staff, so that a great amount of water gushed out, and the congregation and their livestock were able to drink. But the LORD said to Moses and Aaron, "Because you did not trust Me to show My holiness in the sight of the Israelites, you will not bring this assembly into the land that I have given them."

1 Corinthians 10:1-4 ASV

'And did all drink the same spiritual drink: for they drank of a spiritual rock that followed them: and the rock was Christ. and did all eat the same spiritual food; For I would not, brethren, have you ignorant, that our fathers were all under the cloud, and all passed through the sea; and were all baptized unto Moses in the cloud and in the sea; '

When Jesus spoke to the wind and waves: "Peace! Be still!" He was operating in dominion. Another word that is sometimes translated as wind in Hebrew is the word *ruach* which means spirit. So we can interpret it this way: He sent out His Spirit from the East, and His Spirit held back the waters for the

Israelites to Passover.

Prophetic Word

"My Church Will Be Powerful Again, And I Will Show The Enemy That My Church Is A Force To Be Reckoned With Once Again. The Latter Glory Is Going To Be So Much Greater Than The Former Glory, I AM The LORD And There Is No Other, None Other Than Me Can Save. And I Will Show, The Principalities And Powers, The Manifold Wisdom Of God Through My Church Once Again." Says The Lord Jesus Christ, "I AM." Says The Lord Jesus, "Shalom My People, Shabbat Shalom."

Hallelujah!

CHAPTER 23.1: THE POWER OF THE TONGUE AND THE SUPREMACY OF THE WORD

Speaking of the restoration of power to the church, let's talk about the power of the tongue. If you've ever heard the phrase: "Fighting on your knees," it's not an over exaggeration, sometimes it's actually quite literal. *Violence in the spirit looks like submission in the natural.* When it comes to the spirit realm, almost everything is dominated by words and actions. *The words of God's Mouth and the Words of man's mouth are two* of the *most powerful forces on the earth.* So powerful in fact that the Bible says death and life and in the power of the tongue, and it can be steered two ways:

Proverbs 18:21 KJV

"Death and life are in the power of the tongue: And they that love it shall eat the fruit thereof."

James 3:9-10 BSB

"With the tongue we bless our Lord and Father, and with it we curse men, who have been made in God's likeness. Out of the same mouth come blessing and cursing. My brothers, this should not be!"[53]

We battle with our words, and we love with our actions. We've already established that God is a Spirit. And as a Spirit, He spoke the earth and all creation into existence. This means that what the naked human eye cannot see has created that which can be seen by the human eyes. And If you look at Genesis 1 count how many times you see in that chapter: "God said..." and something came to be. Even before God made man, He said: "Let *Us* make man." God said, and then He did. He kept His Word. Does that sound familiar to anyone?

James 1:22 KJV

"But be ye doers of the word, and not hearers only, deceiving your own selves."

John 4:24 ASV

"God is a Spirit: and they that worship him must worship in spirit and truth."

If God is a doer of His own word, who are we not to be? God thinks so highly of His Word that He has magnified His Word above His Own Name—of which He said that anyone who uses His Name in vain would not be guiltless:

Psalm 138:2 KJV

"I will worship toward thy holy temple, and praise thy name for thy lovingkindness and for thy truth: For thou hast magnified thy word above all thy name."

Deuteronomy 5:11 KJV

"Thou shalt not take the name of the LORD thy God in vain: for the LORD will not hold him guiltless that taketh his name in vain."

The Weight of His Word

We can see from Scripture that God values His Word. There

is nothing more powerful in creation than the Word of God spoken in Faith, and the word of man spoken in faith. I say in faith because words can be spoken mingled with faith or futility:

> Hebrews 4:2 KJV
>
> "For unto us was the gospel preached, as well as unto them: but the word preached did not profit them, not being mixed with faith in them that heard it."
>
> Hebrews 4:12 ASV
>
> "For the word of God is living, and active, and sharper than any two-edged sword, and piercing even to the dividing of soul and spirit, of both joints and marrow, and quick to discern the thoughts and intents of the heart."

God honors His Word to the extent that He Himself obeys what He says. There is absolutely no higher authority than the Word of God and the God of the Word.

> Psalm 119:89 KJV
>
> "For ever, O LORD, Thy word Is settled in heaven."

The God of The Word

The book of Jeremiah mentions how the priests of Jeremiah's day knew the Word of God, but they didn't know the God of the Word:

> Jeremiah 2:8 KJV
>
> "The priests said not, Where *is* the LORD? and they that handle the law knew me not: the pastors also transgressed against me, and the prophets prophesied by Baal, and walked after things that do not profit."

They handled the Law, but they didn't handle Him. Even the word *world* has the two words *word* and *LORD* in it. Why? Because the LORD used His Word to create the world. He is the God who speaks it into existence. This is why the Word says:

Job 22:28 KJV

"Thou shalt also decree a thing, and it shall be established unto thee: And the light shall shine upon thy ways."

Peter wasn't walking on the water as much as he was walking on the Word. He never stepped out of the boat until Jesus said the word: "Come," in spite of what was going on around him, the winds, waves, and the storm, he was walking on the Word:

Matthew 14:28-31 BSB

"Lord, if it is You," Peter replied, "command me to come to You on the water." "Come," said Jesus. Then Peter got down out of the boat, walked on the water, and came toward Jesus. But when he saw the strength of the wind, he was afraid, and beginning to sink, cried out, "Lord, save me!" Immediately Jesus reached out His hand and took hold of Peter. "You of little faith," He said, "why did you doubt?"

Psalms 119:105 ASV

"Thy word is a lamp unto my feet, And light unto my path."

CHAPTER 23.2: THE POWER OF PRAISE

Acts 16:25-26 BSB

"About midnight Paul and Silas were praying and singing hymns to God, and the other prisoners were listening to them. Suddenly a strong earthquake shook the foundations of the prison. At once all the doors flew open and everyone's chains came loose."

This is going to be a short chapter, but nonetheless it doesn't mean the topic at hand isn't important. When Paul and Silas were stuck in a prison cell made of what I presume was stone and iron bars, instead of complaining about their situation to others or complaining to the LORD, they praised. Doesn't make sense to carnality, but to those walking in the Spirit, it's the only logical thing to do! The flesh complains, the Spirit praises. And because of their praise God came and opened the prison, and lost not only their shackles, but those who were imprisoned around them. *Their praise not only beckoned God to free them, but even caused the Lord to free those around them*. How many of those prisoners wanted to be freed, and even cried out to God to set them free? And here come Paul and Silas cranking up their praise to the Lord. I don't know if you've ever experienced this before or not, but to a suffering soul who's miserable, a happy person is more irritating to them than someone who is sharing their misery. There's a commonly acknowledged that goes along the lines of *misery loves company*. Paul and Silas very well could have been sent to that prison by the Lord as a *divine appointment* for the prisoners and the jailer. It's like the Pharisees saying can anything good come out of Nazareth? The answer is yes! Yes, it can! God spoke to me one day, saying:

May 17th, 2023

"Don't Despise Your Nazareth."

So don't complain about or despise the Nazareth that God placed you in because you may be the key that unlocks the city and the potential of the lives within it. Don't despise your Nazareth because Jesus didn't despise His. The two apostles and their praises turned out to be the key to their prayers and means for freedom.

CHAPTER 24.1: "WHY GOD, WHY ME?"

You might have sympathized with the title of this chapter, and you may have literally asked the LORD: *"Why God, out of all people, why me?"* You may have even asked: *"Why did God allow that to happen?"* And the simple answer to that question is that the LORD gave Adam and Eve *dominion* of the Earth. And since we're their descendants, we likewise inherit a portion of that dominion, which is amplified when we are born again and draw closer to Christ Jesus. As the children of God, we have an inheritance from our Father, Savior, and His Spirit! Dominion simply means *rulership*. So when the LORD gave that to them, and they willingly submitted to the devil's temptation to eat from the tree, it was in reality a trick for them to legally in the spirit transfer their authority to him. In turn, to every ungodly spirit underneath his authority after he was displaced and kicked out of Heaven. So the Earth is under the devils' authority in part, which is why Satan is called the god of this world in the Scripture. With that being said, however, when the Lord Jesus came he actually exercised authority over the enemy because He carried the authority of the Father, and He inherited the authority that He submitted to from the Father. This is another reason He said:

John 5:19 BSB

"So Jesus replied, "Truly, truly, I tell you, the Son can do nothing by Himself, unless He sees the Father doing it.

For whatever the Father does, the Son also does."

This was one of the reasons that unclean spirits were underneath His authority. The first reason is He was submitted to the Father, but the root reason that the devil was submitted to Jesus was because through Jesus, the world was created:

John 1:1-3 BSB

"In the beginning was the Word, and the Word was with God, and the Word was God. He was with God in the beginning. Through Him all things were made, and without Him nothing was made that has been made."

John 1:14-18 BSB

"The Word became flesh and made His dwelling among us. We have seen His glory, the glory of the one and only Son from the Father, full of grace and truth. John testified concerning Him. He cried out, saying, "This is He of whom I said, 'He who comes after me has surpassed me because He was before me.'" From His fullness we have all received grace upon grace. For the law was given through Moses; grace and truth came through Jesus Christ. No one has ever seen God, but the one and only Son, who is Himself God and is at the Father's side, has made Him known."

And in turn Jesus gave us His Authority and Power over unclean spirits as Christians as a spiritual inheritance because through Him, we have becomes sons and daughters of God:

John 1:12-13 BSB

"But to all who did receive Him, to those who believed in His name, He gave the right to become children of God— children born not of blood, nor of the desire or will of man, but born of God."

Just like you inherit certain genetics from your parents like your hair color, facial features, and eye color to name a few, there is a spiritual inheritance that you receive as a child of God. But what use is an inheritance if the inheritor doesn't know they have one? That's one of the reasons why knowledge is a key, and it's the very thing that is persecuted by the enemy because when you have God's revelation, and Biblical knowledge it sets you up for success. Success is easier when you carry spiritual revelation. And in certain instances where a parent leaves a will for their children, after the death of the parent, the children receive whatever was written in the will for them. When Jesus died for us, the will that the Father, Him, and Holy Spirit have set for us was transferred to us, and are awaiting us to claim it through prayer. And that's something that you can ask God to expand your revelation on, and to teach you how to claim it as well. Now, back to the topic of authority. If people are not Christians they are still underneath a measure of the devils' authority, which varies depending on what the person participates in, says and does. They still in part belong to the devil, and the devil doesn't need to go through God to afflict them. They're easy pickings, but the instant that someone puts their trust in Jesus, their soul and spirit are placed under the covering of His Authority, *and that spiritual covering is strengthened through obedience to Christ.* And it is through the process of deliverance where the Lord starts to transfer more and more of you from the dominion of the old kingdom that used to be a part of, which was the kingdom of darkness. And to the kingdom of light and under His headship, and now you are under.

Colossians 1:13 BSB

> "He has rescued us from the dominion of darkness and brought us into the kingdom of His beloved Son,"

However, there have been some Christians who have experienced hardship and trials even though they were walking with the Lord. This is sometimes because they didn't go through closing unholy spiritual doors and dealing with legal rights in the spirit realm. These are some of the reasons that a number of Christians have suffered the way that they have. And if it's not because of those two criteria, there is one more option of why something would have happened in the life of a believer, and it's to strengthen their faith and to create a testimony. If you've been walking with the Lord and you encountered a trial, that might have happened due to various reasons. The reason that may have happened is that your present testimony might be the very thing that gives hope and saves another person in their future trial. If they experience something very similar to what happened to you, your testimony might be the very thing that keeps that other person from committing suicide. *If you've experienced hardship in your past, just know that those trials might have come because God knows you're strong enough to conquer them and someone who is going to experience that in the future may not be. And your testimony could be the very reason that they don't give up, throw in the towel, file for a divorce, or attempt suicide because they see a living example of someone who's been through it and overcome it. God doesn't waste suffering in the life of a believer.* Don't just take my word for it, take a look at Jesus' life. He endured all kinds of suffering to save millions of people. I've heard the analogy before, *"if you were the only one in the world, Jesus still would've died for you."* So, let me ask you this, *what if the testimony of you overcoming your previous suffering and trials, becomes the very thing that saves another person in the future from committing suicide?* **Would your suffering be worth it if you knew that someone's father, mother, aunt, uncle, cousin, son, or daughter is still alive and chose not to give up in life because they heard the hope of your testimony?**

Revelation 12:11 BSB

"They have conquered him by the blood of the Lamb and by the word of their testimony. And they did not love their lives so as to shy away from death."

Our testimonies can be very powerful, and much more so when we include the Lord in them! Why do you think the first three letters in the word testimony are *test? Sometimes your present tests of life are the reason for someone else's breakthrough, and will to live through their tomorrow...*

CHAPTER 24.2: UNLOCKING THE MYSTERY OF SUFFERING

You're almost through with the teaching part of this book! We are so close to the bloodline cleansing portion of this book, but before we get into that, I want to briefly discuss a topic that I would like to call Unlocking The Mystery of Suffering. Before we get into the prayers. Have you ever noticed a period of time when someone first got saved, and it seemed to be sunshine and rainbows for a season, and seemingly out of nowhere they had unfortunate circumstances that started happening to them? Almost like a spiritual freight train hit 'em? A doctor's diagnosis, sickness, personal attacks and things of the like? Ever heard somebody ask: *"Why did God allow that to happen?"* This question has probably puzzled people for hundreds of years, but I want to discuss and give an answer as to *why*. When we get saved we become a child of God and as we progress into maturity we become the sons and daughters of God. They are walking in power and greater levels of dominion in partnership with the Holy Spirit and the sanctification process. We as human beings, except for Adam, Eve, and the Lord Jesus, everyone else came from an earthly father. This is one of the reasons that you are here, reading this book. Your physical body is a byproduct of the relationship between your mom and dad, which in turn gave you a physical body to dwell in, and our spirit came from heaven once we were born again. When we got saved, our spirit joined the Holy Spirit, and we began inheriting the nature of the One living inside of us. We initially inherited the corrupt nature of Adam but once we got born again, we got a new Father and started inheriting the nature of the Last Adam–Jesus:

Proverbs 13:22 BSB

"A good man leaves an inheritance to his children's children, but the sinner's wealth is passed to the righteous."

Proverbs 19:14 BSB

"Houses and wealth are inherited from fathers, but a prudent wife is from the LORD."

Our Inheritance In Christ

Colossians 1:12 ASV

"giving thanks unto the Father, who made us meet to be partakers of the inheritance of the saints in light;"

Ephesians 2:10 BSB

"For we are God's workmanship, created in Christ Jesus to do good works, which God prepared in advance as our way of life."

We as saints and children of God have an inheritance, and it's helpful to know what that is. We are spirit beings in human bodies that are here to fulfill the assignments we have been predestined for. Our physical bodies descended from our forefathers and foremothers. The reality of it is none of us had a flawless lineage where no one transgressed God's Law except for Jesus because He came from the Seed of His Father–God. One reason some Christians who just got saved and all of a sudden it seemed like they almost were immediately spiritually targeted is because of unresolved legalities in the spirit. Things in the spirit realm don't have a stamped expiration date on them, and this includes words. Before we were saved we lived in the world and did and spoke negative things against ourselves, others and even had other people speak negatively against us. God in His mercy desires us to repent so that He can clear any charges against us in the spirit realm. Whenever God brings things to the surface, it's typically so that it can be repented of, resolved and dismissed. The enemy brings things up to accuse; the Lord brings it up to acquit. That's one of the biggest differences between an advocate and a prosecuting attorney. One of the Lord Jesus' multifaceted roles in Heaven is our Advocate, while the enemy is a prosecuting attorney, hence his title *accuser of the brethren* in Scripture. When we come before God the Father while asking the Lord Jesus Christ to Advocate for us in Heaven's Court System, and we repent and apply the spiritual principle of confession, we will see breakthroughs. For some, they have been long awaited breakthroughs. When we become serious about our walks with the LORD, we become a threat to the kingdom of darkness because the Light of Jesus is radiating through us. We are the light of the world, and a city set on a hill cannot be hidden:

Matthew 5:14 KJV

"Ye are the light of the world. A city that
is set on an hill cannot be hid."

When we go before God as the Righteous Judge and begin to repent of things that we and our ancestors did and start to present our cases, and the Lord Jesus applies His Blood as payment. It starts to take back territory that was taken from our bloodline and take new territory for our bloodline. So the enemy can't operate to the degree he once was able to because there isn't a legal right to do so anymore. *The Blood of Jesus Silences Accusation.* God will not pervert justice because righteousness and justice are the foundation of His Throne:

Psalms 89:14 BSB

"Righteousness and justice are the foundation of Your throne; loving devotion and faithfulness go before You."

However, we can be acquitted justly. Unfortunately, for the most part the enemy has been the one bringing cases against the people of God, but may this book change the churches defensive position to the offensive position. We can gain a spiritual standing with the LORD to where we can present cases on our behalf and more. If we see the enemy overstep, overplay, or manipulate, as God established us as those worthy to present cases before Him. We can secure verdicts from the Throne of God to stop the works of the enemy and advance the Agenda of His Kingdom. We as the people of God, as God grants, can actually live a life and walk a walk worthy of the calling. So what do you say? Let's deal with the outstanding accusations and receive greater freedom together!

CHAPTER 24.3: THE HEART OF THE FATHER

Now, this chapter can be very long because there are multiple aspects of God's Heart, but I want to focus on one key aspect here to share with everybody who is reading: A part of the Kingdom is walking by faith and not by sight:

2 Corinthians 5:7 BSB

"For we walk by faith, not by sight."

Faith is both liberating, and empowering when you put faith in the Lord. However, faith requires humility, and pride is allergic to faith. That's what some of the most brilliant minds have the most difficult time with faith–because they have spent all their life feeding their brain while they have starved their hearts. Faith comes from the earth, not the mind. If you woo the heart of man, you own the man, and I would be shocked if the devil didn't know that–but I for sure know the Lord knows this. We receive by faith, we are supposed to pray from faith, we walk by faith, we see breakthroughs through faith, obedience, and prayer. When it comes to spiritual enemies, you are called to pray in faith because your spiritual standing is automatically above the highest hierarchy of hell. I've heard a man of God say before that the highest part of hell is beneath your feet. Something about children is that you can tell them close to anything, and they'll believe you. However, when a parent isn't honest with their child, as they grow up they learn to question the information they are receiving from their parents, and in turn they do that with school, and even God and His Word. Parents, please do not lie to your kids, because what you're teaching them to do is doubt when they get older, and have trust issues with others. Yes, I'm talking about the Christmas man that likes cookies and milk, the tooth fairy, and elves. Just be honest and upfront about it with them, tell them that you're the ones that get them presents, and if they want presents, then they are rewards for good behavior, and you control the gifting process. If they respect, obey, put in their genuine effort in school, and do the chores they'll get rewarded, but if not, tell them to not expect anything that they don't need to survive. You'll provide the housing, food, water, and other necessities, but they can kiss the Nintendo, Xbox, PlayStations and phones goodbye if they disrespect their parents, and act foolishly. A lot of children would be more respectful, and productive to society if every single parent raised them this way. It's the beautiful balance between unconditional love, and discipline. When a child has both, they are set up for a good life. A part of God's Love is His protective nature. Just take a look at what Jesus said in the Gospel of Matthew:

Matthew 18:1-5 BSB

"At that time the disciples came to Jesus and asked, "Who then is the greatest in the kingdom of heaven?" Jesus invited a little child to stand among them. "Truly I tell you," He said, "unless you change and become like little children, you will never enter the kingdom of heaven. Therefore, whoever humbles himself like this little child is the greatest in the kingdom of heaven. And whoever welcomes a little child like this in My name welcomes Me."

And there is redemption and forgiveness in Christ for those

who have severely abused children of course, I'm just trying to relay the protectiveness of Jesus over His own. We can notice a couple of things in this passage of Scripture. Number one being Jesus' Heart for children, and secondly that He is both very welcoming of children and their child-like faith, and very protective over children. The runner stone of a Millstone weighed about as much as a car did, up to 3,300 lbs. Imagine a stone the weight of your car being wrapped around a person's neck, and then being hurled overboard a ship into the sea. Does that sound like Jesus tolerates abuse of children? Nope, not at all. God's Heart is both so kind and sweet, yet when it comes to protecting His children, He doesn't play–not even a little. The love of a father can melt the hearts of his children. Yet, the wrath of a father might be the last thing a person experiences before they get same-day delivery straight to the Pearly Gates for threatening his child. It's the Lion and the Lamb that we see in Jesus, and it's a beautiful thing that He both cherishes and loves His children, but for those who abuse children, He is the *last person* they want to see...

CHAPTER 25: FOUNDATIONAL SCRIPTURES

The Lord has established the New Covenant on top of the foundation of the work of Christ. Covenants oftentimes are coupled with sacrifices and oaths. In this book, you'll see prayers addressing this very thing. The purpose of this chapter is to compile the necessary Scriptures in one location that are necessary to know during these prayers. I wanted to consolidate these Scriptures into one chapter to avoid a ton of repetition throughout the prayers.

A Call To Give Thanks And Praise

Psalms 100:4-5 KJV

"Enter into his gates with thanksgiving, And into his courts with praise: Be thankful unto him, and bless his name. For the LORD is good; his mercy is everlasting; And his truth endureth to all generations."

Courts of Heaven

Daniel 7:10 BSB

"A river of fire was flowing, coming out from His presence. Thousands upon thousands attended Him, and myriads upon myriads stood before Him. The court was convened, and the books were opened."

Covenants

Hosea 10:4 BSB

"They speak mere words; with false oaths they make covenants. So judgment springs up like poisonous weeds in the furrows of a field."

Scriptures For Repenting For Judging Others

Matthew 7:1-4 BSB

"Do not judge, or you will be judged. For with the same judgment you pronounce, you will be judged; and with the measure you use, it will be measured to you. Why do you look at the speck in your brother's eye, but fail to notice the beam in your own eye? How can you say to your brother, 'Let me take the speck out of your eye,' while there is still a beam in your own eye?"

Scriptures For Personal Forgiveness

Isaiah 43:25-26 BSB

"I, yes I, am He who blots out your transgressions for My own sake and remembers your sins no more. Remind Me, let us argue the matter together. State your case, so that you may be vindicated."

Hosea 14:2 BSB

"Bring your confessions and return to the Lord. Say to Him: "Take away all our iniquity and receive us graciously, that we may present the fruit of our lips."

1 John 1:9 BSB

"If we confess our sins, He is faithful and just to forgive us our sins and to cleanse us from all unrighteousness."

1 John 2:1-2 BSB

"My little children, I am writing these things to you so that you will not sin. But if anyone does sin, we have an advocate before the Father—Jesus Christ, the Righteous

One. He Himself is the atoning sacrifice for our sins, and not only for ours but also for the sins of the whole world."

Scriptures For Justice

Matthew 7:7-12 BSB

"Ask, and it will be given to you; seek, and you will find; knock, and the door will be opened to you. For everyone who asks receives; he who seeks finds; and to him who knocks, the door will be opened. Which of you, if his son asks for bread, will give him a stone? Or if he asks for a fish, will give him a snake? So if you who are evil know how to give good gifts to your children, how much more will your Father in heaven give good things to those who ask Him! In everything, then, do to others as you would have them do to you. For this is the essence of the Law and the Prophets."

Luke 18:1-8 BSB

"Then Jesus told them a parable about their need to pray at all times and not lose heart: "In a certain town there was a judge who neither feared God nor respected men. And there was a widow in that town who kept appealing to him, 'Give me justice against my adversary.' For a while he refused, but later he said to himself, 'Though I neither fear God nor respect men, yet because this widow keeps pestering me, I will give her justice. Then she will stop wearing me out with her perpetual requests.'" And the Lord said, "Listen to the words of the unjust judge. Will not God bring about justice for His elect who cry out to Him day and night? Will He continue to defer their help? I tell you, He will promptly carry out justice on their behalf. Nevertheless, when the Son of Man comes, will He find faith on earth?"

Job 13:18 BSB

"Behold, now that I have prepared my case,
I know that I will be vindicated."

Psalms 103:6 BSB

"The LORD executes righteousness and justice for all the oppressed."

Psalms 146:7 BSB

"He executes justice for the oppressed and gives food to the hungry. The LORD sets the prisoners free,"

James 2:13 BSB

"For judgment without mercy will be shown to anyone who has not been merciful. Mercy triumphs over judgment."

CHAPTER 26: OPENING BLOODLINE CLEANSING PRAYER

DISCLAIMER

Please be mindful that it's important to be actively listening to Holy Spirit while and after praying and these prayers, because the last thing you want is to pray something that has a negative impact on you or your family. However, since I typed these prayers out you don't have to be on guard so much about that, but be mindful whenever you do pray, to pray in alignment with God's Word which is His will revealed. Prayer is a powerful tool, and just like all powerful tools, they can be used to build something beautiful or harm and destroy something that was supposed to be beautiful if used incorrectly. God put the power of redemption in our mouths, and not only that, the very power of life and death within our tongues:

Proverbs 18:21 BSB

"Life and death are in the power of the tongue, and those who love it will eat its fruit."

So this is just a sobering reminder to choose your words carefully, both in prayer and life in general. You sow your own seeds ahead of you by *what you do* and *what you say*, so it's not something to be taken lightly. This is not to steer anyone away from praying these prayers. This is just a reminder that your words have power behind them, and Jesus indeed told us that by our words we'll be justified and by our words we can be condemned. Anyone reminded of the Miranda rights? "Anything you say can and will be used against you in a court of law..." However, don't be a Debbie downer! Don't forget to laugh, make jokes, and have fun in this life! Yes, be mindful of your words, but don't be a killjoy in the process! Enjoy life, create memories, and laugh a little or a lot. Remember, laughter is like good medicine. And not to mention the King is with you, and for those well versed in the Bible you know that the wedding guests cannot mourn while the Bridegroom is with them!

Proverbs 17:22 BSB

"A joyful heart is good medicine, but a broken spirit dries up the bones."

END OF DISCLAIMER

Beginning of Prayer

"Heavenly Father. I come to you in prayer to submit a formal request for the Heavenly Court to be seated, and for the books associated with my destiny to be opened and read. Along with any written documentation of accusations that Satan has filed and charged against me and my bloodline. II further request You LORD to summon heavenly angels and witnesses under your authority and jurisdiction to be witnesses, officers, guardian angels and scribes of the court, in Jesus name."

Opening Declaration

"I declare that through my intercession and repentance that

my family and I as well as the future descendants of my bloodline will be positioned for the blessings of the LORD and be positively affected by the following prayers that go forth. I furthermore decree and declare that all generational curses that You break Heavenly Father will be effective immediately during and after these prayers of repentance, in Jesus name."

Prayer of Dedication

"I dedicate my present and future descendants to You LORD God, Lord Jesus, and Holy Spirit. I place and dedicate myself along with the present and future descendants of my bloodline under Father God's angelic protection and the saving Lordship of Jesus Christ. As for me and my family, we are the LORD's."

Joshua 24:15 KJV

"And if it seem evil unto you to serve the LORD, choose you this day whom ye will serve; whether the gods which your fathers served that were on the other side of the flood, or the gods of the Amorites, in whose land ye dwell: but as for me and my house, we will serve the LORD."

CHAPTER 27: PRAYERS OF REPENTANCE

Daniel 7:10 BSB

"A river of fire was flowing, coming out from His presence. Thousands upon thousands attended Him, and myriads upon myriads stood before Him. The court was convened, and the books were opened."

Revelation 12:10-12 KJV

"Then I heard a loud voice saying in heaven, "Now salvation, and strength, and the kingdom of our God, and the power of His Christ have come, for the accuser of our brethren, who accused them before our God day and night, has been cast down. And they overcame him by the blood of the Lamb and by the word of their testimony, and they did not love their lives to the death. Therefore rejoice, O heavens, and you who dwell in them! Woe to the inhabitants of the earth and the sea! For the devil has come down to you, having great wrath, because he knows that he has a short time."

Opening Prayer

"LORD God, I ask that the records of my genealogy and generations of my father's and mother's bloodline of the family be visualized before the court. Holy Spirit please bring to my attention anything that my ancestors, or I did that needs to be addressed before the court and I request that the Blood of Jesus would be applied to these transgressions according to 1 John 1:9:"

(1)

Scripture For Repentance

2 Timothy 3:2-9 WEB

"For men will be lovers of self, lovers of money, boastful, arrogant, blasphemers, disobedient to parents, unthankful, unholy, without natural affection, unforgiving, slanderers, without self-control, fierce, not lovers of good, traitors, headstrong, conceited, lovers of pleasure rather than lovers of God; holding a form of godliness, but having denied its power. Turn away from these, also. For some of these are people who creep into houses, and take captive gullible women loaded down with sins, led away by various lusts, always learning, and never able to come to the knowledge of the truth. Even as Jannes and Jambres opposed Moses, so do these also oppose the truth; men corrupted in mind, who concerning the faith are rejected. But they will proceed no further. For their folly will be evident to all men, as theirs also came to be."

Prayer (1)

Repentance For Ungodly Character Traits

"I, (say your full name), confess and repent on behalf of myself, my ancestors, and my ancestral bloodline for all love of self, the love of money, boasting, pride, arrogance, blasphemy, greed, disobedience to parents, unthankfulness, unholiness, unlovingness, unforgiveness, slander, lack of self-control, brutality, despising of good, betrayal, murder, committing betrayal, traitorousness, headstrongness, haughtiness, stubbornness, pride, the love of pleasure, the pursuit of pleasure, promiscuity, a form of godliness but denying its power, taking advantage of gullible people, resisting the truth, corrupt-mindedness, double mindedness, and all lack of renewal of the mind, in Jesus name."

(2)

Scriptures For Repentance

Ephesians 4:20-32 WEB

"But you didn't learn Christ that way; if indeed you heard him, and were taught in him, even as truth is in Jesus: that you put away, as concerning your former way of life, the old man, that grows corrupt after the lusts of deceit; and that you be renewed in the spirit of your mind, and put on the new man, who in the likeness of God has been created in righteousness and holiness of truth. Therefore putting away falsehood, speak truth each one with his neighbor. For we are members of one another. "Be angry, and don't sin." Don't let the sun go down on your wrath, and don't give place to the devil. Let him who stole steal no more; but rather let him labor, producing with his hands something that is good, that he may have something to give to him who has need. Let no corrupt speech proceed out of your mouth, but only what is good for building others up as the need may be, that it may give grace to those who hear. Don't grieve the Holy Spirit of God, in whom you were sealed for the day of redemption. Let all bitterness, wrath, anger, outcry, and slander, be put away from you, with all malice. And be kind to one another, tender-hearted, forgiving each other, just as God also in Christ forgave you."

Prayer (2)

Repentance Covering The Above Referenced Scriptures

"I, (say your full name), confess and repent on behalf of myself, my ancestors, and my ancestral bloodline for all theft, generational theft of other people's physical, intellectual and financial property, vehicles, stealing, wasting time and resources, negligent use and unfaithful stewardship of finances and resources, stealing from God by a lack of tithes and offerings (Malachi 3), embezzlement, stealing from the Church and churches, slothfulness, laziness, corrupt words that came out of the mouths of myself and that of my ancestors, cursing, swearing, grieving, agitating, frustrating, insulting, offending, frustrating the Purposes of God and the Spirit of God, and for every time that I and my ancestors spoke negatively against the Holy Spirit, bitterness, wrong thoughts, wrong thinking patterns, unrighteous motives, perverted motives, perverted justice, wrong mindsets, wrath, anger, clamor, evil speaking, malice, covetousness, filthiness, foolish talking, inappropriate crude joking, jokes and words that empowered ungodly activity, and all disobedience to the LORD God, disobedience to adults, our own parents, and the parents of others, in Jesus name."

(3)

Repentance Scriptures

1 Samuel 15:22-23 WEB

"Samuel said, "Has Yahweh as great delight in burnt offerings and sacrifices, as in obeying Yahweh's voice? Behold, to obey is better than sacrifice, and to listen than the fat of rams. For rebellion is as the sin of witchcraft, and stubbornness is as idolatry and teraphim. Because you have rejected Yahweh's word, he has also rejected you from being king."

Proverbs 17:11 WEB

"An evil man seeks only rebellion; therefore a cruel messenger shall be sent against him."

Messenger[54]

Hebrew: מלאך ⟺ מַלְאָךְ

Transliteration: mal'âk

Strong's Definition

"From an unused root meaning to despatch as a deputy; a messenger or an angel."

Prayer (3)

Prayer of Repentance Concerning Rebellion

"I, (say your full name), confess and repent on behalf of myself, my ancestors, and my ancestral bloodline for all rebellion that has negatively impacted and or has been a source of affliction towards me and or my family in any way, shape, and form. I now permanently break agreement and break covenant with all the unclean spirits connected to and or associated with rebellion, stubbornness, iniquity, and idolatry. And I ask You LORD to heal any wounds of rejection, including any connected to any rebellion that my ancestors and I and my ancestors have personally walked in and that my ancestors were guilty of committing against You as well as godly and ungodly authority. Heavenly Father, I repent for all sins, transgressions, and iniquities including rebellion that I have ever walked in personally and that my ancestors walked in as well. LORD, I now ask that any unclean spirits that had assignments against me and my family would be subpoenas before us in court to face You as the Righteous Judge. I repent for every time I personally walked in disobedience and rebellion, and I forgive everyone who has wronged me. I request for a judgment and verdict of a cease and desist order along with a permanent order of protection against all the assignments of the enemy, all unclean spirits and including any associated with rebellion. According to Isaiah 54:17 and 1 John 3:8, in Jesus Name:

Isaiah 54:17 KJV

"No weapon that is formed against thee shall prosper; and every tongue that shall rise against thee in judgment thou shalt condemn. This is the heritage of the servants of the

LORD, and their righteousness is of me, saith the LORD."

1 John 3:8 KJV

"...For this purpose the Son of God was manifested, that he might destroy the works of the devil."

(4)
Scriptures For Forgiveness

Matthew 18:21-22 BSB

"Then Peter came to Jesus and asked, "Lord, how many times shall I forgive my brother who sins against me? Up to seven times?" Jesus answered, "I tell you, not just seven times, but seventy-seven times!"[55]

The Lord Jesus made it pretty clear about the importance of forgiveness, primarily for our sake. I personally apologize to everyone who is reading this for everyone who hurt, offended, physically and mentally abused you or didn't see the value in you. I ask you to forgive them for what they did because by forgiving them you're not saying that what they did was right, you're doing it for your own freedom. We always forgive for our sake because unforgiveness only keeps the person holding onto it bound. So what do you say? Let's forgive together.

Prayer (4)

Forgiving And Releasing Those Who Have Wronged You And Breaking Agreement With The Spirit of Accusation

Beginning of Prayer [56]

"Heavenly Father, I confess, repent and break agreement on behalf of myself, my ancestors, and my ancestral bloodline for all agreements made with accusation, unforgiveness, offense, bitterness and all of their associated spirits that my ancestors and I ever agreed with, partnered in, partook in, made, confirmed, established, bore false witness to or walked in lies and falsehood. I repent and break agreement with all true and false accusations that I agreed with and was a part of in any way against another brother or sister in Christ, people, cities, governments, churches, nations, my family, and even myself. I now choose to bless, forgive and release myself and those who have spoken curses, negativity, witchcraft, spells, potions, spells, potions, hexes and vex on me or my family and I ask that they all would be revoked by the Blood of Jesus."

(5)

Scriptures For Repentance

Colossians 3:5-11 WEB

"Put to death therefore your members which are on the earth: sexual immorality, uncleanness, depraved passion, evil desire, and covetousness, which is idolatry; for which things' sake the wrath of God comes on the children of disobedience. You also once walked in those, when you lived in them; but now you also put them all away: anger, wrath, malice, slander, and shameful speaking out of your mouth. Don't lie to one another, seeing that you have put off the old man with his doings, and have put on the new man, who is being renewed in knowledge after the image of his Creator, where there can't be Greek and Jew, circumcision and uncircumcision, barbarian, Scythian, bondservant, freeman; but Christ is all, and in all."

Prayer (5)

Prayer of Repentance For Sexual Immorality And Pride

"Heavenly Father, I, (say your full name), confess, repent and break agreement on behalf of myself, my ancestors, and my ancestral bloodline for all adultery, fornication, marital unfaithfulness, spouses who cheated, emotional affairs, acts of physical and emotional intimacy outside of marriage, kissing outside of marriage, fornication, sexual immorality, self-gratification, uncleanness, unholy passions, evil desires, covetousness, idolatry, iniquity, self-imposed religion, neglect of the body, lack of self-control, self-indulgence, false comforts, false refuges, self-gratification, sexual self-gratification, spiritual bunnies, the spirit of Ishtar, and every unclean spirit that is linked to sexual sin. I also renounce and repent for any and all anger, wrath, malice, bad intentions, murder, jealousy, hatred, strife, debate, disunity, anti-harmony, pride, Biblical debates, contentions about words, upholding and establish ungodly doctrines and demonic wisdom, the love of philosophy, the love of worldly wisdom, all forms of pride including intellectual, physical, pride of possessions, beauty, financial, pride of socio-economic status, envy, heresy, mental confusion, confusion connected to rebellion and witchcraft, manipulation, and every other form of confusion, blasphemy, ungodly language that my ancestors and I partook of, and all lies for your Living Word says:

Psalms 51:6 WEB

"Behold, you desire truth in the inward parts. You teach me wisdom in the inmost place."

1 Corinthians 14:33 WEB

"for God is not a God of confusion, but of peace, as in all the assemblies of the saints."

(6)

Scriptures For Repentance Against False Religion

Colossians 2:13-23 KJV

"And you, being dead in your sins and the uncircumcision of your flesh, hath he quickened together with him, having forgiven you all trespasses; blotting out the handwriting of ordinances that was against us, which was contrary to us, and took it out of the way, nailing it to his cross; and having spoiled principalities and powers, he made a shew of them openly, triumphing over them in it. Let no man therefore judge you in meat, or in drink, or in respect of an holyday, or of the new moon, or of the sabbath days: which are a shadow of things to come; but the body is of Christ. Let no man beguile you of your reward in a voluntary humility and worshiping of angels, intruding into those things which he hath not seen, vainly puffed up by his fleshly mind, and not holding the Head, from which all the body by joints and bands having nourishment ministered, and knit together, increaseth with the increase of God. Wherefore if ye be dead with Christ from the rudiments of the world, why, as though living in the world, are ye subject to ordinances, (touch not; taste not; handle not; which all are to perish with the using;) after the commandments and doctrines of men? Which things have indeed a shew of wisdom in will worship, and humility, and neglecting of the body; not in any honour to the satisfying of the flesh."

Prayer (6)

Renouncing False Religions And False Belief Systems

"Heavenly Father, Lord Jesus, Holy Spirit, I, (say your full name), confess, repent and break agreement on behalf of myself, my ancestors, and my ancestral bloodline for all self-imposed religion, false humility, neglect of the body, following false religions, including self-made and man made religion, asceticism, religious rules, religious regulations, worship of angels, legalism, satanism, and worship of saints that didn't line up with your Word. I repent for my ancestors forever having been associated with, connected to and or were engaged in the new age movement, ancient and modern new age philosophies whether named or unnamed.

Ancient or modern Islam, Hinduism, Buddhism, Druidism, Agnosticism, Atheism, and all other false belief systems and religious systems that contradict the teachings and Word of God, the Holy Bible. I confess, break agreement, repent and ask for Your forgiveness for anyone who prayed and or worshiped saints, demons, idols, mother Mary, love of wisdom and false philosophy, debate and religious debate, religious discussions according to the elementary principles of the world such as *don't handle, don't taste, don't touch* and all unclean spirits, personal iniquity, and generational iniquities associated with or connected to these practices as well as unclean spirits operating under these false religions and aliases, in Jesus name."

Prayer (7)

Repentance And Surrender of Passions To The LORD

"I, (say your full name), confess, repent and break agreement on behalf of myself, my ancestors, and my ancestral bloodline for everybody who willingly yielding to temptation out of boredom, selfish desires, unholy desires and unholy passions. Lord Jesus, I surrender my physical, mental, emotional, sexual, intimate and spiritual passions and cravings to You, and may they be in alignment with your Word, purity and Your Holy Spirit. Please remove any ungodly and unholy passions and desires along with impure motives from my heart and mind. I ask you to purify and align my passions to be in perfect alignment with You. And I ask you to renew my mind to be in perfect alignment with your Holy Spirit and your Living Word, the Holy Bible, in Jesus name."

(8)

Scripture Against Witchcraft

Numbers 23:23 LSV

"For no enchantment is against Jacob, Nor

divination against Israel; At the time it is said of Jacob and Israel, O what God has worked!"

Isaiah 54:17 BSB

"No weapon formed against you shall prosper, and you will refute every tongue that accuses you. This is the heritage of the servants of the LORD, and their vindication is from Me," declares the LORD."

Prayer (8)

Renouncing Witchcraft And Cleansing The Bloodline

Joel 3:21 LSV

"And I have declared their blood innocent, That I did not declare innocent, And YHWH is dwelling in Zion!"

"Heavenly Father, Lord Jesus, I, (say your full name), confess, repent and break agreement on behalf of myself, my ancestors, and my ancestral bloodline for all involvement and participation of black magic, white magic, gray magic, witchcraft, voodoo, sorcery, child sacrifice, human sacrifice, abortion, human trafficking, shamanism, ethnic cleansing, ethnic hatred, religious wars, bloodshed from the Revolutionary War, the American Civil War, World War I, World War II, "holy war," jihad, wars and religious wars that broke out from my homeland that my ancestors partook in, ethnic cleansing, all bloodshed connected to occult activity, murder in war, war crimes, unethical and unbiblical use of human and animal blood, and all types of DNA that was connected or associated with occult activity, spells, hexes, vexes, interpretation of omens, tarot card readings, sacrifices to unclean spirits, ancestors, necromancy, curses cast on other people, people groups, and nations, especially those spoken out of anger, bitterness, resentment and or jealousy of others by myself and by my ancestral bloodline. I also stand in the gap on behalf of myself and my ancestors and I confess, repent, ask for forgiveness and break agreement with any anger, bitterness, resentment, jealousy and hatred, offense, strife along with any spirits that have tried or might try taking advantage of such things as these along with any supervising spirits of such things, in Jesus name. I repent on behalf of my ancestors and myself for any oaths, vows, covenants, contracts, and agreements made and or sworn by my ancestors that might have affected and afflicted us, our lives, our marriages, our family, our finances, in any negative way, shape, or form and in any way that the LORD God did not intend, in Jesus name. I also break agreement with any dedications to false religions, religious groups and religious systems. I renounce Mormonism, Jehovah's witnesses, Catholicism, the Greek Orthodox, as well as the Serbian religious structures, along with all unbiblical teachings and unbiblical theology, false and demonic wisdom, I also renounce the idolization of apostles, prophets, pastors, teachers, evangelists, saints, popes, priests, deacons, ancestral worship, the lighting of candles on behalf of the deceased, all beliefs in purgatory and works based salvation, and as well as all idolatry that has been rooted and associated with such religious organizations and their associated unclean, religious, and legalistic spirits, as well as legalistic doctrine and all associated spiritual, soulish, mental, emotional, and physical strongholds, false belief systems, extra biblical revelations that were not from the Spirit of God, but rather from the enemy, in Jesus name. I ask for the total deliverance and complete deliverance from all extra-biblical as well as unbiblical demonic strongholds, false revelations, false visions, and false convictions, in Jesus name."

Prayer Continued...

"I further renounce, repent, and break agreement for all tithes, church offerings, offerings, meat offerings, drink offerings and all other forms of sacrifices made to ungodly spirits and or occultic religious organizations especially those that were rooted in extra biblical revelations and religions. I now place a formal request from the Courts of Heaven to blot my name and my family's names off of ungodly altars and out of all records of financial giving that pertains to me and my ancestors given to ungodly religious organizations. Ungodly religious institutions of all kinds, including Jehovah's Witnesses, and all Serbian Orthodox religious structures. I break agreement with all unclean spirits and spirits of false religion, religious spirits, that have had legal ground, legal footing, and legal rights along with legal claims to operate in the lives of myself, our family, our finances, our children's lives, our home, and our bloodline due to the sins, transgressions, iniquities, covenants, contracts, agreements, dedications, trades, oaths, vows, sworn in curses, spirits of infirmity and infirmity attached to curses, sacrifices to demons and satanic beings, financial sacrifices, blood sacrifices, sacrifices of time, gifts and talents, along with any and all covenants made by our forefathers and foremothers confessed and repenting of in this prayer, including anything ungodly done and committed in ignorance, in Jesus name."

Breaking Agreement With Ungodly Oaths

"I also break agreement with all ungodly and unrighteous oaths, vows, agreements, false dedications, agreements, contracts, covenants, false baptisms, ungodly baptisms, baptisms of blood, ungodly altars and their supervising spirits along with the idols attached to them, unholy family altars, ancestral family altars, religious structures, day of the dead altars, and all other altars that have occultic roots, and all soul ties made with former spouses, partners, unclean spirits, satanic spirits, political movements, spiritual spouses, witches, witch covens, wizard covens and with the enemy by our ancestors and relatives all the way back to Adam and Eve and every ancestor in between that has included my earthly mother's bloodline and my earthly fathers' bloodline including all oaths that would, if not repented of, would have the purpose and assignment to negatively impact, affect, and or afflict future generations in any negative way, shape, or form including any dedication from the womb of future descendants, and false covenants taken by myself and my ancestors that were not godly or in alignment with the Word of God, The Holy Bible, in Jesus name."

(9)
Scripture Against Substance Abuse And Calling Forth the LORD's Plans And Purposes

Jeremiah 29:11-13 WEB

"For I know the thoughts that I think toward you," says Yahweh, "thoughts of peace, and not of evil, to give you hope and a future. You shall call on me, and you shall go and pray to me, and I will listen to you. You shall seek me, and find me, when you search for me with all your heart."

Prayer (9)
Renouncing Substance Abuse

"Heavenly Father, confess, repent and break agreement on behalf of myself, my ancestors, and my ancestral bloodline for all use of psychedelics, drugs, alcohol, and every known and unknown drugs and or substances introduced into my family lineage by myself personally and or the lives of my ancestors up until this present moment. Lord Jesus, I ask You to shut every ungodly door that has been opened because of the use of foreign substances, whether in my life, the lives of my family members, and the lives of my ancestors, in Jesus name. I ask you to deliver me and all of my family members from any and all use of alcohol, drugs, cigarettes, cigars, psychedelics, addictions, watching or viewing inappropriate explicit adult content. And every unclean spirit that might be attached to them, or that might try to exploit such actions and substance abuse that they might be currently engaged in, in Jesus name. And may I, and they, walk in the prophetic destiny and calling of God and the absolute fullness of Your plans that You have planned LORD for them to walk in according to Jeremiah 29:11, in Jesus name."

Note

It would be helpful to know your family, cultural history or background a little before going into this part of prayer because it can help hit specifics. If you don't know, that's okay, we'll continue:

Prayer (10)

Prayer of Renouncing Associations To Ancient And Modern Altars Built By Ancestors In The Bloodline

"Heavenly Father, I, (say your full name), confess, repent and break agreement on behalf of myself, my ancestors, and my ancestral bloodline for all who erected ungodly altars built to sacrifice, worship creation, rocks, saints, apostles, land, earth, trees, plants, herbs, the sun, moon, stars, the queen of heaven, demons, satanic entities, emperors, ancestors, and those in former or current positions of authority, and every sacrifice that was made upon these unrighteous altars. I confess, repent, give up and release permanently every personal benefit, demonic gifts, demonic mantles, demonic mandates, demonic assignments, personal gains, demonic gifts, that my ancestors and I gained through these transactions and trades with demons and satanic powers including, false gifts, false gifts, demonic intelligence, satanic intelligence, demonic mantles, psychic abilities, false "holy spirits," "spirit guides," and demonic "spirit guides" even those disguised as previous ancestors, animal spirits that would have an assignment to try to mimic the voice of the Holy Spirit of the LORD God. I permanently renounce, release, and give up all demonic inheritances that came from these transactions made in the spiritual, soul, and the physical realm, and with the seed and children of wickedness as well, including all transactions made on ungodly altars and those connected as collateral within ungodly covenants and contracts, and agreements, in Jesus name."

Prayer (11)

Renouncing Idols And The Love of Money

"Heavenly Father, I, (say your full name), confess, repent and break agreement on behalf of myself, my ancestors, and my ancestral bloodline for all idols, idolatry, covenants, contracts, agreements, transfers of ownership and legal claims of ownership and spiritual and physical trades initiated with mammon (greed), ancient Mesopotamian fertility idols, ancient Mesopotamian gods, ancient roman idols, ancient Greek idols, as well as all the idols mentioned in the Hebrew Old Testament Bible, Greek New Testament, including any and all ancient and modern Philistine idols, fertility idols as well as the unclean spirits attached and associated with these idols that have operated under aliases. I pledge my sole allegiance to my true Heavenly Father, the Lord Jesus Christ, and the Holy Spirit of God. I declare I want absolutely *nothing* to do with ungodly spirits. I belong to the Lord Jesus!"

Prayer (12)

Prayer of Repentance For Ancient Altars

"I repent on behalf of myself and my ancestral bloodline all the way back to Adam and Eve for sacrificing on ancient unholy altars and satanic altars, especially any spiritual and physical principalities, spiritual and physical powers, spiritual rulers, spiritual armies or hosts of wickedness, spiritual idols and demonic "gods," mentioned in the Hebrew Old Testament Bible, those worshiped in Ancient Rome, and in the Middle East, in Jesus name."

"Heavenly Father, I, (say your full name), ask you to

forgive me and my ancestors and break the influences, chains, ungodly inheritances, and ungodly and demonic strongholds, satanic strongholds, inherited iniquity, transgressions, and sin within my DNA that was passed down to me, and I renounce them in Jesus name. I repent and renounce all the offerings and sacrifices that my ancestors made to roman pagan idols and roman emperors. They were worshiped during the time of the Roman Empire's reign over and around the Mesopotamian area we know today as the Mediterranean, modern day Europe, the Middle East, Egypt, Africa, and India, including incense burned to Roman emperors. I confess, repent, and ask forgiveness for all sacrifices made to the roman idols and false so-called *gods* that they worshiped before, during, and after the Roman Empire reigned over that geographical region and beyond. And I break agreement with those idols and the demon spirits associated and standing behind them and I declare that I want NOTHING to do with them any longer, in Jesus Name, amen!"

Prayer (13)

Repentance For Modern Altar

Jeremiah 32:29 BSB

> "And the Chaldeans who are fighting against this city will come in, set it on fire, and burn it, along with the houses of those who provoked Me to anger by burning incense to Baal on their rooftops and by pouring out drink offerings to other gods."

"I, (say your full name), confess, repent, break agreement and forsake on behalf of myself, my ancestors, and my ancestral bloodline for all modern ungodly altars and their supervising spirits, and their associated spirits, even altars associated with technological addictions, all altars of video games, and ungodly video games, and altars of entertainment. LORD, please forgive me and my ancestors for all incense offering, burnt offering, animal blood offerings, animal sacrifices, human blood offerings, human sacrifice, every building of wooden, clay, and metal images which are demonic idols, and we repent for every oath, promise, vow, and covenant made and sworn to these demonic idols all sacrifices, including financial sacrifices and sacrifices of time to these ancient and modern altars, in Jesus name."

Prayer (14)

Ancestral Repentance Became Human Attendants To These Wicked Altars

"Heavenly Father, I confess and repent along with that I also ask for forgiveness for all my ancestors who became human hosts, human attendants, priests, high priests, high priestesses, priestesses, kings, queens, all my ancestors who wore a false demonic crown in the spirit realm and in the spirit, soul, and physical realm as well, male and female cult prostitutes, temple prostitutes and anything associated with the aforementioned things either willingly or unwillingly at unholy altars, with idols, and every unclean spirit, especially false unholy spirits that disguised themselves as *spirit guides* or *good spirits*. I repent for every blood sacrifice and blood covenant, male seed sacrificial offerings and male seed covenants, female seed sacrificial offerings, female seed covenants. I repent for any DNA that was sacrificed on any ungodly altars, and to principalities in the heavenly places, powers, rulers of darkness, and spiritual wickedness in high places. I declare that I want nothing in common and nothing to do with them. I repent for every sacrifice of animal blood, chicken blood, pigeon blood, dove blood, human blood, children blood, children, and every other kind of sacrifice and sacrificial offering given and made to demons and satanic forces of wickedness. Especially idols and demons connected to and believed to be associated with influencing the harvest in any way, shape, or form. LORD God, I now ask you to forgive all of my ancestors who partook of these wicked acts and abominations and lift any curse that came because of these unrighteous acts according to the Finished Work of the Cross of my Lord Jesus Christ at Calvary and Galatians 3:13-14, in Jesus name."

Galatians 3:13-14 BSB

"Christ redeemed us from the curse of the law by becoming a curse for us. For it is written: "Cursed is everyone who is hung on a tree." He redeemed us in order that the blessing promised to Abraham would come to the Gentiles in Christ Jesus, so that by faith we might receive the promise of the Spirit."

Prayer (15)

Repenting For Legal Claims of Ownership

"LORD God, Heavenly Father, I ask for any legal claims of ownership that the devil and his wicked army have had and might currently have on me and my bloodline through the sins, transgressions, iniquities, habitual and willful sins, blood covenants, blood sacrifices, human seed covenants, meal covenants, meal agreements, meal sacrifices, oaths, contracts, and agreements and vows made and or signed verbally or through writing or agreed to with the kingdom of darkness. I now ask that they would be revoked immediately and rendered legally null and void, never to be established again, in Jesus name. I request that any legal paperwork associated with these agreements be nailed to the cross of the Lord Jesus Christ according to Colossians 2 for I claim that *It Is Written*:

Colossians 2:11-15 WEB

"In whom you were also circumcised with a circumcision not made with hands, in the putting off of the body of the sins of the flesh, in the circumcision of Christ; having been buried with him in baptism, in which you were also raised with him through faith in the working of God, who raised him from the dead. You were dead through your trespasses and the uncircumcision of your flesh. He made you alive together with him, having forgiven us all our trespasses, wiping out the handwriting in ordinances which was against us; and he has taken it out of the way, nailing it to the cross; having stripped the principalities and the powers, he made a show of them openly, triumphing over them in it."

1 Corinthians 6:19-20 WEB

"Or don't you know that your body is a temple of the Holy Spirit who is in you, whom you have from God? You are not your own, for you were bought with a price. Therefore glorify God in your body and in your spirit, which are God's."

Prayer (16)

Prayer Renouncing Secret Societies, Curses, And Oaths Through The Blood of Jesus

"Heavenly Father, I now repent for anybody who was in my ancestry and my bloodline who was a part of and or had ties with freemasonry, illuminati, the KKK, the black hand, skull and bones, the daughters of the eastern star, knights Templar, the mafia, the Celtic druids, druids, I renounce and repent for every financial tithe and offering given to these organizations and those similar to them in nature and every other secret society that practices ungodly rules, ungodly rituals, ungodly rites, ungodly initiations, including any that pronounce ungodly curses not mentioned in this prayer. I renounce every oath, curse, covenant, sacrifice, dedication of future descendants through the laying on of hands on the womb. Verbal contracts, legally binding words, legal contracts written in the spirit and the natural physical realm that were signed and or sealed with human blood. I renounce these oaths, covenants, and curses that were made if these ancestors left or disclosed secret information about these secret societies. I repent for any acts of violence, sinful, transgressions, and iniquitous behavior that my ancestors partook in, and were guilty of committing in order to be successfully initiated into these secret societies. I declare today on, (insert the date you are praying this prayer), that *I want absolutely nothing to do with these secret societies.* And if there were any curses, verbal and or written contracts that were made that have negatively impacted and affected my physical, mental, emotional, my soul, and spiritual health, I now renounce them and ask that all curses to be rendered legally null and void through the Lord Jesus' Atoning Sacrifice, through and by verdicts of the Courts of Heaven, in Jesus name."

Prayer (17)

Petitioning The LORD To Dissolve Curses According To Galatians 3

"Heavenly Father, I now petition You and make a formal appeal to Your Heavenly Court to break and dissolve all curses that have negatively affected and or effected me, my physical, mental, emotional and spiritual health, and even my relationship with You LORD God, Lord Jesus, and You Holy Spirit."

"LORD, I now move upon You and Your Court to dissolve every curse that has hitched a ride in or on my bloodline and DNA, according to Psalms 103:6 and Galatians 3:13-14. And I now formally request that every demonic curses and demonic covenants would be dissolved and rendered legally null and void on the basis and Foundation of the Finished Work of the Lord Jesus' cross according to Psalms 103:6, Galatians 3:13-14 and Colossians 2:13-14, in Jesus name. For it is written,

Psalms 103:6 BSB

"The LORD executes righteousness and

justice for all the oppressed."

Galatians 3:13-14 BSB

"Christ redeemed us from the curse of the law by becoming a curse for us. For it is written: "Cursed is everyone who is hung on a tree." He redeemed us in order that the blessing promised to Abraham would come to the Gentiles in Christ Jesus, so that by faith we might receive the promise of the Spirit."

"I now ask for these curses and demonic covenants to be dissolved, diminished, and legally rendered null and void, never to be re-established ever again, on the basis and Foundation of the Finished Work of the Lord Jesus' Atoning Sacrifice upon His cross by righteous verdicts from the Courts of Heaven according to Psalms 103:6, Galatians 3:13-14 and Colossians 2:13-15:

Colossians 2:13-15 BSB

"When you were dead in your trespasses and in the uncircumcision of your sinful nature, God made you alive with Christ. He forgave us all our trespasses, having canceled the debt ascribed to us in the decrees that stood against us. He took it away, nailing it to the cross! And having disarmed the powers and authorities, He made a public spectacle of them, triumphing over them by the cross."

"I ask now personally for a Divine decree of judgment against the enemy and for release, breakthrough, restoration, redemption, rejuvenation, and active refreshment for me and my family, in Jesus Name, amen!"

Prayer Concerning DNA And Behavioral Issues

"LORD, I receive everything that the Lord Jesus' atoning sacrifice paid for me to receive, including my healing, deliverance, breakthrough, soundness of mind, healing, and deliverance from rejection, the spirit of rejection, the orphan spirit, healing from orphan-heartedness and as well as the healing of my own heart. I appeal to Your court for the Redemption of my DNA. I ask You Heavenly Father for the complete restoration, healing, and realignment of my personal DNA. I repent for all the sins, transgressions, iniquities, dedications, vows, covenants, sacrifices, ungodly words, word curses, self-inflicted word curses along with any generational curses including all illegitimate and sinful behavior that I and my ancestors have been guilty of partaking in and or committing against You, ourselves and others, in Jesus name."

"LORD, I ask You for the realignment and healing of my DNA and for deliverance from any ungodly forces that attached themselves to my DNA. I dedicate my DNA to You LORD God to sanctify it and protect it and may the blood coursing through my veins and that of my family sing of Your praise. I ask if there are any genetic codes within my DNA or my families that would try to entice us into sin, transgressions, rebellion, iniquities, self-gratification, sexual sins, unhealthy relationships, sin cycles, sinful patterns, behaviors, behavioral issues, ADD, ADHD, Obsessive Compulsive Disorder (OCD), generational illnesses, infirmities and every other genetic glitch and alteration that sinful behavior, transgressions, iniquities, and demonic covenants made by my ancestors that have negatively impacted that they be reversed completely by Your power according to Galatians 3:13-14, Colossians 2:14-15 and 1 John 1:9 previously quoted within these prayers. I receive the healing of my DNA and I thank You for my healing and restoration in Jesus Name, amen!"

Prayers To Break Unhealthy And Ungodly Spiritual Ties Associated With Father And Mother

James 2:13 WEB

"For judgment is without mercy to him who has

shown no mercy. Mercy triumphs over judgment."

"Heavenly Father, I ask for a personal severing of any unhealthy spiritual, soulish, and bodily bridges, that the enemy might have had, or currently might have access through, to try to afflict, affect, torment, bring temptation towards me in any way, shape, or form. And I renounce the iniquities of my forefathers and foremothers, in Jesus name."

Prayer #18:

Prayer of Repentance For Father

"Heavenly Father, I repent and ask for forgiveness for any participation of my father's sins, transgression, and iniquitous behavior in both time past and in time present. LORD, Judge, I appeal to You for Your forgiveness and I further appeal to the mercy of Your Court for every time I dishonored my parents in any way that displeased Your Heart, in Jesus name."

"Heavenly Father, I make a formal appeal and petition for You to cut and sever any ungodly spirit, soul and body ties to and from my earthly father in every area of my life. And I ask You to sever any ties that would permit temptation in any given area of the life that You have graciously given me. I forgive my parents for being less than perfect and I acknowledge that all have sinned and fallen short of the glory of God except for Jesus, and I ask mercy for them and for myself, in Jesus name."

Prayer #19:

Prayer of Repentance For Mother

"Heavenly Father, I ask for your forgiveness for every sin, transgression, and iniquity that my mother and her bloodline has been guilty of partaking in previously, or presently engaged in. I now appeal to You to cut any unholy spiritual umbilical cord from my earthly mom. I acknowledge that Your Word says:

Deuteronomy 5:16 BSB

"Honor your father and your mother, as the LORD your God has commanded you, so that your days may be long and that it may go well with you in the land that the LORD your God is giving you."

"LORD, please forgive me for any time I dishonored my father and my mother. I ask You to help me honor You by honoring them in a healthy and godly way. I now formally ask You and make an appeal for You to set me free from any spirit, soul and or body ties to and from my mother and father that would give the enemy any access to me personally–especially from any unhealthy codependency and any ties that would allow temptations, in Jesus name."

Prayer #20:

Applying The Blood of Jesus

"Lord Jesus, I (say your full name) make a formal appeal before You and the authority of the court, as Heaven's High Priest, to apply Your Holy Blood to everything I confessed as well as every other unconfessed sins that were not specifically covered in this prayer as well."

Hebrews 12:24 KJV

"And to Jesus the mediator of the new covenant, and to the blood of sprinkling, that speaketh better things than that of Abel."

"I appeal to Your Holy Blood to speak a better word, answer, and silence all the accusations of the enemy on my behalf. I also ask that You would grant me the grace to be an overcomer, walk in freedom, purity, and holiness with a heart of first love, in Jesus Name, amen."

Prayer #21:

Garments of Salvation, Robe of Righteousness, And Pursuing Godly Character

Isaiah 61:1-11 BSB

"The Spirit of the LORD GOD is on Me, because the LORD has anointed Me to preach good news to the poor. He has sent Me to bind up the brokenhearted, to proclaim liberty to the captives and freedom to the prisoners, to proclaim the year of the LORD's favor and the day of our God's vengeance, to comfort all who mourn, to console the mourners in Zion— to give them a crown of beauty for ashes, the oil of joy for mourning, and a garment of praise for a spirit of despair. So they will be called oaks of righteousness, the planting of the LORD, that He may be glorified. They will rebuild the ancient ruins; they will restore the places long devastated; they will renew the ruined cities, the desolations of many generations. Strangers will stand and feed your flocks, and foreigners will be your plowmen and vinedressers. But you will be called the priests of the LORD; they will speak of you as ministers of our God; you will feed on the wealth of nations, and you will boast in their riches. Instead of shame, My people will have a double portion, and instead of humiliation, they will rejoice in their share; and so they will inherit a double portion in their land, and everlasting joy will be theirs. For I, the LORD, love justice; I hate robbery and iniquity; in My faithfulness I will give them their recompense and make an everlasting covenant with them. Their descendants will be known among the nations, and their offspring among the peoples. All who see them will acknowledge that they are a people the LORD has blessed. I will rejoice greatly in the LORD, my soul will exult in my God; for He has clothed me with garments of salvation and wrapped me in a robe of righteousness, as a bridegroom wears a priestly headdress, as a bride adorns herself with her jewels.

> For as the earth brings forth its growth, and as a garden enables seed to spring up, so the LORD GOD will cause righteousness and praise to spring up before all the nations."

"Lord Jesus, I ask you to clothe me with the garments of salvation, the royal robe of righteousness, fill me with Your love, joy, peace, patience, kindness, tender mercies, goodness, humility, meekness, long-suffering, forbearance, forgiveness, patience, and self-control. And if I ever have a complaint against anyone, help me to be quick to forgive them, even as God in Christ forgave me. May I live *in* the peace of God and *with* the God of peace. May I live and love with a thankful heart and mind. I ask You to help me to be quick to listen and not get unrighteously angry. May the Word of Christ dwell in me richly, with all wisdom, and may we as believers have the opportunity to teach and sharpen one another, in Jesus name."

Prayer #22:

Petitioning For Financial Blessing

"Heavenly Father, I ask you to bless the finances that I have and will receive. May you grant me the heart of wisdom to use finances in a way that pleases You and may the blessing flow of Abraham, Isaac, and Jacob and the favor of the LORD rest upon every aspect of the life You have given me in obedience and submission to You LORD God, in Jesus name."

Closing And Opening Doors

Revelation 3:7-8 BSB

> "To the angel of the church in Philadelphia write: These are the words of the One who is holy and true, who holds the key of David. What He opens no one can shut, and what He shuts no one can open. I know your deeds. See, I have placed before you an open door, which no one can shut. For you have only a little strength, yet you have kept My word and have not denied My name."

Prayer #24:
Prayer of Repentance For Closing Doors

"Lord Jesus, I, (say your full name), confess and repent for all disobedience, rebellion, and resistance to the Holy Spirit and His voice. Including all words and anything else, known and unknown, that might have opened up any negative doors in the past that the enemy has had access to me and my family through. I now ask You Lord Jesus to shut every door that the enemy has had access through and seal it with Your Blood permanently–never to be opened again in accordance with Father God's will, for You have the Key of David and what You shut no man can open and what You open no man can shut, in Jesus Name, amen!"

Prayer #25:
Opening Doors In Accordance To God's Will

"LORD God, Lord Jesus, Holy Spirit, I ask you to open the doors of Your Will in Your perfect, pleasing and acceptable will at the proper timing that you want me to walk through as well as for my friends and family. I ask You to prepare me to be ready at the appointed time that you open the correct doors, in Jesus name."

Prayer #26:
Asking For Divine Orders of Protection From The Courts of Heaven

"Lord Jesus, I petition You as my Heavenly Advocate and Heaven's High Priest to petition the Father for a supernatural and physical permanent order of protection to be set and put in place against the enemy over my life and every aspect of my life and my family's lives–from the youngest to the eldest, in Jesus name."

"LORD God, I ask You, through the help and empowerment of Your Holy Spirit, please help my family and I to fulfill the prophetic callings and destinies given to us by you. May my family fulfill their prophetic destinies and the call of God upon their lives as well through the power of your Holy Spirit, in Jesus name. For it is not by might nor by power but by Your Spirit:

Zechariah 4:6 BSB

"So he said to me, "This is the word of the LORD to Zerubbabel: Not by might nor by power, but by My Spirit, says the LORD of Hosts."

"I ask You Lord Jesus to apply Your Holy Blood to all of my prayers of confession and repentance as well as everything not covered within these prayers according to 1 John 1:9:

1 John 1:9 BSB

"If we confess our sins, He is faithful and just to forgive us our sins and to cleanse us from all unrighteousness."

Prayer #27:

Sealing These Prayers

"I now seal these prayers in the Blood of Jesus. Lord, You have my consent and to open the scroll of this prayer and read it before the Father to petition Him on my behalf for the fulfillment of His will. And I ask that you bring the Father's Will to come to pass for my life. May You grant me the desires of Your Heart in accordance with your timing and will. I thank you LORD for hearing me, and I thank you that I have what I've asked for, in Jesus name."

Note

It's okay to wait to pray this prayer below until you mean it. I would recommend not praying it until you can say it and mean it from your heart.

Prayer (28)

Surrendering To The Call Of God Upon Your Life

"Heavenly Father, Lord Jesus, Holy Spirit, I surrender to the Call of God upon my life. And I say yes to You, LORD God. Help me fulfill the prophetic destiny that You have already placed and ordained for my life through the power of your Holy Spirit, in Jesus name."

"And now like David of old I say let my vindication come from Your Presence, in Jesus Name, amen!"

Psalms 17:2 BSB

"May my vindication come from Your presence; may Your eyes see what is right."

This Concludes The General Bloodline Cleansing Prayers Section

---

End Note

Congratulations! You have just prayed through quite a bit of bloodline cleansing prayers. You will more than likely feel lighter and even a sense of relief now that you've gone through the general bloodline cleansing prayers section. I would like to encourage you to just worship the LORD in your way, whether that's singing, playing a musical instrument, dancing, loving Him or just simply talking to Him. I would personally recommend turning on some worship music, but do what works for you to get to that intimate place with the Lord and just enjoy His Presence. There is no script or prayer for this, as this is something that flows from your heart to His.

Personal Note

Now that you have gone through these prayers, please be careful of the words that you speak over yourself and others. Ask the Holy Spirit to help your heart, words and actions be in alignment with God's Heart and will for your life. Don't give the enemy ammunition with the words you speak, speak the Word of the Lord!

CHAPTER 28: REST AND REPLENISH

Below are some prayers that are geared towards protection, walking in victory and some focus on deliverance as well. Once God gives freedom and deliverance, you have a part to play now, and it's simply renewing your mind and obedience, because it's important what we dwell on. This is why the Bible says:

Proverbs 23:7 BBE

"For as the thoughts of his heart are, so is he: Take food and drink, he says to you; but his heart is not with you."

Colossians 3:2 ASV

"Set your mind on the things that are above, not on the things that are upon the earth."

The Word doesn't say: "Visit your mind on the things that are above…" But rather to *set* your mind on things above. In other words: *Let your mind dwell in Heaven, not on the things that are upon the earth.* Even after the deliverance takes place with the prayers in the second part of this book of targeted prayers, there is a renewing of the mind that you directly partake in through soaking the Word of God into your spirit, heart, mind, and soul. Whether that's reading or listening to the Bible that's up to you but renewing the mind is a part of the process:

Ephesians 4:23 KJV

"and be renewed in the spirit of your mind;"

Remember that passivity and complacency isn't Kingdom. There are times when we are still and know that He is God, but there is also an active partnership with the LORD that takes place. A healthy marriage isn't just one-sided, there are two sides to the equation. We are His Bride and He is our Bridegroom:

Ephesians 5:28-32 ASV

"Even so ought husbands also to love their own wives as their own bodies. He that loveth his own wife loveth himself: for no man ever hated his own flesh; but nourisheth and cherisheth it, even as Christ also the church; because we are members of his body. For this cause shall a man leave his father and mother, and shall cleave to his wife; and the two shall become one flesh. This mystery is great: but I speak in regard of Christ and of the church."

CHAPTER 29: SPEAKING BIBLICAL DECLARATIONS OVER YOURSELF

After you are done with the general bloodline cleansing prayers, I've included Biblical declarations that you can speak and pray over yourself:

Job 22:28 ASV

"Thou shalt also decree a thing, and it shall be established unto thee; And light shall shine upon thy ways."

Speaking The Word of God Over Yourself

"I decree that I am the head and not the tail, I am a child of God, I am blessed coming in and blessed going out, no weapon formed against me shall prosper, every tongue that rises up in judgment against me shall be condemned as unrighteous, for this is my inheritance as a servant of the Living God. Blessed is the fruit of my spiritual and physical womb, my bread basket, my kneading bowl, and my source of provision is blessed. I shall not lack. I will live in abundance. I decree that the LORD is my Refuge, my Strength, a very present help in time of need. I decree that I live under the shadow of the Most High and I abide in the Shadow of the Almighty. I decree and declare that the LORD has heard, and I shall not lack, I declare that my God will supply all my needs according to His riches in grace, I decree that I have all that I need, as well as abundant provision. I decree that things always go right for me from here on out, I decree unexpected blessings to come to me, I decree that I am blessed to be a blessing, I decree that I am accepted in the beloved, that I am being restored in the image of God in Christ Jesus My Savior, I decree that the LORD is my shield, I decree that I am dearly loved, I decree that I am a child of God, I decree that I'm fearfully and wonderfully made, I decree that my life has purpose, I decree that I'm taken care of, I decree that I am blessed, I decree that I have all that I need and more, I decree that the LORD fights my battles according to Deuteronomy 3:22, in Jesus Name, amen!"

Deuteronomy 3:22 KJV

"Ye shall not fear them: for the LORD your God he shall fight for you."

THIS CONCLUDES PART I OF THE BOOK

PART II : TARGETED PRAYERS

Below are bonus targeted prayers that deal with specific topics if you want to go further in cleansing your bloodline, or would like further freedom and deliverance. Or if you just want to cover something that maybe the general prayers didn't quite include in enough detail. Now that you've gone through the general bloodline cleansing prayers, you can take a minute, breathe and just enjoy the goodness of God and His presence. And if you want to continue with the prayers, be my guest, but I also want to take a minute to remind you that the prayers have been prayed through. And you can lay the Sword down for a minute and light your heart and your hands in worship to the King. Please don't neglect intimacy with the King for the battlefield. After you read this book, I would like you to intentionally choose to focus on the LORD's goodness and choose to ignore the wickedness of the enemy. The enemy is not deserving of our attention other than what is strictly necessary. Decide to focus on Jesus and be so in love with Him that nothing else matters like He matters to you. God bless you and for the next section is for those who need something specifically addressed and desire freedom from it. However, you are welcome to check the prayers out as you please, and there are a few starting prayers of protection that everyone who reads this book should pray. Shalom.

Psalms 119:45 BSB

"And I will walk in freedom, for I have sought Your precepts."

Introduction

Welcome to part two of this book. I decided to establish this part of the book as its own separate section because these are specific prayers for spiritual issues not everyone has dealt with or needs to deal with. They are there for those that do need to. This part starts with some prayers of protection and a daily covering to pray over yourself that anyone can and should pray. The rest of the prayers are aimed for a specific audience desiring freedom on various topics, along with a few chapters that are extended teachings as well. So if you're still looking for freedom from something that hasn't been hit yet, then please feel free to look through the table of contents. These prayers are formatted in a way where they can be prayed individually and won't require incredible amounts of time to pray one by one. Please don't skip the next section with the foundational Scriptures because you're going to need to know them for the rest of the prayers. May the prayers below prove to be a source of breakthrough, freedom, healing and deliverance, in Jesus Name, amen.

CHAPTER 30.1: PRAYER TO RECEIVE YOUR SPIRITUAL INHERITANCE

"Heavenly Father, I come before You to receive my spiritual inheritance. I ask that the Heavenly Courtroom to be seated to be witnesses to my hearing today as I present my case as Your Word states in Isaiah:

Isaiah 41:21 BSB

"Present your case," says the LORD. "Submit your arguments," says the King of Jacob."

"Heavenly Father, I come before You today to receive the spiritual, physical, and financial inheritance that belongs to me. I renounce the sins, transgressions, iniquities, enemy altars, and false religions that my ancestors and I partook of, and I chose to embrace Your Lordship over my life. I ask the Blood of Jesus to be applied as the full ransom payment to release my spiritual, physical, and financial inheritance to me now in Jesus Name. Furthermore, I receive and accept my spiritual, physical, and financial inheritance in all shapes and forms that originated from You Heavenly Father. I receive all the good things that You have planned for me, and simultaneously reject the inheritance of wickedness. I ask for deliverance from the inheritance of wickedness, and I pray these things in Jesus name, believing Your Word says:

Matthew 7:7 BSB

"Ask, and it will be given to you; seek, and you will find; knock, and the door will be opened to you."

"I ask that You would send your angels on assignment to receive, and deliver my spiritual inheritance to me, in Jesus name I receive, amen!"

CHAPTER 30.2: PRAYER FOR PROTECTION

Psalms 121:1-8 BSB

"I lift up my eyes to the hills. From where does my help come? My help comes from the Lord, the Maker of heaven and earth. He will not allow your foot to slip; your Protector will not slumber. Behold, the Protector of Israel will neither slumber nor sleep. The Lord is your keeper; the Lord is the shade on your right hand. The sun will not strike you by day, nor the moon by night. The Lord will guard you from all evil; He will preserve your soul. The Lord will watch over your coming and going, both now and forevermore."

Note

I welcome you to pray this over yourself and to petition the LORD to assign heavenly hosts (angels) to guard you on the earth while you are fulfilling your destiny. May the LORD bring about miraculous deliverances in the present and future for you and those you are tied to, in Jesus Name, amen!

Psalms 100:2 BSB

"Serve the LORD with gladness; come into His presence with joyful songs."

Daniel 7:10 BSB

"A river of fire was flowing, coming out from His

presence. Thousands upon thousands attended Him, and myriads upon myriads stood before Him. The court was convened, and the books were opened."

"Heavenly Father, as I now appear before You in prayer I now request for the activation of the ministry of Your heavenly hosts (Your angels) to be in, around, over and upon my life all the days that you have apportioned towards me. Heavenly Father, Your Word says in Psalms 91:

Psalms 91:1-16 BSB

"He who dwells in the shelter of the Most High will abide in the shadow of the Almighty. I will say to the LORD, "You are my refuge and my fortress, my God, in whom I trust." Surely He will deliver you from the snare of the fowler, and from the deadly plague. He will cover you with His feathers; under His wings you will find refuge; His faithfulness is a shield and rampart. You will not fear the terror of the night, nor the arrow that flies by day, nor the pestilence that stalks in the darkness, nor the calamity that destroys at noon. Though a thousand may fall at your side, and ten thousand at your right hand, no harm will come near you. You will only see it with your eyes and witness the punishment of the wicked. Because you have made the LORD your dwelling— my refuge, the Most High— no evil will befall you, no plague will approach your tent. For He will command His angels concerning you to guard you in all your ways. They will lift you up in their hands, so that you will not strike your foot against a stone. You will tread on the lion and cobra; you will trample the young lion and serpent. "Because he loves Me, I will deliver him; because he knows My name, I will protect him. When he calls out to Me, I will answer him; I will be with him in trouble. I will deliver him and honor him. With long life I will satisfy him and show him My salvation."

"Heavenly Father, I now ask the covenant promise of angelic protection to be activated here on earth and beyond, for the purpose of protection, deliverances from any malicious situation, including any possible encounters with enemies of the Gospel, religious extremists, extremists, demonically possessed individuals with at would have the intent to harm in any way, in Jesus name.

"Heavenly Father, I ask that You would give Your Heavenly Hosts (Your angels) the mandate, authority, and power to guard, watch over, protect, bind, cast down, detain, arrest and drag into the abyss any and all unclean spirits that would ever have any intent to hurt, harm, destroy, or cause anything of that nature to me whether through people or the spirits themselves, in Jesus name.

Prayer of Petition For Divine Angelic Protection Concerning Astral Projection

"Heavenly Father, I also ask that guardian and warring angels would be assigned over me to guard, protect, defend, war, bind, cast down, and detain any physical harm, or spiritual harm that people who would try to astral project against me and or family, in Jesus name.

"LORD, I also ask that You would give Your heavenly hosts (angels) a permanent injunction, charge, and command to seize, overtake and detain, astral projected human spirits and human souls and to send them back to their rightful human bodies, in any possible circumstance of that happening, in Jesus name.

"LORD GOD, I proclaim, agree, accept, declare and establish the covenant promise of angelic protection for me and my family according to Psalm 91, in Jesus name.

"LORD GOD, I receive Your protection and the Holy Spirit's Protection. And I ask that You would defend, protect, and fight for me all the length of my appointed days and beyond into when I step into eternity, in Jesus name, love You LORD, in Jesus Name, amen!"

CHAPTER 31.1: PRAYER OF PETITION FOR GOD TO REDEEM YOUR TIMELINE

Ephesians 5:15-16 BSB

"Pay careful attention, then, to how you walk, not as unwise but as wise, redeeming the time, because the days are evil."

Few things are more precious than time. It's a limited resource that God created, which I believe began after the fall because death was never in the picture of God's perfect plan or His perfect will. You see, God has given us all a destiny and attached to that destiny is time. God has appointed you and I to be alive for such a time as this!

Esther 4:14 BSB

"For if you remain silent at this time, relief and deliverance for the Jews will arise from another place, but you and your father's house will perish. And who knows, if perhaps you have come to the kingdom for such a time as this?"

You were not an accident. Your life has purpose and meaning. When we ask the LORD to redeem the time, we're essentially asking Him to bring into our present what should have been in the past. God has declared that He watches over His Word to accomplish it, and God has also declared that He knows the thoughts and plans that He has for us:

> Jeremiah 1:12 BSB
>
> "You have observed correctly," said the LORD, "for I am watching over My word to accomplish it."
>
> Jeremiah 29:11 BSB
>
> "For I know the plans I have for you, declares the LORD, plans to prosper you and not to harm you, to give you a future and a hope."

This prayer is an important one not because I wrote it, but because this prayer is redemptive in nature. How cool is it that God is able to bring into your *present* what should've already been in your *past*? Redemption is a double edge sword in a sense because the things you wished you had not done get covered in the Blood of Jesus as they are confessed. The things you wished you had done God can bring into your present-double redemption. I want to introduce this prayer with something very fitting that the LORD spoke to me that I released back in 2022. I want to encourage you to not take this Word lightly but rather to take it to heart because I might have been the one who typed it out, by no means was I the One who said it:

The Prophetic Word of The Lord

"I AM The Redeemer. Do I Not Redeem The Time? Stop Focusing On Wasted Years. Do You Not Think I Can Redeem It? It Is A Light Thing For Me, To Do So." Says The Lord Jesus, "I AM, And There Is None Besides Me. Shalom, My People, Shalom. Says The LORD Who Made Heaven And Earth And Everything In It, The Sea And All That Is Within Them…AM I Not The God Of Restoration? I Can Redeem The Time, You Don't Have To Regret Over Your Past Mistakes. They Didn't Take Me By Surprise. I Covered

Them In My Blood. You Just Need To Forgive Yourself. As I Have Forgiven You, So You Also Must Do…"[57]

Prayer of Personal Repentance

"Heavenly Father, I come before You at this moment to repent for any time that I resisted Your plans and purposes for me or another person. I repent for any time I said no to You and for any time that I caused hurt to Your Heart. I repent and declare that any time I have personally done that, it was wrong, and I ask You to forgive me. I also repent for any time that I knowingly or unknowingly missed a *kairos* moment that You ordained for me in times past. I repent, and I ask You to forgive me based on the finished work of the Cross and Your Word, for the Scriptures declare that You are not a man that you should lie, for it is written:

Isaiah 43:25 BSB

"I, yes I, am He who blots out your transgressions for My own sake and remembers your sins no more."

Numbers 23:19 KJV

"God is not a man, that he should lie; Neither the son of man, that he should repent: Hath he said, and shall he not do it? Or hath he spoken, and shall he not make it good?"

Petitioning For The Redemption of Your Timeline And God's Purposes

"Heavenly Father, Your Honor, I now petition you for the redemption of my timeline and Your purposes for me including innocence, the prophetic words You have destined to release through me, the prayers that You want to pray through me, the books that You want to write through me, the words of wisdom that you want to release through me, the divine connections and divine relationships that you want to introduce into my path, the places you've ordained for me to visit and minister, the friendships that You desire to establish and everything else you want to redeem I ask You to fully redeem it in Jesus name."

Prayer Petitioning God To Permanently Shut Down Any Assignments Against You And Your Timeline

Isaiah 43:26 BSB

"Remind Me, let us argue the matter together. State your case, so that you may be vindicated."

"Heavenly Father, Your Word says to state my case and put You in remembrance, so LORD I now remind You of the assignments against Your purposes and the destiny that You have ordained for me here upon the earth to fulfill, and I ask You according to Jeremiah 29:11, Psalm 103:6, Isaiah 49:25, and Isaiah 54:16, for a verdict of permanent cease and desist from the Courts of Heaven against any legal, spiritual, and physical entity trying to resist me fulfilling Your will here on this Earth for it is written:

Psalms 103:6 BSB

"The LORD executes righteousness and justice for all the oppressed."

Jeremiah 29:11 BSB

"For I know the plans I have for you, declares the LORD, plans to prosper you and not to harm you, to give you a future and a hope."

Isaiah 49:25 BSB

"Indeed, this is what the LORD says: "Even the captives of the mighty will be taken away, and the plunder of the tyrant will be retrieved; I will contend with those who contend with you, and I will save your children."

Isaiah 54:17 BSB

"No weapon formed against you shall prosper, and you will refute every tongue that accuses you. This is the heritage of the servants of the LORD, and their vindication is from Me," declares the LORD."

Prayer Continued...

"LORD, Your Word says that You watch over Your Word to perform it:

Jeremiah 1:12 BSB

"You have observed correctly," said the LORD, "for I am watching over My word to accomplish it."

"I now remind You of Your Word over my life, and I ask You to accomplish Your Word according to Your predestined council about me. I ask according to Jeremiah 29:11 that you would fulfill Your thoughts of Peace. I ask according to Isaiah 49:25 that you would deliver me from the mighty, and that You would contend against the demonic forces that have contended against me. I ask that you would save my children. I ask according to Isaiah 54:17 that you would permanently destroy the weapons that have been formed against me. I ask that you destroy the negative words that have been spoken against me and my family, as well as any that are being spoken or might be spoken in time to come.

Psalms 103:6 BSB

"The LORD executes righteousness and justice for all the oppressed."

"I ask according to Psalm 103:6 that You would execute righteousness and judgment on my behalf against all the oppression that has come against me and any that might be attempted in the future. I ask that You would let nothing stand against the destiny that You have ordained for me to fulfill. I ask that any people who have or might try to resist Your will in my life would be saved and filled with the Holy Spirit. Furthermore, I ask for anything that would try to resist Your plans and purposes, that You would restrain them from resisting Your purposes and will for my life. I bless and forgive those who have resisted Your purposes as well as spoken negativity against me. LORD, I receive Your Redemption of my timeline and Your Purposes, in Jesus Name, amen!"

CHAPTER 31.2: PRAYER FOR FAMILY'S SALVATION

Genesis 7:1 BSB

"Then the LORD said to Noah, "Go into the ark, you and all your family, because I have found you righteous in this generation."

Acts 16:31 BSB

"They replied, "Believe in the Lord Jesus and you will be saved, you and your household."

Matthew 18:12-14 BSB

"What do you think? If a man has a hundred sheep and one of them goes astray, will he not leave the ninety-nine on the hills and go out to search for the one that is lost? And if he finds it, truly I tell you, he rejoices more over that one sheep than over the ninety-nine that did not go astray. In the same way, your Father in heaven is not willing that any of these little ones should perish."

1 Timothy 2:3-5 BSB

"This is good and pleasing in the sight of God our Savior, who wants everyone to be saved and to come to the knowledge of the truth. For there is one God, and there is one mediator between God and men, the man Christ Jesus,"

Beginning of Prayer

"Heavenly Father, I come before You on the Foundation of Your Word to pray for the salvation of my family. I ask You to send angels on assignment to do the ministering work that you assign them to do in order for my family members to be saved. As You have said in Your word that it is your will that no one perish, but that everyone be saved. I ask that You would assign angels to break any demonic barriers established by the enemy or any blindness inflicted on anyone by the enemy to try to prevent them from seeing the glory of the Gospel:

2 Corinthians 4:4 BSB

"The god of this age has blinded the minds of unbelievers so they cannot see the light of the gospel of the glory of Christ, who is the image of God."

Acts 9:17-19 BSB

"So Ananias went to the house, and when he arrived, he placed his hands on Saul. "Brother Saul," he said, "the Lord Jesus, who appeared to you on the road as you were coming here, has sent me so that you may see again and be filled with the Holy Spirit." At that instant, something like scales fell from Saul's eyes, and his sight was restored. He got up and was baptized, and after taking some food, he regained his strength. And he spent several days with the disciples in Damascus."

"Heavenly Father, I ask for the healing, deliverance, and permanent removal of any scales superimposed or put in place by the devil against the members of my family that have been afflicted by these scales. I ask that every one of my family members get saved, born again, and baptized with fire from on High and fulfill their destiny and purpose here on earth, in Jesus name."

"Lord, I repent for any time that I spoke something negative against any one of my family members. I repent for any time I called a family member stubborn. I ask for your forgiveness, and I chose to speak life instead. Lord, I receive the salvation of their souls as part of my inheritance in Christ. Just like You saved Noah and his entire household, I ask that you would do the same for mine. Thank You, Lord, in Jesus name I pray. I receive what I have prayed for in accordance with Matthew 7:7, amen!"

Matthew 7:7 BSB

"Ask, and it will be given to you; seek, and you will find; knock, and the door will be opened to you."

CHAPTER 32: NULLIFYING WORD CURSES FROM THE HEAVENLY COURTS AND ADDRESSING BITTER-ROOT JUDGEMENTS

Opening Prayer

"Heavenly Father, I (say your full name), begin by confessing, repenting, and asking for forgiveness for all the negative words and word curses that I have spoken against others and that my ancestors spoke all the way back to Adam and Eve against another entity, person, government, or business for your Living Word says in the book of James:

James 3:9-10 BSB

"With the tongue we bless our Lord and Father, and with it we curse men, who have been made in God's likeness. Out of the same mouth come blessing and cursing. My brothers, this should not be!"

"I, (say your full name), confess, repent, come out of

agreement and ask for forgiveness for speaking any and every bitter-root judgment internally in my heart and out loud with my mouth and for all the negative and ungodly words spoken against other people, myself and even you LORD. Especially negative words that have empowered witchcraft against others, myself, cities, states, churches, nations and governments, in Jesus name.

"Heavenly Father, I now formally appeal to You to legally render null, void, and fruitless all the negative words and bitter root judgements made by me and by my ancestors against anyone or anything outside your will. I now out of an act of my own free-will break agreement with any and all negative words and word curses [try to be specific and ask Holy Spirit to bring to your remembrance any time you internally made a judgment against someone or yourself that needs to be confessed and repented of], that were spoken out of my mouth against [if you're able to name them I recommend doing so], myself, another person, and You LORD God, especially negative words that the enemy has been using as legal testimony that has enabled and or empowered the enemy to resist someone else's breakthrough or my own breakthrough, destiny, victory, and freedom. Forgive me for speaking any and all such negative words against others or me, especially word curses that I've spoken against others up until this present moment in time and especially words that have empowered witchcraft to operate against me, my family, and my God-given destiny. I ask You to help me to speak in alignment with your Heart, your Word, and your will from here on out, Lord, in Jesus name.

Forgiving Those Who Have Cursed And Spoken Against You

Matthew 18:21-22 BSB

"Then Peter came to Jesus and asked, "Lord, how many times shall I forgive my brother who sins against me? Up to seven times?" Jesus answered, "I tell you, not just seven times, but seventy-seven times!"

Luke 6:28 BSB

"Bless those who curse you, pray for those who mistreat you."

Romans 12:14 BSB

"Bless those who persecute you. Bless and do not curse."

1 Peter 3:9 BSB

"Do not repay evil with evil or insult with insult, but with blessing, because to this you were called so that you may inherit a blessing."

"I now choose to forgive, release and bless those who have spoken against me and my Prophetic Destiny, in Jesus name."

Prayer of Release

"LORD GOD, I choose to forgive, release and bless everyone who has spoken false prophecy, false prophetic words, manipulative shepherds and leadership that I was previously under for all the negative words and things that they were guilty of saying and doing against me. I now ask you to forgive and release them of any wrong that they have done. I now appeal to You by the authority of Your court and the Blood of Jesus to legally render null, void, ineffective and fruitless all of the negative words and word curses that were spoken against me. My family, my loved ones, and my God-given destiny, and especially those spoken out of jealousy, anger, wrath, strife, envy, hatred, murder, covetousness. Including words spoken by those who have held or currently hold a position of spiritual and or physical authority over me that hurt me rather than helped me:

Note

If you've been under manipulative leadership now would be

the time to name, forgive and release them from any debt they've owed you and bless them—even if you feel like that debt is a simple apology. Forgiveness isn't saying what they did was right, but it does grant the one wronged personal freedom.

Continued Prayer of Release

"I forgive, [try to name them if you can and if you don't know their names just think of the person or people and substitute their names with 'them'] and I release them into my forgiveness under the Blood of the Lamb, in Jesus Name."

"Heavenly Father, I, (say your full name), come before you as the Righteous Judge and I petition You to dissolve, render null, void, and fruitless all curses, vexes, hexes, spells, incantations, divination, and all forms of low, medium, high and advanced level witchcraft. As the redeemed of the LORD, I now petition You Heavenly Father to dissolve, condemn, bring to a permanent halt and dismantle these unrighteous weapons. Issue a permanent order of protection by the authority of Your court against all forms of witchcraft. Weapons of warfare that would try to work against the earthly manifestation of or bring to a premature halt the purposes of God for my life according to Isaiah 54:17:

Isaiah 54:17 BSB

"No weapon formed against you shall prosper, and you will refute every tongue that accuses you. This is the heritage of the servants of the LORD, and their vindication is from Me," declares the LORD."

Proverbs 26:2 WEB

"Like a fluttering sparrow, like a darting swallow, so the undeserved curse doesn't come to rest."

"Heavenly Father, Your Word states that a curse without cause doesn't come to rest, so I ask you to forgive me for any sins, transgressions, and generational iniquities that I have been guilty of partaking in directly and those of my ancestors that might have given any legal right for the enemy to land a curse on me or my family line. I now formally and officially appeal to the courts of Heaven and my Heavenly High Priest and Advocate, the Lord Jesus Christ. To apply His righteous blood and His finished work on the cross to atone and destroy all sins, transgressions, iniquities, demonic strongholds, curses, word curses completely rendering them useless and void. Your Living Word states that Christ became the curse of the law for me. So I no longer have to live under the curse, *for it is written*:

Galatians 3:13-14 BSB

"Christ redeemed us from the curse of the law by becoming a curse for us. For it is written: "Cursed is everyone who is hung on a tree." He redeemed us in order that the blessing promised to Abraham would come to the Gentiles in Christ Jesus, so that by faith we might receive the promise of the Spirit."

"Based upon these two Scriptures and the Finished Work of The Cross of the Lord Jesus Christ, I now formally enter a plea to Your Court to legally annul and render void every curse that came because of generational iniquity, generational issues, idolatry, negative words and witchcraft that I or my ancestors partook in which also includes any witchcraft that came against me or my family and any other reason that legally might have given room for a curse to land. Forgive us for any disobedience to You LORD, and because of the Work of Jesus on the cross I no longer have to live under a curse but rather live blessed, in Jesus name. I now, like King David, say:

Psalms 17:2 WEB

"Let my sentence come out of your presence.
Let your eyes look on equity."

"Thank you for hearing me, and I accept your Righteous Verdict of release and breakthrough from curses. I now ask for goodness and mercy to follow me all the days of my life according to Psalm 23:6 for *it is written*:

Psalm 23:1-6 KJV

"The LORD is my shepherd; I shall not want. He maketh me to lie down in green pastures: He leadeth me beside the still waters. He restoreth my soul: He leadeth me in the paths of righteousness for his name's sake. Yea, though I walk through the valley of the shadow of death, I will fear no evil: for thou art with me; Thy rod and thy staff they comfort me.

Thou preparest a table before me in the presence of mine enemies: Thou anointest my head with oil; my cup runneth over. Surely goodness and mercy shall follow me all the days of my life: And I will dwell in the house of the LORD for ever."

"Thank you, Father God, I love you, in Jesus Name, amen!"

END OF THE PRAYER

Word of Wisdom

If you're wondering: "Okay. I've prayed through this prayer. But what do I do if someone says something negative to me or about me down the road? And how do I handle that while maintaining peace and without causing unnecessary conflict or offense?" Good question. Number one, the goal is to nullify what this person said while maintaining peace, and without creating unnecessary conflict or offense. Here are some things you can do to deal with what someone said in a way that honors the LORD:

A Hypothetical Example

Let's say you came to a family gathering, sat down on the

couch, and while you got up to go to the kitchen, bumped into a family member who hasn't seen eye to eye with you. Or just doesn't like you because of your faith in Jesus. A conversion started and during the conversation this person says: "You know you're just wasting your time with this religious thing, you're not going to amount to anything." Now, this is a hypothetical scenario, but I want to use this to help teach us how to properly handle situations like this in a way that doesn't defile our witness for Christ. Maintains the peace while simultaneously deals with the situation in authority and love, because the Word says it says:

Matthew 5:9 ASV

"Blessed are the peacemakers: for they shall be called sons of God."

This is a good way to deal with that: "Please excuse me, I'm going to go to the restroom." Go to the bathroom, lock the door, turn the bathroom fan on and begin to pray:

"Heavenly Father, I choose to forgive this person for what they said about me. LORD Your Word says in Isaiah 54:17:

Isaiah 54:17 KJV

"No weapon that is formed against thee shall prosper; and every tongue that shall rise against thee in judgment thou shalt condemn. This is the heritage of the servants of the LORD, and their righteousness is of me, saith the LORD."

"LORD, according to Your Word I permanently annul, render useless and permanently unfruitful every single negative word spoken about me and against me by this person and everyone else. LORD, I declare that I will amount to *everything* that You have created me to be, as Your Living Word says about me:

Psalms 139:14 BSB

"I praise You, for I am fearfully and wonderfully made.

Marvelous are Your works, and I know this very well."

Jeremiah 29:11 BSB

"For I know the plans I have for you, declares the LORD, plans to prosper you and not to harm you, to give you a future and a hope."

Exodus 23:26 BSB

"No woman in your land will miscarry or be barren; I will fulfill the number of your days."

Philippians 1:6 BSB

"Being confident of this, that He who began a good work in you will carry it on to completion until the day of Christ Jesus."

"I declare that You will fulfill the number of my days. I decree that the good work You have begun in me, You will see it through until it's completed. You will never give up on me. I decree and declare that no weapon formed against me shall prosper, and every accusing tongue will be shut down in Jesus name. I decree and declare that I will be fruitful and multiply, as You have commanded numerous times in Your Word. And LORD, I also choose to bless and release this person for what they said because Your Word tells me:

Romans 12:21 KJV

"Be not overcome of evil, but overcome evil with good."

1 Peter 3:9 KJV

"not rendering evil for evil, or railing for railing: but contrariwise blessing; knowing that ye are thereunto called, that ye should inherit a blessing."

"LORD, I bless and release this person into my forgiveness. I choose to agree with Your Word for me and about me, and I decree this in Jesus Name, amen!"

END OF PRAYER

Do you see how this can be handled in a way that allows the person after the night is over while they are in bed about to fall asleep? Holy Spirit can start to replay that moment they said something to their family member and start to feel bad about realizing that they were too harsh for no good reason. And the other person gets a phone call in the middle of the night from that same family member who apologizes for what they said and that they were out of line for saying that. The reason they explain the reason that they were so emotional was because of a personal issue in their life that they were dealing with. All the while, the person on the phone starts to feel compassion for them and says the golden words I forgive you. And the other person says thank you, starts to get emotional and asks, *how are you so forgiving? I see you in family reunions all the time and people talk bad about you because you're a Christian, yet you somehow still show love to us. How? How can you do that?* And the Christian has a wide open door to share their faith in Jesus and share the Gospel with that family member, prays for them, and the Holy Spirit starts moving in the prophetic and touches the heart of that family member. At this point, they're weeping while God is in the room healing their heart. A year and a half later, that person is saved and walking with Jesus, and now there are two of you in the family. Do you think that could happen if you as the believer would've put up a fight, called the other person names and stormed off in anger? Nope. They just ruined their witness for Christ because they couldn't keep their cool. Do you see why love covers a multitude of offenses?

CHAPTER 33: SCRIPTURES FOR DAILY COVERING

Turning Scripture Into Your Daily Prayer

As you read the following Scriptures below, instead of just reading them, personalize them. I'll start by giving an example just to show you:

Sample Prayer

"Heavenly Father, Your Word says that I shall decree a thing, and it shall be established. I decree that I dwell in the Secret Place of the Most High and I abide in the Shadow of the Almighty. You are my refuge and my fortress, my God in whom I trust. Your faithfulness is my shield…"[58]

Job 22:28 KJV

"Thou shalt also decree a thing, and it shall be established unto thee: And the light shall shine upon thy ways."

Psalms 91:1-16 BSB

"He who dwells in the shelter of the Most High will abide in the shadow of the Almighty. I will say to the LORD, "You are my refuge and my fortress, my God, in whom I trust." Surely He will deliver you from the snare of the fowler, and from the deadly plague. He will cover you with His feathers; under His wings you will find refuge; His faithfulness is a shield and rampart. You will not fear the terror of the night, nor the arrow that flies by day, nor the pestilence that stalks in the darkness, nor the calamity that destroys at noon. Though a thousand may fall at your side, and ten thousand at your right hand, no harm will come near you. You will only see it with your eyes and witness the punishment of the wicked. Because you have made the LORD your dwelling— my refuge, the Most High— no evil will befall you, no plague will approach your tent. For He will command His angels concerning you to guard you in all your ways. They will lift you up in their hands, so that you will not strike your foot against a stone. You will tread on the lion and cobra; you will trample the young lion and serpent. "Because he loves Me, I will deliver him; because he knows My name, I will protect him. When he calls out to Me, I will answer him; I will be with him in trouble. I will deliver him and honor him. With long life I will satisfy him and show him My salvation."

Isaiah 54:10 BSB

"Though the mountains may be removed and the hills may be shaken, My loving devotion will not depart from you, and My covenant of peace will not be broken," says the LORD, who has compassion on you."

Isaiah 54:13-15 BSB

"Then all your sons will be taught by the LORD, and great will be their prosperity. In righteousness you will be established, far from oppression, for you will have no fear. Terror will be far removed, for it will not come near you. If anyone attacks you, it is not from Me; whoever assails you will fall before you."

Isaiah 54:17 BSB

"No weapon formed against you shall prosper, and you will refute every tongue that accuses you. This is the heritage of the servants of the LORD, and their vindication is from Me," declares the LORD."

Proverbs 28:1 BSB

"The wicked flee when no one pursues, but the righteous are as bold as a lion."

Romans 8:28-34 BSB

"And we know that God works all things together for the good of those who love Him, who are called according to His purpose. For those God foreknew, He also predestined to be conformed to the image of His Son, so that He would be the firstborn among many brothers. And those He predestined, He also called; those He called, He also justified; those He justified, He also glorified. What then shall we say in response to these things? If God is for us, who can be against us? He who did not spare His own Son but gave Him up for us all, how will He not also, along with Him, freely give us all things? Who will bring any charge against God's elect? It is God who justifies. Who is there to condemn us? For Christ Jesus, who died, and more than that was raised to life, is at the right hand of God—and He is interceding for us."

Romans 8:37-39 BSB

"No, in all these things we are more than conquerors through Him who loved us. For I am convinced that neither death nor life, neither angels nor principalities, neither the present nor the future, nor any powers, neither height nor depth, nor anything else in all creation, will be able to separate us from the love of God that is in Christ Jesus our Lord."

CHAPTER 34: PRAYER FOR FREEDOM FROM SPIRITUAL ACCUSATIONS FROM A DIVORCE

Introduction

If you have been through a divorce which could have been for various reasons, maybe your spouse was abusive or there was unfaithfulness involved, and you've personally felt accusations, this prayer is for you. Of course, there are some instances where Scripture excuses divorce. The first one being one of the partners was unfaithful and slept with another person, or the other partner was an unbeliever and wanted the divorce. Those are the two that Scripture excuses. In this prayer, my goal is not to bring something to your remembrance to cause condemnation because as a child of God, that is not your inheritance:

Romans 8:1 BSB

"Therefore, there is now no condemnation for those who are in Christ Jesus."

But rather my aim is to provide a prayer to help guide you to deal with any legal resistance from the adversary against you because of previous decisions that were made and words that were said. Especially more so if you are a minister of God and are desiring the deeper things that He has for you. You are not your past, and God has a plan and future planned for you:

Jeremiah 29:11-13 BSB

"For I know the plans I have for you, declares the LORD, plans to prosper you and not to harm you, to give you a future and a hope. Then you will call upon Me and come and pray to Me, and I will listen to you. You will seek Me and find Me when you search for Me with all your heart."

In this prayer, we will be bringing up this topic not to dwell in the past, but rather to deal with it for good and have the accusations and any legal resistance removed. This way, you can pursue all that God has for you. If you've felt spiritual accusations concerning a previous divorce, and you want to deal with this for good and move on from it, then the prayer below is for you.

Beginning of Prayer

"Heavenly Father, I (insert your name) come before You to seek freedom from the accusations of the enemy concerning a previous divorce. I acknowledge that Your Word says that you hate divorce:

Malachi 2:16 BSB

"For I hate divorce," says the LORD, the God of Israel. "He who divorces his wife covers his garment with violence," says the LORD of Hosts. So guard yourselves in your spirit and do not break faith."

"Lord, You know everything that happened and lead up to that divorce and I recognize and confess that it was wrong, and I ask You to forgive me as I stand on Your Word that says you are faithful to forgive and that there is no condemnation for those who are in Christ:

1 John 1:9 BSB

"If we confess our sins, He is faithful and just to forgive us our sins and to cleanse us from all unrighteousness."

Romans 8:1 BSB

"Therefore, there is now no condemnation for those who are in Christ Jesus."

1 Corinthians 7:15 BSB

"But if the unbeliever leaves, let him go. The believing brother or sister is not bound in such cases. God has called you to live in peace."

Note

Although this part below is pre-typed, this would be a perfect time for you to have a heart-to-heart to God about this and then resume with the written prayer. Your prayer may sound like: "LORD, I just want peace again. I'm sorry for what happened and took place. I'm tired spiritually, and I just want my joy back again, please help me." Take your time, there's no rush.

Prayer Continued...

"I come before You now standing on Your Word and the hope of redemption. I confess my faults and I repent for them, Lord, and I now ask according to these Scriptures: [60]

Psalms 103:12-13 BSB

"As far as the east is from the west, so far has He removed our transgressions from us. As a father has compassion on his children, so the LORD has compassion on those who fear Him."

1 John 1:9 BSB

"If we confess our sins, He is faithful and just to forgive us our sins and to cleanse us from all unrighteousness."

Isaiah 43:25-26 BSB

"I, yes I, am He who blots out your transgressions for My own sake and remembers your sins no more. Remind Me, let us argue the matter together. State your case, so that you may be vindicated."

"Heavenly Father, I ask You to acquit me of all the accusations of the enemy and reestablish me stronger than before as the man of God (or woman of God) that You have called me to be. Help me be everything that You have destined me to become. I ask You Lord Jesus to advocate for me on my behalf in the courts of Heaven and may You contend with the spirits that have contended with me in the spirit, in Jesus Name."

Petitioning For An Order of Protection

"Heavenly Father, I now ask for a verdict of judgment against spirits of accusation and an immediate cease and desist order to be released in the spirit and a permanent order of protection against the spirits of accusation and torment, as well as all other unclean spirits that have accused and afflicted due to a previous divorce. I receive your order of protection against these spirits and I declare by faith You are releasing freedom, for where the Spirit of the Lord is there is freedom, and where can I go from Your Presence?

2 Corinthians 3:17 BSB

"Now the Lord is the Spirit, and where the Spirit of the Lord is, there is freedom."

Psalms 139:7 BSB

"Where can I go to escape Your Spirit? Where can I flee from Your presence?"

"I receive these verdicts in my favor and I thank you for Your peace in my life, in Jesus Name, amen."

END OF PRAYER

My Prayer For You

Father, my prayer for those reading this chapter in particular is that you would restore the pep in their step and the joy that they maybe once had or have yet to experience. I ask that You would restore the glimmer of hope in their eyes and hearts, and may they come out on the other side of this victorious, stronger than ever and more intimate with You than ever before. May You guard them and keep them safe from temptations, and I speak live over these precious souls in Jesus Name, amen.

Note

For those who have been disqualified for ministry because of a previous divorce. I want to share with you that I have seen a man of God who went through a divorce, took a break from ministry, remarried a woman of God and bounced back into what God called him to. You are not disqualified by any means, and your life is valuable, remember that!

CHAPTER 35: PRAYER OF DELIVERANCE FROM JEALOUSY

Jealousy can be a dangerous thing if the person doesn't know how to let things go, and *especially* if they don't have self-control. If you've found yourself feeling jealous of other people's achievements, their spouse, or even their life, I want to encourage you to take a look at your own blessings that you've probably taken for granted. Jealousy is not something that should be harbored:

Proverbs 14:30 BSB

"A tranquil heart is life to the body, but envy rots the bones."

The Enemy's Way

James 3:14-16

"But if you harbor bitter jealousy and selfish ambition in your hearts, do not boast in it or deny the truth. Such wisdom does not come from above, but is earthly, unspiritual, demonic. For where jealousy and selfish ambition exist, there will be disorder and every evil practice."

Instead of being jealous over another person's accomplishments, spouse or even their life, learning to rejoice and be happy for other people when they succeed will position your heart in a better place. You will not only be happy for them, but you'll also be happy yourself. Why would God want to bless someone with an attitude and heart that thinks like this? "Whatever, I deserve that more than she does. She got everything handed to her, and she's not even that pretty. What does he see in her that I don't have?" God can hear everyone's thoughts. Instead of that, it's better to have the attitude: "Wow. She is blessed. I'm happy for her, praise God! I don't know everything that she's gone through, but she's in a good place, she's blessed and highly favored. I'm going to go ask her what she did to get to where she's at today. Maybe I can learn a thing or two from her. May she be blessed coming in, blessed going out, and may she be a blessing to others as well all the days of her life." When God hears you think and speak like that, you set yourself up for His reward. He wants to reward that attitude. He's a Father, how could He not?

God's Way

James 3:17-18 BSB

> "But the wisdom from above is first of all pure, then peace-loving, gentle, accommodating, full of mercy and good fruit, impartial, and sincere. Peacemakers who sow in peace reap the fruit of righteousness."

Do you see how much better God's way is? May we rejoice in one another's accomplishments because their accomplishments might even benefit you one day. Don't hate the ones who are doing great things, *especially* if what they're doing is God ordained.

Beginning of Prayer

"Heavenly Father, I come before You in prayer to lift my heart to You. I declare that all jealousy and envy that I have harbored against anyone is wrong, as I clearly saw in

Your Word. I choose to humble myself and apologize for the wrong I have committed and the wrong attitude I chose to have. I'm sorry and ask for Your forgiveness. I confess and break all levels of agreement with spirits of jealousy that have influenced envy and things of similar manner. I repent for every time that I and my ancestors had hateful or murderous thoughts towards somebody due to jealousy, personal accomplishments, blessings and any good thing that came their way. I repent for committing murder in my heart towards another person through hatred or jealousy for any time I didn't even realize it. I renounce any covenants made with jealousy and any spirits associated with it, and help me to be happy and rejoice with those who rejoice and to be happy for those who are doing great things for Your Kingdom and those who experience blessings. I pray that you would give me Your Heart and attitude to see people's accomplishments in a positive light and to speak life. Thank you for hearing me and thank you that I have what I've asked for, in Jesus Name, amen."

END OF PRAYER

CHAPTER 36.1: PRAYER OF DELIVERANCE FROM HOMOSEXUALITY

In a culture where homosexuality and the spirit of homosexuality has gained more of a cultural acceptance, people have started to think that homosexuality is somehow okay, even though it's actually not. The covenant that God created was between a man and a woman. There are different levels of maturity in the Body of Christ, so I want to address it in this manner. As children, sons, and daughters of God, we have to understand that He has not made man and woman for homosexual relationships. It's one thing for two men to be friends and two women to be friends. However, when the sacred boundary is crossed between two men and two women, it has become a perversion of what God intended for mankind and becomes sin. Let's take a look at what Scripture has to say about this topic:

1 Timothy 1:8-10 BSB

"Now we know that the law is good, if one uses it legitimately. We realize that law is not enacted for the righteous, but for the lawless and rebellious, for the ungodly and sinful, for the unholy and profane, for killers of father or mother, for murderers, for the sexually immoral, for homosexuals, for slave traders and liars and perjurers, and for anyone else who is averse to sound teaching"

Maybe you haven't personally partaken of this, but maybe you had some ancestors who did. One way you can know if you had ancestors who did is if you have had impulses, urges and desires for the same gender. This is more than likely due to iniquity within the bloodline, and some may have actually been born with iniquity in their bloodline. I'm speculating here, but I wonder if this iniquity actually alters the person's DNA and gets passed down to their children. The good news is that because Jesus did His part all it takes on our part is repentance, confession, a willingness to change and the power of God sets free and delivers. God has been in the business of freedom and deliverance for a while, and if anyone knows a thing or two about it, it's Him. If you can relate to what I said above, and you have a desire for freedom, here is a prayer to deal with it:

Asking The Court To Be Seated

"LORD GOD, I now ask according to Daniel 7:10 that the Heavenly Court would be seated to hear my case, in Jesus name. I ask You to call Your heavenly angels under your authority and jurisdiction to be witnesses, scribes and officers of the Court to protect me, keep the peace of the Court, and execute Your righteous decrees and commands, in Jesus name."

Prayer of Repentance For Judgments Made On Others

"Heavenly Father, I repent, renounce, break agreement and ask for forgiveness for every bitter-root judgment that my ancestors and I made on others in the area of homosexual relations, acts, deeds, thoughts, and intentions. I repent. I ask for You to forgive me and my ancestors for judgments that were made. I ask You to lift any possible negative repercussions off of me and my family that came as a result of those judgments made on others. I repent for all the hypocrisy that has been in my family line and in my personal life."

Repentance And Asking For Personal Forgiveness

"Heavenly Judge, I confess, renounce, denounce, break agreement with and cast down all acts of homosexuality that my forefathers and I have been previously and presently involved in. I declare that it's wrong, as I have seen in the Scriptures. Forgive me and my ancestors for every homosexual act committed including, some sexual relations, acts of intimacy done with males and males, and females with females. LORD, Your Word says that if I confess my sins, You are faithful and just to forgive me of our sins, and to cleanse us of all unrighteousness. So now LORD, You are not a man that You should lie, as Your Word plainly declares:

Numbers 23:19 BSB

"God is not a man, that He should lie, or a son of man, that He should change His mind. Does He speak and not act? Does He promise and not fulfill?"

Asking For A Verdict of Pardon

Job 13:18 BSB

"Behold, now that I have prepared my case, I know that I will be vindicated."

Renouncing Altars And Spirits of Homosexuality

"LORD GOD, in the Name of Jesus I renounce and break agreement with every oath, vow, covenant, sacrifice, acts of homosexuality committed by myself, my forefathers, foremothers and all of my ancestors. I renounce the spirits of lesbianism, homosexuality, perversion, bestiality, pornography, fornication, adultery, confusion and transgenderism, in Jesus name.

Addressing Altars

"Heavenly Judge, I ask that my name, the names of my ancestors, and my family's first, middle, and last names to be blotted out and blotted off of unholy altars and demonic records connected to homosexuality, lesbianism, bestiality, pornography, perversion, gods, and goddesses of sex, sexuality, gods, and goddesses of quote on quote "love," lust, sexuality, and perverted sexuality, in Jesus name."

Renouncing Soul Ties Made With Spirits of Perversion

"Heavenly Judge, I renounce every soul tie made with satanic and unclean spirits made by myself and my ancestors, including any ungodly legal claims of ownership that the enemy has had over me and my family line, in Jesus name. I now ask You LORD, to send Your angels to blot out my name, the names of my ancestors, and my families names off of every demonic altar, never to be written on or in any unholy altars ever again, in Jesus Name, amen!"

Prayer Asking For Justice

"I now ask for the court according to Matthew 7:7-12, Luke 18:1-8, Job 13:18, Psalms 103:6, and Psalms 146:7 to render a sentencing of judgment against all demonic spiritual oppressors from the kingdom of darkness and for an order to protection be placed immediately against them on my behalf. I also request accordion to 1 John 1:9 for the court to issue a verdict rendering me forgiven and cleansed based upon the blood of Jesus and His finished work on His Cross at Calvary, I ask now that all my sins, transgressions, and iniquities be blotted out of Heaven and hell's records, in Jesus name."

"Like David of old, I now say:

Psalms 17:2 WEB

"Let my sentence come out of your presence.
Let your eyes look on equity."

"In Jesus Name, amen!"

END OF PRAYER

CHAPTER 36.2: PRAYER OF DELIVERANCE FROM THE SPIRIT OF TRANSSEXUALITY

1 Corinthians 14:33 KJV

"For God is not the author of confusion, but of peace, as in all churches of the saints."

Proverbs 14:12 BSB

"There is a way that seems right to a man, but its end is the way of death."

A concept that has been heavily promoted by mainstream media, educational systems, social media, and even certain activists is the ideology of transgenderism. In reality, the forces behind this push are not aligned with godly principles. This ideology is often rooted in confusion and lacks a spiritual foundation grounded in faith. Our relationship with God the Father, the Lord Jesus, the Holy Spirit, and the Bible forms our foundation. Just like an experienced construction worker knows that to topple a building, it's not necessary to destroy every brick; targeting the foundation causes the entire structure to collapse. Consider why the

Bible and prayer were removed from schools first. The enemy strategically attacked the foundation, leaving young people without strong morals, spiritual guidance, or the tools to defend their faith. Once the truth of God's Word is removed, lies and manipulation can easily take root. This is not a new tactic. Historically, regimes like Hitler's, the Chinese government, North Korea, and many predominantly Muslim nations have used similar methods. They suppressed the Bible, arrested Christians, and forced their populations into conformity—either with their leaders or with the dominant faith, as in the case of Islam. Those who did not conform often faced persecution. Whenever there is an attack on the Bible or Christians, there are always destructive forces behind it, whether that manifests through Islam, transgenderism, homosexuality, or other ideologies. These agendas often seek to undermine the traditional family unit —defined as a father, a mother, and their children. In today's world, what used to be common sense seems less prevalent, and that shift is partly due to a spiritual attack on the minds of this generation. There is a purposeful attempt to confuse people about their gender and sexuality, which ultimately disrupts the divine purpose for their lives. If the enemy can convince someone of a false identity, it affects their potential future—especially in the context of marriage. For example, if a woman is led to believe she is attracted to other women, the man who God intended for her will not be a part of her life. The potential for a godly marriage and the spiritual work they could have accomplished together will never come to fruition. When confusion clouds one's sense of identity, it prevents God's intended plans from being realized. Transgenderism and homosexuality can, in a way, serve as an early form of birth control, blocking the natural creation of future generations of ministers and spiritual leaders who are meant to emerge from a family unit with a mother and father. The enemy's goal is not to acknowledge good intentions, but rather to stop anything that may contribute positively to the Kingdom of God and the world. History shows that whenever positive change begins, there is opposition. This attempt to hinder the birth of children, and thereby the spread of God's Kingdom, is something the enemy continues to target, as seen in biblical events such as King Herod's actions:

Matthew 2:16-18 BSB

"When Herod saw that he had been outwitted by the Magi, he was filled with rage. Sending orders, he put to death all the boys in Bethlehem and its vicinity who were two years old and under, according to the time he had learned from the Magi. Then what was spoken through the prophet Jeremiah was fulfilled: "A voice is heard in Ramah, weeping and great mourning, Rachel weeping for her children, and refusing to be comforted, because they are no more."

I wouldn't be surprised if the same political spirit that influenced Herod to order the massacre of the innocents, is the same political spirit that is trying to promote abortion rights in America. We are in a spiritual war, and how can someone win a war if you don't know they're in one? And there is no condemnation for those who have succumbed themselves over to what I'm talking about here because the Good News is that there is freedom and forgiveness in Jesus from all of these things. And all you have to do is simply ask the Lord to free you from these things. I hope this prayer below serves as a helpful guide on petitioning the Lord for your freedom.

Beginnings of Prayer

"Heavenly Father, I come before You as I ask for a court proceeding to repent and prosecute the spirits responsible for gender confusion, transgenderism, and spirit of the like because Your Word says in 1 Corinthians that You are not the author on confusion but of peace:

1 Corinthians 14:33 KJV

"For God is not the author of confusion, but of peace, as in all churches of the saints."

"On this Scriptural foundation I come before You today. I break agreements, covenants, partnerships, and sacrifices made to, for, and with the spirits of confusion, sexual promiscuity, sexual confusion, pedophilia, and transgenderism. I ask that You would note before the Court that I have confessed these things and according to 1 John 1:9 that You are faithful and just to forgive me:

1 John 1:9 BSB

"If we confess our sins, He is faithful and just to forgive us our sins and to cleanse us from all unrighteousness."

"Lord, I ask You to forgive me in alignment with Your Word. Your Word also states that You do not lie, and that you are faithful to fulfill Your promises:

Numbers 23:19 BSB

"God is not a man, that He should lie, or a son of man, that He should change His mind. Does He speak and not act? Does He promise and not fulfill?"

Petitioning For Deliverance

Psalms 68:20 BSB

"Our God is a God of deliverance; the Lord GOD is our rescuer from death."

"Heavenly Father, Your Word says that You are a God of deliverance. I ask You Father, Lord Jesus, and Holy Spirit for a heavenly verdict of deliverance to be issued at this moment and enforced by You Lord God. I renounce my past ways, and I choose to follow The Way–You, Lord Jesus.

Requesting An Order of Protection

"Heavenly Father, I now ask for a divine order of protection against the spirit of transgenderism, confusion, trans-sexuality, gender confusion, and every other spirit associated with them according to the fullness of Psalm 91, and specifically verses nine through eleven, which state:

Psalms 91:9-11 BSB

> "Because you have made the LORD your dwelling— my refuge, the Most High— no evil will befall you, no plague will approach your tent. For He will command His angels concerning you to guard you in all your ways."

"I ask for a divine permanent order of protection to be enforced by Your heavenly angels against these spirits as well as people that would try to engage in a relationship with me that is influenced by these spirits and have influence for unholy things listed within this chapter. I ask for this order of protection to be enforced in both the physical, soulish, and spiritual realms. I ask that the names of the members of my bloodline be removed from enemy altars associated with transgenderism, transsexuality, gender confusion, and confusion. I receive Your freedom, Lord, in Jesus name, amen!"

END OF PRAYER

CHAPTER 36.3: PRAYER OF DELIVERANCE FROM THE SPIRIT OF LUST

Proverbs 6:25 BSB

"Do not lust in your heart for her beauty or let her captivate you with her eyes."

2 Timothy 2:21-22 BSB

"So if anyone cleanses himself of what is unfit, he will be a vessel for honor: sanctified, useful to the Master, and prepared for every good work. Flee from youthful passions and pursue righteousness, faith, love, and peace, together with those who call on the Lord out of a pure heart."

This one's for the men of God, especially those who are young men of God waiting to be married to their future wife, however this prayer can also apply for women as well. Something in modern day society that has been almost normalized is lust. I don't want to spend too much time discussing it, but if you're wanting freedom, the prayer below is for you.

Beginning of Prayer

"Heavenly Father, I come before You today to ask for complete deliverance and permanent freedom from both lust and the spirit of lust. I renounce all lust, pornography, the spirit of Jezebel, witchcraft, idolatry, and objectifying men and women. I ask that You would enable me to walk in a manner that is pleasing to You and holy because Your Word declares:

1 Peter 1:15-16 BSB

"But just as He who called you is holy, so be holy in all you do, for it is written: "Be holy, because I am holy.""

"Heavenly Father, I renounce, break agreement, and repent for all the sins, transgressions, iniquities, and covenants of my forefathers and that I myself also partook in and committed, whether knowingly or unknowingly. I ask for Your forgiveness according to 1 John 1:9 which states:

1 John 1:9 BSB

"If we confess our sins, He is faithful and just to forgive us our sins and to cleanse us from all unrighteousness."

"Heavenly Father, I ask according to Your Scriptures that You would forgive me and my bloodline for all the sins, transgressions, iniquities, and covenants that were made with the kingdom of darkness on all levels. I now ask You Heavenly Father, and You Lord Jesus that Your Blood would be applied as the payment on the behalf of myself and my family's behalf according to the Scripture:

John 19:30 BSB

"When Jesus had received the sour wine, He said, "It is finished." And bowing His head, He yielded up His spirit."

Requesting An Order of Protection

"Heavenly Father, I ask for a permanent order of protection against the spirit of lust, spiritual spouses, and false spouses. I ask that You would bring the person in Your perfect will that You handpick for me Lord. I ask as well that You would keep those who would be agents of the enemy to attempt to cause temptation away from being near me. I ask that You would assign angels to guard me in all things, Lord, according to Psalm 91. I ask that a part of the commission You give those heavenly angels to guard and protect me is to keep people away from me that would try to tempt me to do something out of Your will or to be with somebody outside Your will. Your Word says that You will give me the desires of my heart if I take delight in You. So I ask that You would place Your desires in my heart and remove the desires that are not of you from me. I ask You to guard my heart and mind, Lord Jesus. I ask the heavenly court records that contained evidence would be marked as paid in full, and I ask as well that hell records that contained evidence and accusations be cleared of my name and that of my family's names. I ask that my name and that of my family would be removed from enemy altars in the natural and supernatural realms. I renounce the idols of my ancestors and like Joshua I declare, as for me and my house, we serve the LORD:

Joshua 24:15 BSB

"But if it is unpleasing in your sight to serve the LORD, then choose for yourselves this day whom you will serve, whether the gods your fathers served beyond the Euphrates, or the gods of the Amorites in whose land you are living. As for me and my house, we will serve the LORD!"

"Thank You, Lord, for hearing me. I receive Your freedom, deliverance, healing, and protection, in Jesus name, amen!"

END OF PRAYER

CHAPTER 36.4: PRAYER OF DELIVERANCE FROM THE SPIRIT OF JEZEBEL

If you believe that this prayer applies to you, or if you've had people around you that were influenced by this spirit, and you just want freedom from it, I welcome you to use the prayer below. These prayers are meant to be a helpful blueprint, but ultimately letting Holy Spirit move in the midst of the prayer is a good goal to have. So yes, use the prayer but also listen to where God leads you to add or address something specific to you.

Beginning of Prayer

"Heavenly Father, as I come before You in prayer at this moment, I begin by asking for the blood of Jesus to cover me. I renounce, repent, break agreements, covenants, and contracts made by everyone attached to my bloodline. I declare that I want nothing to do with the spirits of Ahab, Jezebel, witchcraft, sorcery, idolatry, or manipulation. I renounce and repent for any time that anyone in my bloodline, and even if I participated in those things, I repent and renounce those things, and I ask for Your forgiveness. I ask that the Blood of Jesus would be applied to those sins, transgressions, iniquities, and those covenants associated with the list that is mentioned within this prayer.

Order of Protection

"Heavenly Father, I now ask for a divine order of protection against the spirit of Ahab, Jezebel, witchcraft, manipulation, idolatry, religion, and every other spirit associated with Ahab and Jezebel according to the fullness of Psalm 91, and specifically verses nine through eleven, which state:

Psalms 91:9-11 BSB

"Because you have made the LORD your dwelling— my refuge, the Most High— no evil will befall you, no plague will approach your tent. For He will command His angels concerning you to guard you in all your ways."

"I ask for a divine permanent order of protection to be enforced by Your heavenly angels against the spirits, sleeper cells, vessels, *decoy spouses*, people that would try to engage in a relationship with me that are not my future spouse that You have ordained for me, and unholy things of the enemy listed within this chapter. I ask for this order of protection to be enforced in both the physical and spiritual realms. I ask that the names of the members of my bloodline be removed from enemy altars associated with Jezebel, Ahab, witchcraft, idolatry, Islam, and false holy spirits. I receive Your freedom, Lord, in Jesus name, amen!"

END OF PRAYER

CHAPTER 37.1: PRAYER OF DELIVERANCE FROM FALSE HOLY SPIRITS

Something I know that some believers–especially new believers, have dealt and possibly even struggled with are the voices of false holy spirits. Now, you might be wondering: *"What is a false holy spirit?"* And if you're wondering that, you probably have never dealt with one, and for that you can thank God because they are nasty. The devil doesn't play fair. A false holy spirit is an unclean spirit that tries to speak to new believers to do or say things, and the person thinks it's God talking to them. Now you might be wondering how is that possible and do some people really deal with that? And the answer is yes. We have to remember that thirty-three percent of the angels who were once in heaven got kicked out because they sided with the devil, and they knew what the Father, Jesus, and Holy Spirit sounded and spoke like. They have the responsibility of mimicking the voice of God to new believers, and making it seem like God is speaking to them. They try to make them live in fear and condemnation, because that's where these spirits thrive. The Bible says there is therefore now *no condemnation for those who are in Christ*:

Romans 8:1

"Therefore, there is now no condemnation
for those who are in Christ Jesus,"

We walk by faith, not by sight. God does not contradict His Scripture. Although they once knew His Voice, they no longer obey the Father like they used to, and instead of Heaven being their eternal home, they have forfeited Heaven for hell. Misery loves company, and now some of these spirits try to prey on the consciences of new believers. And especially those who love Jesus and are willing to do almost anything that He would ask them to do with Him and for Him. You might be wondering: *"How can I know that it's God speaking to me, and not a false holy spirit?"* The answer is simple, ask yourself:

A."Does it line up with **Scripture**?"

B. "Does the voice carry a holy **weight**?"

C. "Is there **peace** associated with the voice?"

If the answer to those three questions is a yes in all three categories, then it is very likely the Voice of God. You also begin to recognize the Voice of God over time, but those three tests are pretty solid indicators to help you identify the Voice of the Shepherd, and the voice of strangers. Remember what Jesus said:

John 10:3-5 BSB

"The gatekeeper opens the gate for him, and the sheep listen for his voice. He calls his own sheep by name and leads them out. When he has brought out all his own, he goes on ahead of them, and his sheep follow him because they know his voice. But they will never follow a stranger; in fact, they will flee from him because they do not recognize his voice."

And if you're wondering how you can identify a false holy spirit, a few ways you can identify it are:

How To Identify The Voice of A False Holy Spirit

> A. Does the voice prohibit you to do something that the Bible says is okay?
>
> B. Is the voice belittling you, and bringing condemnation?
>
> C. Does the voice tell you to do things that violate your conscience?
>
> D. Is the voice controlling?
>
> E. Is the voice threatening if you refuse to do something that violates your conscience?

F. Is the voice forbidding you or encouraging legalistic mindsets?

These are some tell-tale signs it's an unclean, false holy spirit or religious spirit. One important spiritual tool that God has given us is the ability to bind and loose. Jesus mentioned this not just once, but twice when He was speaking to His disciples, which includes us:

> Matthew 16:19 BSB
>
> "I will give you the keys of the kingdom of heaven. Whatever you bind on earth will be bound in heaven, and whatever you loose on earth will be loosed in heaven."
>
> Matthew 18:18 BSB
>
> "Truly I tell you, whatever you bind on earth will be bound in heaven, and whatever you loose on earth will be loosed in heaven."

If God is repeating Himself, whatever He is saying is something that carries double importance. We can find this principle in both Deuteronomy 17, and 2 Corinthians 13. I hope this prayer helps you articulate, and provide the words for you to pray to overcome this spirit, and give the enemy a good kick, you know where.

Prayer Asking The Court To Be Seated In Session

"LORD GOD, I now ask according to Daniel 7:10 that the Heavenly Court would be seated to hear my case. I ask You to call heavenly angels under your authority and jurisdiction to be witnesses, scribes, and officers of the Court to protect me, keep the peace of the Court, and execute Your righteous decrees and commands. As it is written:

Psalms 103:20 BSB

"Bless the LORD, all His angels mighty in strength who carry out His word, who hearken to the voice of His command."

Prayer of Repentance For Judgments Made On Others

"LORD GOD, I repent, renounce, break agreement, and ask for forgiveness for every bitter-root judgment that my ancestors and I made upon others in the area of hearing voices, and instances where others were dealing with false Holy Spirit's. I repent, and I ask for You to forgive us for those judgments that were made, and I ask You to lift any negative repercussions that came as a result of those judgments made on others. I repent for all the hypocrisy that has been in my family line and in my personal life, in Jesus name."

Asking For Personal Forgiveness

"LORD, Judge, I come before You to state my case against all deceptive spirits, false Holy Spirit's, and false spirit guides. LORD Your Word says that Holy Spirit I will lead and guide me into all truth, because He is the Spirit of Truth:

John 16:13 BSB

"However, when the Spirit of truth comes, He will guide you into all truth. For He will not speak on His own, but He will speak what He hears, and He will declare to you what is to come."

Prayer of Renouncement

"Heavenly Father, I renounce all false spirits, false spirit guides, deceptive spirits, false holy spirits, all spirits that would try to act and or imitate the Spirit of God's Voice, personality, person, and presence. Heavenly Father, I renounce and repent for any and all written, verbal, and blood agreements, affiliations, covenants, contracts, trades, including physical bodily, soul, and spiritual transactions and trades. This includes trades of books of destiny that were ever made with these spirits. And every other deceptive spirit that was not walking in obedience to the LORD that was ever made in my family line with these false and deceptive spirits, in Jesus name. I repent for all the sins, transgressions, iniquities, rebellion that my ancestors and I ever walked in and committed. And I ask You and Your Court to dismiss any and all charges against me and my family line because Your Word says, and you are not a man, that You should lie:

Numbers 23:19 BSB

"God is not a man, that He should lie, or a son of man, that He should change His mind. Does He speak and not act? Does He promise and not fulfill?"

"LORD, Lord Jesus, and Holy Spirit I choose to forgive everybody who has wronged me, because I have been forgiven as You have forgiven me, I am card to do likewise. I forgive myself, and I also receive Your forgiveness, in Jesus name."

Prayer Asking For Justice

"LORD, Your Word says that you will avenge your elect speedily. Your Word also says that You execute righteousness and judgment for all that are oppressed. So I now ask you to execute judgment against every false and unholy spirit that has ever tried to mimic the Holy Spirit's Voice. I ask for a judgment against these spirits, and I also ask for a verdict of permanent cease and desist against these false holy spirits. I also ask for a verdict from Your Court to forbid these spirits from speaking to me at all ever again, in Jesus name. Furthermore, I also repent for any time that I lied. No manger how big or small I repent, for Your Word says that You desire truth in the inwards parts:

Psalm 51:6 KJV

"Behold, thou desirest truth in the inward parts: And in the hidden part thou shalt make me to know wisdom."

"Your Honor, Your Word also says that the mouths of liars will be stopped:

Psalms 63:11 ASV

"But the king shall rejoice in God: Every one that sweareth by him shall glory; For the mouth of them that speak lies shall be stopped."

"Heavenly Father, I ask now that You would permanently shut the mouths of every false holy spirit that has been assigned to me and my family line. I ask for a verdict from the Courts of Heaven issuing an immediate, permanent order of protection against these unclean spirits, in Jesus name. Your Word says that whatever I ask for I will receive, so I ask for this by faith, in Jesus name. I now ask LORD that a judicial decree and verdict from Your Throne would come as vindication for me, and I also ask for a verdict of deliverance from all false holy spirits, false spirit guides, especially all unclean spirit guides that came through the Navajo Indian tribe and every other Indian tribe, as well as every other form of falsehood, false religion, and all religious spirits associated with Eastern Orthodoxy, I renounce them and I ask You to sever their ties from me completely, I am Yours LORD GOD, in Jesus name.

2 Corinthians 3:17 ASV

> "Now the LORD is the Spirit: and where the
> Spirit of the LORD is, there is liberty."

Psalms 17:2 BSB

> "May my vindication come from Your presence;
> may Your eyes see what is right."

"Heavenly Father, I now ask for my vindication to come from Your Presence and may Your eyes Behold what is right, and I receive Your Freedom, in Jesus Name, amen!"

END OF PRAYER

CHAPTER 37.2: PRAYER OF DELIVERANCE FROM ISLAM

If you have had ancestors or family members who practiced or currently practice Islam, and you have come to faith in Jesus, you may have noticed that some of those close to you have changed or even distanced themselves since you embraced Christ. I understand that this can be painful, but I want to encourage you not to take it personally. They may have treated you differently because of your new faith, but this reaction would likely not have occurred if you were still Muslim. They may struggle with the Christ in you, the hope of glory. Remember, Jesus Himself said:

John 15:18 BSB

"If the world hates you, understand that it hated Me first."

It's easy to be upset with them and angry at what they have done, and you'd be justified in feeling that way however, you'd only negatively affect and rob yourself of joy because of the hate harbored in the heart. I would encourage you to pray for them to be saved, and for them to come to the Light.

Matthew 5:44 BSB

"But I tell you, love your enemies and pray

for those who persecute you,"

Why would Jesus say that? Because vengeance belongs to Him, and He would much rather see the person who persecuted His people repent, convert, and be saved, than face judgment like those who have harmed His followers. Remember, having a clean conscience is one of the greatest gifts you can possess. Before we dive into this prayer, I'd like to briefly share some thoughts on Islam. The black cube, known as Mecca, located in Saudi Arabia, is, from a spiritual perspective, an altar. Every time someone prays towards it, visits it, or walks around it, they are expressing their allegiance to it and participating in that altar of Islam.

Beginning of Prayer

"Heavenly Father, I come before You, renouncing Islam and its principles. I renounce the spirits, powers, and principalities associated with Islam, and I repent for every time my ancestors, family, or I have prayed to the spirits behind it. I renounce the false god Allah, Mecca, Muhammad, and all the spirits, powers, and principalities connected to Islam and the spirit of Islam. I renounce every sacrifice, prayer, and all bloodshed that has occurred through Jihad. I renounce all acts of terrorism against people, the Jewish people, and American lives by Islamic extremists. I renounce any ancient hatred towards the Jewish people, Americans, and Christians that my ancestors and I have ever held or participated in. Heavenly Father, I ask, according to 1 Kings 13:5, that these spiritual altars be destroyed in accordance with the word of the LORD.:

1 Kings 13:5 BSB

"And the altar was split apart, and the ashes poured out, according to the sign that the man of God had given by the word of the LORD."

"Heavenly Father, I ask for Your protection against any

extremists, family members, and unclean spirits that may try to hinder or prevent the destiny You have placed on my life from being fulfilled. I ask for angelic protection for myself and for all those in my family who will come to faith in Christ, according to Psalms 91, which says:

Psalms 91:8-12 BSB

> "You will only see it with your eyes and witness the punishment of the wicked. Because you have made the LORD your dwelling— my refuge, the Most High— no evil will befall you, no plague will approach your tent. For He will command His angels concerning you to guard you in all your ways. They will lift you up in their hands, so that you will not strike your foot against a stone."

"Heavenly Father, I receive the promises of protection in Your Word. I ask for the salvation of those who were steeped in other religions to turn to You Lord Jesus as their Lord and Savior. I ask that You would visit them and open the eyes of their hearts and expand their understanding that You are not just a prophet, or a godly man. But that You are Messiah, that You are God wrapped in flesh. I thank you, and I receive Your freedom and protection, in Jesus name, amen."

END OF PRAYER

CHAPTER 37.3: PRAYER TARGETING GATEKEEPER SPIRITS OF MENTAL STRONGHOLDS

1 Chronicles 9:23-27 BSB

"So they and their descendants were assigned to guard the gates of the house of the LORD—the house called the Tent. The gatekeepers were stationed on the four sides: east, west, north, and south. Their relatives came from their villages at fixed times to serve with them for seven-day periods. But the four chief gatekeepers, who were Levites, were entrusted with the rooms and the treasuries of the house of God. They would spend the night stationed around the house of God, because they were responsible for guarding it and opening it every morning."

Psalms 119:160 BSB

"The entirety of Your word is truth, and all Your righteous judgments endure forever."

There are many things in the Bible that serve as physical representations of spiritual truths, and I wouldn't be surprised if this portion of Scripture is one of them. Have you ever met someone who is very religious, and no matter how much you tried to share the truth with them, they just couldn't accept it? They might have wanted to discuss their views, believing they were right, and you were wrong for believing in Jesus. Sometimes, people who grow up outside of Christ's influence may be influenced by other spirits. One example of this is the spirit of Islam, which, in its teachings, does not acknowledge Jesus as the Christ:

1 John 2:22 BSB

"Who is the liar, if it is not the one who denies that Jesus is the Christ? This is the antichrist, who denies the Father and the Son."

There was an interview done with a Christian man who was on a podcast who was at one point in the military. He had asked an ISIS member that he made contact with, who was captured, but he asked him the following question and I quote:

Man On Podcast

"What's gonna happen to you when you die?"

ISIS Fighter

The ISIS fighter responded with: "Inshallah."

Man On Podcast

"Do you mind if I share with you what I consider my security of salvation when I die?"

ISIS Fighter

He goes, 'no, go ahead.'

Man On Podcast

"And then I share the Gospel, I share the Cross what Jesus did and how He's the One that can forgive and pardon any one of our sins, and I explained the thieves on the Cross who were criminals, and one of them wanted to enter into Paradise, and I said *do you want to know you have that assurance of life after death?*"

ISIS Fighter

"He goes, '*yes.*'"

Man On Podcast

"Do you want to pray with me to receive Christ?"

ISIS Fighter

"He's like, '*yes.*'"

Man On Podcast

"It's an ISIS fighter. I'm literally stunned this is happening. So he starts praying to receive Christ, and right at the end, I'll show you a picture of em, I said in Jesus Name, and he stopped and he shook his head, '*no.*' I mean, it was out of nowhere, just, '*no.*' And I literally saw evil come upon this man, like an evil entity come upon him, and just like that he broke out of his hand ties, his face contorted, and his ears pinced up like a troll or something…"

This is a brief excerpt from a much longer interview. In the interview, when the Name of Jesus was mentioned during prayer, the spirit of Islam that had a hold on that man seemed to take control and prevented him from finishing the prayer in Jesus' Name. After this moment, the individuals present were able to subdue him and tie him up, and shortly after, the man regained his composure. A further conversation took place, but that's all I wish to share about this particular encounter in this book. Had that man been fully open to receiving Jesus at that time, the power of the Lord would have been more than sufficient to deliver him. The reason I mention this story is to illustrate how a spirit acted as a gatekeeper for this individual. The Bible teaches that our battle is not just physical, but also spiritual..

Beginning of Prayer

"Heavenly Father, I come before You on the foundation of Your Word for the promise of freedom and a sound mind according to Psalm 119:45, and 2 Timothy 1:7:

Psalms 119:45 BSB

"And I will walk in freedom, for I have sought Your precepts."

2 Timothy 1:7 LSV

"for God did not give us a spirit of fear, but of power, and of love, and of a sound mind;"

"Heavenly Father, I come before You, seeking freedom from any spirits that may be oppressing my spirit, soul, body, or mind. I ask, according to Your Word, that You would bring judgment against every unclean spirit that has caused oppression in any way, including any gatekeeper spirits. I renounce and repent for all sins, transgressions, and iniquities of myself and my ancestors, as well as the unclean spirits that have acted as gatekeepers over my heart, mind, body, soul, or spirit, preventing me from receiving the truth of Your Word. I renounce religious practices such as Eastern-Orthodox Christianity, Islam, Buddhism, Hinduism, Antichrist religions, and the worship of idols. I ask for deliverance and freedom from these influences and any similar entities that are against You and the Gospel of Christ."

Asking For An Order of Protection

"Heavenly Father, I ask for a permanent divine order of protection against every unclean gatekeeping spirit, and spirits associated with Islam, Buddhism, Hinduism, and other false religions. I ask that You would assign angelic officers to enforce my safety against those spirits, as well as gatekeeping spirits. I receive Your righteous verdict, release, freedom, and breakthrough in Jesus name, thank You father, amen!"

END OF PRAYER

CHAPTER 37.4: PRAYER OF DELIVERANCE FROM THE SERBIAN ORTHODOX RELIGION

Before I begin the prayer, I want to take a moment to explain this a little more. You might be thinking, "Isn't Orthodox Christianity Christian?" And the answer is no, not exactly. At its best, it's a mix of New Testament traditions, pagan ancestral worship, and idolatry, all wrapped up in a blend of tradition. If you grew up in a Serbian family like I did, you might have noticed the festivals and traditions you either participated in or observed, whether you understood them fully or not. If you've ever asked yourself, "What do these practices mean? Why are we lighting candles and honoring our family patron saint?" you're not alone. If you're Serbian and have wondered why your family celebrates these things, here's some insight:

Pagan Origins And Explaining The Serbian

Traditions Of The "Slava"

When Christianity came to the Balkans in the 9th century, it mixed with old pagan beliefs. This blend made it easier for people to accept the new religion. The Balkans Slavic tribes, including Serbians, practiced something called animism. Which is basically holding reverence or worship of nature believing that rocks, animals and plants hold consciousness and spirits which is not Biblical–rocks don't have spirits. Serbians believed that trees, rivers, animals, and yes, even mountains were inhabited by spirits. Serbs thought that these spirits had their own personalities and powers that influenced the world. One of the traditions such as the *slava* engaged in the worship of a patron *saint*. Each family picks a saint, often tied to the saint's special day, to honor and celebrate. These ancestral spirits were believed to have protected and guided alive family members. Fire was used in purification ceremonies and symbolized connection to divinity and rituals were also a part around fire to honor spirits–newsflash this was not the Spirit of the Lord but demons and occasionally dead believers. This is why lighting candles is almost always included in Serbian Orthodox tradition. Occasionally, families would leave offerings such as food or symbolic items on mountains and other sites as offerings to these spirits and to seek their spiritual blessings.

Rituals For Protection

Many Serbians have used, and unfortunately still use, incense around the home and in their "churches," which I would refer to as pagan temples, as that's what they truly are —not churches. Incense was believed to purify the space it was used in (though this is a belief, not a Biblical truth). They placed their faith in the smoke, which cannot protect, rather than trusting in the Lord. It was believed that incense created a protective barrier around the home where it was burned.

Additionally, incense was used to attract benevolent spirits and ancestors. Yes, I know this may sound unusual, but bear with me. They believed burning incense invited these spirits' presence and protection to keep the household "safe." They also thought incense cleansed icons and talismans. Now that you understand this, I encourage you never to partake in these practices, as you now know what they truly represent.

Beginning of Prayer

"Heavenly Father, I come before You with a humble heart, acknowledging the unbiblical and pagan spiritual practices of my ancestors. I repent for any involvement in rituals or beliefs that have strayed from Your light. I renounce all ties to animism, ancestral worship, and any customs that do not align with Your truth. I confess the actions of my forebears that may have called upon spirits or sought protection apart from You. I ask for Your forgiveness and for Your cleansing power to wash over me and my family, breaking any bonds to these practices. According to Your Word in Psalm 91:1-2, I seek refuge in You, Lord, as my fortress and my deliverer. I ask that You deliver and shield my home and family from any unholy spirits. May Your presence fill our lives, dispelling any darkness and bringing peace to our hearts and homes. I lift up my family and pray that they, too, would come to know Your truth and find freedom in Your love. May they choose to turn away from past practices and embrace a life rooted in Your grace. Thank You, Lord, for the freedom that comes through Your redemption. I claim this freedom for myself and my bloodline, trusting in Your protection and guidance. I renounce Orthodox traditions and its religion, along with its pagan beliefs, and choose to serve and worship You and You alone. In Jesus' name, I pray, amen."

END OF PRAYER

CHAPTER 38: PRAYER OF DELIVERANCE FROM FALSE CONVICTIONS

False convictions only disrupt a person's peace and place an unnecessary burden on them, distracting them from what truly matters. That is not the Lord's heart for His people. It mirrors what the Egyptians did to the Israelites before the Lord intervened on their behalf, even though they were initially upset when the Lord began to intervene, as we can read about in Exodus. This prayer is a simple petition for freedom from just that.

Matthew 11:28-30 BSB

"Come to Me, all you who are weary and burdened, and I will give you rest. Take My yoke upon you and learn from Me; for I am gentle and humble in heart, and you will find rest for your souls. For My yoke is easy and My burden is light."

John 8:36 BSB

"So if the Son sets you free, you will be free indeed."

2 Corinthians 3:17 BSB

"Now the Lord is the Spirit, and where the Spirit of the Lord is, there is freedom."

Beginning of Prayer

"Heavenly Father, I come before You, standing on the foundation of Your Word, to ask for deliverance from false convictions that did not come from Your Spirit, as well as any unclean spirits that have influenced or caused these false convictions and burdens. Lord, You created me to be free to serve You with joy and freedom. I receive Your freedom, Lord Jesus. Thank You. Amen!"

END OF PRAYER

CHAPTER 39: PRAYER OF DELIVERANCE FROM ANXIETY

Few things are more paralyzing than anxiety. Jesus was very clear about worry and anxiousness. Some people might think that worry and anxiousness are a normal part of life, but they are not. In fact, it is very abnormal in the life of a believer because anxiousness is not of the Lord:

> Matthew 6:34 ASV
>
> "Be not therefore anxious for the morrow: for the morrow will be anxious for itself. Sufficient unto the day is the evil thereof."
>
> Philippians 4:6-7 ASV
>
> "In nothing be anxious; but in everything by prayer and supplication with thanksgiving let your requests be made known unto God. And the peace of God, which passeth all understanding, shall guard your hearts and your thoughts in Christ Jesus."

There is a difference between *feeling* anxious and *being* anxious. This is why the Word of God says to take every thought and imagination captive to the obedience of Christ:

> 2 Corinthians 10:3-6 ASV

> "For though we walk in the flesh, we do not war according to the flesh (for the weapons of our warfare are not of the flesh, but mighty before God to the casting down of strongholds); casting down imaginations, and every high thing that is exalted against the knowledge of God, and bringing every thought into captivity to the obedience of Christ; and being in readiness to avenge all disobedience, when your obedience shall be made full."

Anxiety does not have to be tolerated in the life of a believer, it has to bow through the authority of the believer in Christ Jesus the LORD:

Matthew 18:18 ASV

> "Verily I say unto you, What things soever ye shall bind on earth shall be bound in heaven; and what things soever ye shall loose on earth shall be loosed in heaven."

Anything unbiblical that opposes Jesus is in essence antichrist. That's literally what the word means: anti which means *against*, Christ meaning *Christ*:

Prayer Asking The Court To Be Seated In Session

"LORD GOD, I now ask according to Daniel 7:10 that the Heavenly Court would be seated to hear my case, in Jesus name. I ask You to call heavenly angels under your authority and jurisdiction to be witnesses, scribes, and officers of the Court to protect me, keep the peace of the Court, and execute Your righteous decrees and commands, in Jesus name."

Prayer of Repentance For Judgments Made On Others

"LORD GOD, I repent, renounce, break agreement, and ask for forgiveness for every bitter-root judgment that my ancestors and I made upon others in the area of anxiety and anxiousness. I repent, and I ask for You to forgive us for those judgments that were made, and I ask You to lift any negative repercussions that came as a result of those judgments made on others. I repent for all the hypocrisy that has been in my family line and in my personal life, in Jesus name."

Addressing And Repenting For Altars of Anxiousness

"LORD GOD, I renounce all spirits of anxiety, anxiousness, fear, ungodly timidity, and doubt because your Word says:

2 Timothy 1:7 KJV

"For God hath not given us the spirit of fear; but of power, and of love, and of a sound mind."

Prayer of Repentance For Anti Anxiety Medications And Pharmakeia

"Heavenly Father, I confess and repent before You on the Scriptural foundation of Isaiah 43:25-26, 1 John 1:9, and 2 John 2:1-2 for every time I took medication to try to relieve anxiety. I repent for having ever taken anti-anxiety medications such as benzodiazepines and all its variants, Diazepam, Lorazepam, Alprazolam, Clonazepam, Buspirone, Sertraline, Paroxetine, Escitalopram, Fluoxetine, Venlafaxine, Duloxetine, Gabapentin, Pregabalin, Propranolol, Hydroxyzine, Clonidine, Tiagabine, Mirtazapine, Bupropion, Valium, Xanax, Ativan, Librium, Klonopin, and all SSRIs, SNRIs, beta blockers, MAOIs, and all forms of experimental drugs such as Ketamine, eye movement desensitization drugs, reprocessing drugs (EMDR), as well as neuropeptides including neuropeptide-Y/NP and all other anti-anxiety medications."

Prayer of Repentance And Petition For Deliverance

"Heavenly Father, I repent for every time I turned to doctors, pharmacies, drugs and medications to try to relieve anxiousness. I repent for coming to them instead of coming to You. I repent for all spiritual adultery that I've committed by turning to everyone but You for help. I now request according to Isaiah 22:22 and Revelation 3:7 for You to permanently shut every single demonic door, access point, and every legal access point to any demonic oppression of anxiousness, anxiety, fear, doubt and all of their associated spirits for it is written:

Isaiah 22:22 BSB

"I will place on his shoulder the key to the house of David. What he opens no one can shut, and what he shuts no one can open."

Revelation 3:7 BSB

"To the angel of the church in Philadelphia write: These are the words of the One who is holy and true, who holds the key of David. What He opens no one can shut, and what He shuts no one can open."

"LORD GOD, Lord Jesus, Holy Spirit, I declare that I want absolutely nothing to do with demonic oppression, pharmaceutical drugs and its associated spirits. I ask You to deliver me and set me free from any urges for pharmaceutical drugs, prescription drugs, legal and illegal drugs as well as all forms of substance abuse including alcohol, for it is written:

Romans 11:26 BSB

"And so all Israel will be saved, as it is written: "The Deliverer will come from Zion; He will remove godlessness from Jacob."

Petition of Deliverance

"Heavenly Father, I renounce the world, the lusts of the flesh, anxiety medications as well as prescribed medications that didn't fix the problem but just served as an access point. I now petition You for deliverance from all anxiety, panic attacks, paralyzing fears, low self-esteem, low self-worth, condemnation, tormenting thoughts, constant replaying thoughts like a song stuck on repeat, beating myself up or being hard on myself. Self condemnation as it is written:

Romans 8:1 BSB

"Therefore, there is now no condemnation
for those who are in Christ Jesus."

"Heavenly Father, I now ask You, according to Isaiah 22:22 and Revelation 3:7 to slam shut, lock, and *permanently* seal in Jesus' Holy Blood all demonic doors and entryways, never to be opened ever again, in Jesus name."

Prayer Requesting For Justice

"Heavenly Father, I choose to remind You and Your Court of all the hurt, pain, death, loss, destruction, grief, sorrow, ungodly sorrow, and all thefts that the devil, demons, and satanic powers have caused to me and my family. Heavenly Father, Lord Jesus, Holy Spirit, I declare that Your Word states:

Isaiah 61:8 ASV

"For I, Jehovah, love justice, I hate robbery with iniquity;
and I will give them their recompense in truth, and I
will make an everlasting covenant with them."

Prayer Asking For Justice

"Heavenly Father, Lord Jesus, Holy Spirit, I now ask for a sentence of judgment against every demonic entity, including the spirit of death, spirits of anxiety, panic attacks, anxiety related disorders, constant worry, loss, destruction, ungodly grief, tormenting grief, ungodly sorrow, hopelessness, and a sick heart that has oppressed me in every way, shape, or form, in Jesus name."

Asking For An Order of Protection

"LORD GOD, I also request for an order of protection of the spirits listed above that would try or have oppressed, caused depression, suicide, seasonal depression, false weights, unjust measures, anxiety, worry, constant worry, rampant thoughts, ungodly thoughts constantly repeating and meditated upon. I ask You to give your angels charge over me, and I declare like King David:

Psalms 103:6 BSB

"The LORD executes righteousness and justice for all the oppressed."

Psalms 17:2 WEB

"Let my sentence come out of your presence. Let your eyes look on equity."

"LORD GOD, I receive Your mercy for myself, and I also receive Your righteous verdicts of judgment against the demonic, in Jesus Name, amen!"

END OF PRAYER

CHAPTER 40: HOUSE CLEANSING PRAYER

Dominion, A Gift From God

I want to briefly revisit an earlier chapter within this book to discuss and teach about the dominion that man and woman were given over this earth. Flip with me to the first book of the Bible, the Book of Genesis:

> Genesis 1:26 KJV
>
> "And God said, Let us make man in our image, after our likeness: and let them have dominion over the fish of the sea, and over the fowl of the air, and over the cattle, and over all the earth, and over every creeping thing that creepeth upon the earth."

God is a Spirit and when He said let *them* have dominion He spoke and released a universal Law in the spirit realm that now even He Himself is submitted to. God's Word is so powerful that when God speaks, He obeys His own Word.

> John 4:24 KJV
>
> "God is a Spirit: and they that worship him must worship him in spirit and in truth."

Prior to the fall of Adam he had full dominion to take that serpent that was speaking to his wife Eve and throw that thing into kingdom come, but he felt the enticement and lustful desire for the tree and probably love for his wife, Adam knew what she did and he more than likely understood the repercussions that she would experience that he ate of the tree also. When he took the fruit from the tree, yielding to the voice of his wife and the voice of the enemy he willing submitted himself under the serpents' authority, and we can see this was a very big problem because Romans give us insight into dominion and obedience:

Romans 6:12-18 KJV

"Let not sin therefore reign in your mortal body, that ye should obey it in the lusts thereof. Neither yield ye your members as instruments of unrighteousness unto sin: but yield yourselves unto God, as those that are alive from the dead, and your members as instruments of righteousness unto God. For sin shall not have dominion over you: for ye are not under the law, but under grace. What then? shall we sin, because we are not under the law, but under grace? God forbid. Know ye not, that to whom ye yield yourselves servants to obey, his servants ye are to whom ye obey; whether of sin unto death, or of obedience unto righteousness? But God be thanked, that ye were the servants of sin, but ye have obeyed from the heart that form of doctrine which was delivered you. Being then made free from sin, ye became the servants of righteousness."

Houston We Had A Problem

Some translations say the word *slaves,* which is a more accurate rendering of the Greek word used there. When Adam and Eve submitted to the enemy, they became a servant, slave to sin and the enemy. That is where the transfer of dominion initially happened. Since God said: "Let *them* have dominion," and dominion was transferred willingly to the rebellious spirit that the Bible, and we call, Satan and his rebellious angels. Because of this, a giant problem emerged. This is the reason a lot of suffering had taken place in history, because dominion was given to a spirit who is literally rebelling against the LORD GOD, and the enemy absolutely hates mankind. *It was never God's fault.*

Houston We Have The Solution

But this is where it gets superb. God was looking for a man to use to shift the earth. The LORD couldn't find a sinless man to partner with for the transfer of dominion for the earth: because remember we've established that God spoke: "Let them have dominion over the earth," and when God speaks, He Himself obeys. Now God was looking for a man to stand in the gap to use, but here was the issue, no one was sinless. Everyone was under the dominion of the enemy through sin. That is, until Jesus came. Some have thought that JESUS didn't even exist until Mary gave birth to Him. But this is most certainly not the case.[61]

John 17:1-5 BSB

"When Jesus had spoken these things, He lifted up His eyes to heaven and said, "Father, the hour has come. Glorify Your Son, that Your Son may glorify You. For You granted Him authority over all people, so that He may give eternal life to all those You have given Him. Now this is eternal life, that they may know You, the only true God, and Jesus Christ, whom You have sent. I have glorified You on earth by accomplishing the work You gave Me to do. And now, Father, glorify Me in Your presence with the glory I had with You before the world existed."

John 8:51-58 KJV

"Verily, verily, I say unto you, If a man keep my saying, he shall never see death. Then said the Jews unto him, Now we know that thou hast a devil. Abraham is dead, and the prophets; and thou sayest, If a man keep my saying, he shall never taste of death. Art thou greater than our father Abraham, which is dead? and the prophets are dead: whom makest thou thyself? Jesus answered, If I honour myself, my honour is nothing: it is my Father that honoureth me; of whom ye say, that he is your God: yet ye have not known him; but I know him: and if I should say, I know him not, I shall be a liar like unto you: but I know him, and keep his saying. Your father Abraham rejoiced to see my day: and he saw it, and was glad. Then said the Jews unto him, Thou art not yet fifty years old, and hast thou seen Abraham? Jesus said unto them, Verily, verily, I say unto you, Before Abraham was, I am."

The very next verse is the Jewish leaders picking up stones to stone Him for what He just said. Do you want to know the significance of what He said when He said: "I AM." Flip with me to Exodus 3:

Exodus 3:13-14 KJV

"And Moses said unto God, Behold, when I come unto the children of Israel, and shall say unto them, The God of your fathers hath sent me unto you; and they shall say to me, What is his name? what shall I say unto them? And God said unto Moses, I AM THAT I AM: and he said, Thus shalt thou say unto the children of Israel, I AM hath sent me unto you."

Isaiah 48:12-13 KJV

"Hearken unto me, O Jacob and Israel, my called; I am he; I am the first, I also am the last. Mine hand also hath laid the foundation of the earth, and my right hand hath spanned the heavens: when I call unto them, they stand up together."

Revelation 1:17 KJV

"And when I saw him, I fell at his feet as dead. And he laid his right hand upon me, saying unto me, Fear not; I am the first and the last:"

Our Messiah did not just come into existence one day. He already existed before the world began, because He was with the Father and Holy Spirit and helped create the world. Jesus laid aside the *Garments of Divinity* to take up the garments of a Servant, in order to help the Father and Holy Spirit redeem humanity back to a pre-fall condition. This is why the Book of Psalms, and the Book of Hebrews say:

Psalms 40:6-8 BSB

"Sacrifice and offering You did not desire, but my ears You have opened. Burnt offerings and sin offerings You did not require. Then I said, "Here I am, I have come — it is written about me in the scroll: I delight to do Your will, O my God; Your law is within my heart."

The BSB translators added a note at the end of verse 6 mentioning that some Hebrew and LXX manuscripts say: "But a Body You have prepared for Me." The Book of Hebrews reiterates this and shows that the Hebrew language renders this verse as indeed: "Body you have prepared for Me;"

Hebrews 10:5-7 BSB

"Therefore, when Christ came into the world, He said: "Sacrifice and offering You did not desire, but a body You prepared for Me. In burnt offerings and sin offerings You took no delight. Then I said, 'Here I am, it is written about Me in the scroll: I have come to do Your will, O God.'"

Why did the LORD come down in a body? There were multiple reasons, but we see one in revelation being dominion related. This is where we see that our Jesus reclaimed the dominion of not just the Earth, but death and hell itself. Why? Because He has the keys!

Revelation 1:17-18 KJV

"And when I saw him, I fell at his feet as dead. And he laid his right hand upon me, saying unto me, Fear not; I am the first and the last: I am he that liveth, and was dead; and, behold, I am alive for evermore, Amen; and have the keys of hell and of death."

One of the reasons that Jesus, The Messiah, came was to

reclaim the dominion that Adam lost. This is one of the reasons why the Lord Jesus is called *The Last Adam* in Scripture:

1 Corinthians 15:45 ASV

"So also it is written, The first man Adam became a living soul. The last Adam became a life-giving spirit."

And the same One that has the keys to death, hell, and the grave said to you and me:

Luke 10:19 KJV

"Behold, I give unto you power to tread on serpents and scorpions, and over all the power of the enemy: and nothing shall by any means hurt you."

The Lord Jesus is currently waiting for the Word from the Father: "Son, go get Your bride–she's ready." But until that day, Jesus told us to occupy until He comes:

Luke 19:13 KJV

"And he called his ten servants, and delivered them ten pounds, and said unto them, Occupy till I come."

We are His governing Bride on earth. We have dominion because He has given us the authority. Through revisiting this teaching, I wanted us to gain a fresh perspective of dominion over the homes that we live in and that unclean spirits don't just get to do whatever they want. In Christ Jesus, we can stand and say: *"Not in my metron, and most certainly not in my house. As for me and my house, we serve the LORD!"*

Joshua 24:14-15 KJV

"Now therefore fear the LORD, and serve him in sincerity and in truth: and put away the gods which your fathers served on the other side of the flood, and in Egypt; and serve ye the LORD. And if it seem evil unto you to serve the LORD, choose you this day whom ye will serve; whether the gods which your fathers served that were on the other side of the flood, or the gods of the Amorites, in whose land ye dwell: but as for me and my house, we will serve the LORD."

Below is a prayer to cleanse your home. May the prayer bring about such a beautiful breakthrough, peace, and invite the Presence of God to permeate the atmosphere of your humble abode, in Jesus name. Jesus is Lord. Amen!

Beginning of House Cleansing Prayer

Proverbs 3:33 BSB

"The curse of the Lord is on the house of the wicked, but He blesses the home of the righteous."

"Heavenly Father, I renounce and repent for all acts of witchcraft, occultic activity, religious rites, initiating, rituals, all magic, tarot card readings and the practice of unholy religions. I renounce all idols and false gods of false religions as well as all the legal rights that were given to all unclean spirits through the burning of incense, the burning of sage, prayers to false gods, the devil, unclean spirits and the spirits of the dead. I renounce and repent for all necromancy that happened in this home, I renounce and repent for rituals that included blood sacrifice in this home. Furthermore, I come out of agreement with every act of disobedience, occultic activity, rebellion, and the occult that happened in this home and around its property. Heavenly Father, I ask You to dispatch heavenly angels to bind, arrest, escort, and bind in everlasting chains the presence of every single unclean spirit that has occupied never to return again as a familiar spirit to harass me, my family, or anyone else in Jesus name."

"Heavenly Father, Your Word clearly declares that the curse of the Lord is on the house of the wicked, but You bless the home of the righteous. So I ask You to lift and curse off of my home from previous owners if there are any present, as well as to remove it from my bloodline and my spouse's bloodline if it is present. I ask You to release the scroll of your protection, favor, divine and physical blessing into the timber of my home and the rest of its material as well as the soil that my house stands on because we are built upon the true foundation—Jesus. And I declare that our house will remain standing and I ask for Your divine protection and angels to be assigned to protect us and our home from any calamity foreseen and unforeseen including spiritual causes or in any potential future times of unforeseen and aggressive weather in Jesus name, amen."

Obtaining Freedom For Your Property

"Heavenly Father, I now request for a permanent divine order of protection to be established indefinitely and permanently against all the powers of darkness against my home in Jesus name. I repent for all occultic activity and ask that the Blood of Jesus would be supernaturally applied to my home and the residents of my home as well. I desire my home to be a safe and holy space, and I ask that You would dispatch Your angels to come and remove any evil presence off the home's property and the home itself. And for any evil presence to be banished into the bottomless pit, never to return to earth. Or my current home, my future home and any other property I may own or live in the future, in Jesus name. I received Your righteous verdict, and I thank You for freeing my home."

Declare By Faith

"I command that every evil presence in and around my

home's property to leave NOW in the Name of Jesus. I take dominion of my property and I give it to the LORD. I command every evil presence to never return to my home again or face the judgment of the Lord, in Jesus name, amen!"

END OF PRAYER

CHAPTER 40.1: PRAYER OF DELIVERANCE FROM POVERTY

Malachi 3:8-12 BSB

"Will a man rob God? Yet you are robbing Me! But you ask, 'How do we rob You?' In tithes and offerings. You are cursed with a curse, yet you—the whole nation—are still robbing Me. Bring the full tithe into the storehouse, so that there may be food in My house. Test Me in this," says the LORD of Hosts. "See if I will not open the windows of heaven and pour out for you blessing without measure. I will rebuke the devourer for you, so that it will not destroy the fruits of your land, and the vine in your field will not fail to produce fruit," says the LORD of Hosts. "Then all the nations will call you blessed, for you will be a land of delight," says the LORD of Hosts."

Proverbs 13:21 BSB

"Disaster pursues sinners, but prosperity is the reward of the righteous."

I'm just going to be honest here, *poverty is not piety.* And poverty is not God's will for His children. God is the God of exceedingly abundantly above what we can ask or think. Do you think that sounds like poverty to you?

Ephesians 3:20 WEB

"Now to him who is able to do exceedingly abundantly above all that we ask or think, according to the power that works in us,"

And bear with me for a moment here, as I know that some were taught that that poverty is somehow attributed to piety and godliness, but I'm going to present to you Scripture that literally says otherwise. The reason I'm going to be posting these scriptures is to break down the strongholds that churches and the devil have exalted in the minds of some believers. To make them believe that poverty is somehow of God and okay, which it's not!

Psalms 25:13 BSB

"His soul will dwell in prosperity, and his descendants will inherit the land."

Psalms 37:10-11 BSB

"Yet a little while, and the wicked will be no more; though you look for them, they will not be found. But the meek will inherit the land and delight in abundant prosperity."

Proverbs 28:25 BSB

"A greedy man stirs up strife, but he who trusts in the LORD will prosper."

Job 36:10-11 BSB

"He opens their ears to correction and commands that they turn from iniquity. If they obey and serve Him, then they end their days in prosperity and their years in happiness."

Deuteronomy 28:11-14 BSB

"The LORD will make you prosper abundantly—in the fruit of your womb, the offspring of your livestock, and the produce of your land—in the land that the LORD swore to your fathers to give you. The LORD will open the heavens, His abundant storehouse, to send rain on your land in season and to bless all the work of your hands. You will lend to many nations, but borrow from none. The LORD will make you the head and not the tail; you will only move upward and never downward, if you hear and carefully follow the commandments of the LORD your God, which I am giving you today. Do not turn aside to the right or to the left from any of the words I command you today, and do not go after other gods to serve them."

Deuteronomy 30:9 BSB

"So the LORD your God will make you abound in all the work of your hands and in the fruit of your womb, the offspring of your livestock, and the produce of your land. Indeed, the LORD will again delight in your goodness, as He delighted in that of your fathers,"

But there's a common aspect in these

promises and it has everything to do with the heart, and that is obedience:

Deuteronomy 30:8 BSB

"And you will again obey the voice of the LORD and follow all His commandments I am giving you today."

No doubt someone will think to themselves: "Well, what about 1 Timothy 6:10, 'The love of money is the root of all evil?'" And this is true, but notice Paul the apostle said the love of money, not money itself. You give a righteous man wealth he will build God's Kingdom, you give a wicked man wealth he will start wars, and cause destruction for personal gain. Poverty sounds so noble to some, but you'll never hear a rich person praise poverty, it is only those living in it with a religious mindset that try to justify it as a blessing. Go ask children in Kenya, Zambia, Zimbabwe, and other parts of poor countries what poverty is like, they won't praise it. Poverty is not a blessing, it's a curse. You understand that better if you've seen the living conditions that poverty causes, not to mention the crime and drug problems it helps create and foster.

Beginning of Prayer

Isaiah 45:21 BSB

"Speak up and present your case— yes, let them take counsel together. Who foretold this long ago? Who announced it from ancient times? Was it not I, the Lord? There is no other God but Me, a righteous God and Savior; there is none but Me."

"Heavenly Father, I come before You today to prosecute the spirit of poverty. Your Word says that through obedience You prosper me. So I now begin with asking for forgiveness for all of my family's, and I's sins, transgressions, and iniquities and even those that are attached to my bloodline. I ask that the Blood of Jesus would be applied to me and my family, and I ask that through Your Power that the curse of poverty would be forever and permanently broken off of my family line. I renounce poverty. I declare it is not God's will for His children to walk in lack, but that Your Scriptures declare I shall not lack, as David states in the book of Psalms:

Psalms 23:1 WEB

"A Psalm by David. Yahweh is my shepherd:
I shall lack nothing."

"I renounce and break covenants, oaths, curses, vows, voodoo, witchcraft, contracts, physical ties, soul ties, spiritual ties, emotional ties, and agreements made that would give legal rights to the spirit of poverty, the enemy's camp, and or the kingdom of darkness in any way, shape, and or form. I now request that Jesus' Blood would be applied to and silence every negative voice in the spiritual realm as well as any negative financial testimony being spoken in the natural and in the spiritual realm, in Jesus name.

"I, myself, renounce any ancestral ties to Mammon, unholy financial altars, the love of money, putting faith, hope, and trust in material wealth, materialistic gains, and everything to do with lusting for power, authority, paper money, gold, silver, platinum, copper, and other precious metals, and other forms of currency, as well as any bloodshed and violence because of financial reasons as well.

1 Samuel 18:15 BSB

"When Saul saw that David was very successful, he was afraid of him."

"I not ask that my name, the names of my children, and even up to my grandchildren for all future generations, as well as the names of my family members to be erased from demonic records and unholy altars for anyone who had ties to them in my ancestry, including but not limited to, with the Freemasons, the Daughters of the Eastern Star, the Illuminati, the Ku Klux Klan, and other organizations that were displeasing to You. I renounce them, and I declare I don't want anything to do with them anymore. I am Yours Lord, set me free.

"I repent for any of my ancestors who didn't sow financially into Your Kingdom Lord whether through blood or marriage ties. For those who never tithed or gave offerings into Your Kingdom work here on this Earth or to churches that were Houses of the LORD. And I renounce the sins, iniquities, and transgressions of my forefathers. I ask that the Blood of Jesus would cleanse, free me, and release me from any spiritual debts that I have owed. I release and forgive everyone who was indebted to me through financial, natural, emotional, soulish, and spiritual means. Your Word says, as I have been forgiven, so also I must forgive:

Ephesians 4:31-32 WEB

"Let all bitterness, wrath, anger, outcry, and slander, be put away from you, with all malice. And be kind to one another, tender hearted, forgiving each other, just as God also in Christ forgave you."

"I forgive those who have wronged and owed me Lord, and I likewise now ask for Your forgiveness for me and my family lineage as well, according to 1 John 1:9 which states:

1 John 1:9 BSB

"If we confess our sins, He is faithful and just to forgive us our sins and to cleanse us from all unrighteousness."

Empower me to change, and be a better version of myself through the working of Your Hands upon my life. As a pot is shaped by the potter, may You be the Potter that shapes the clay of my heart, in Jesus name, amen!"

END OF PRAYER

CHAPTER 41: PRAYER OF DELIVERANCE FOR SEXUAL ABUSE

"Heavenly Father, I come before You today to seek for the full healing and deliverance from previous physical and sexual abuse and its spirits. LORD, I declare what was done by those who decided to take advantage was wrong, and I chose to forgive them for my own freedom. I now ask for deliverance and freedom from any spirits that have taken advantage of the trauma that happened to me or my ancestors, and especially those spirits who have attached themselves to trauma in my bloodline and DNA. I ask for complete and total healing and deliverance.

"Lord Jesus, I ask for complete deliverance, freedom, and healing from trauma, memories, and every spirit that has taken advantage of previous abuse. I declare that oppression ends today and today is the day that I receive freedom, in Jesus name."

Galatians 5:1 BSB

"It is for freedom that Christ has set us free. Stand firm, then, and do not be encumbered once more by a yoke of slavery."

END OF PRAYER

CHAPTER 42: RENOUNCING TRADES MADE WITH HUMAN DNA AND BOOKS OF DESTINY

Psalms 139:16 BSB

"Your eyes saw my unformed body; all my days were written in Your book and ordained for me before one of them came to be."

"Heavenly Father, I come before You today to address any legal and illegal spiritual trades done in my bloodline in partnership with demonic, satanic, witches and warlocks and unclean spirits. I renounce every trade and any that included a book of destiny, whether it be mine or one of my family members. As a member of my bloodline I now renounce every spiritual trade done with the kingdom of darkness and its ambassadors and associates and I now appeal to You Heavenly Father to dispatch heavenly angels to retrieve these books of destiny of both myself and my family's, in Jesus name.

"I ask that a divine judgment would be rendered against these forces of evil by you for these illegal trades and I ask that the Blood of Jesus would cover me, my books of destiny, my family's books of destiny and our DNA as well. I ask that You would heal, redeem and take back claim over our individual and collective DNA in Jesus name.

"Heavenly Father, I invoke the protection and purchasing power of the blood of Jesus (Yeshua my Messiah) to purchase me and my bloodline back for the Kingdom of God, to unlock our books of destiny and that through the power of your Holy Spirit that we would all fulfill the destinies you've placed on our lives. I receive Your freedom, healing, redemption and forgive Lord Jesus. Consecrate me and my family for Your purposes and the Father's will, and may we be a headache to the enemy and an asset to Your Kingdom and Your people. We receive You, Lord Jesus, amen!"

END OF PRAYER

CHAPTER 43: PRAYER AGAINST DNA RIDERS AND CANCER

"Heavenly Father, I ask according to Jesus' sacrifice that the redemption power of His blood would be applied to my blood and DNA. I come before you to prosecute potential DNA riders off of my bloodline and DNA, in Jesus name.

"Heavenly Father, I ask for the deliverance for every genetic anomaly including cancer to be issued for me immediately. I declare that You have not created me to be sick, but You have created me to be in good health according to the truth of Your Word:

Exodus 23:25 BSB

"So you shall serve the LORD your God, and He will bless your bread and your water. And I will take away sickness from among you."

Acts 10:38 BSB

"how God anointed Jesus of Nazareth with the Holy Spirit and with power, and how Jesus went around doing good and healing all who were oppressed by the devil, because God was with Him." [62]

"Lord Jesus, I now according to the Scriptures request from

the Father's Court in Heaven a verdict of judgment against every cancer cell in my body as well as spiritual DNA riders, genetic DNA riders, and DNA typos to be restored back to perfect condition for You are the architect of the human body. I ask for healing, restoration and refreshing to take place and I receive those things, in Jesus name, amen!"

END OF PRAYER

CHAPTER 44: PRAYER OF DELIVERANCE FROM THE ORPHAN SPIRIT

John 14:18 BSB

"I will not leave you as orphans; I will come to you."

Galatians 4:6-7 BSB

"And because you are sons, God sent the Spirit of His Son into our hearts, crying out, "Abba, Father!" So you are no longer a slave, but a son; and since you are a son, you are also an heir through God."

"Heavenly Father, I come before You today as Your son (or daughter). I acknowledge that I may have felt like I was an orphan, but today I clearly have read in the Scripture that regardless of what my feelings say Your Word speaks louder than my emotions. I accept that I am a son (or daughter) and that I am loved, chosen, redeemed, righteous, holy, unstoppable and that I'm growing up into everything that You have for me and called me to be. Today I ask for deliverance from the orphan heart, the orphan mentality and the orphan spirit along with the healing of my soul. I ask for Your judgment to be poured out on my behalf against the orphan spirit and every other unclean spirit attached to it. May You make Your love a reality in my heart and show me that You are for me and that You are my Father. Show me that it didn't matter what my earthly parents were like if they were around and even if I don't know who they were, may You be my pursuit and show me that You deeply care for me. I welcome Your Presence into right where I'm at, and I accept Your love today, in Jesus name, amen.

END OF PRAYER

CHAPTER 45: PRAYER OF DELIVERANCE FROM OCCULTIC SPIRITS, ACTIVITIES, AND PRACTICES

Renouncing Occult Activities

"Heavenly Father, I repent for every occultic activity that my ancestors and I have ever partaken in. I renounce every coven, witch sisterhood, warlock brotherhood and all forms of witchcraft and occult activities. I confess the sins of my ancestors for partaking in these things, and I desire total and complete freedom from the works of darkness and the spirits of darkness. I ask You to redeem and free me from any and all ties to and from any of these things that I just mentioned."

"Heavenly Father, according to Psalm 103:6 I ask that You would pour out Your judgment against the unclean spirits that have afflicted me and my family in any way shape or form in connection to witchcraft and occult activities. I ask for deliverance and healing for me and my entire bloodline, which includes my family. I thank you for their lives:

1 Timothy 2:3-4 BSB

"This is good and pleasing in the sight of God our Savior, who wants everyone to be saved and to come to the knowledge of the truth."

"I ask according to 1 Timothy 2:3-4 that my entire family would come to salvation and even today Lord, may my family choose to receive You as their Lord and Savior. Thank You, Lord, for freedom and I revive Your freedom in Jesus name, amen!"

END OF PRAYER

CHAPTER 46: PRAYER RENOUNCING FREEMASONRY

If you're wondering: "How do I know if I had ancestors who were Freemasons?" One really strong indicator is if you find items in their home, rings, stickers on their cars, pictures on their laptops, phones, phone cases and other belongings with this:

Prayer Asking The Court To Be Seated In Session

"LORD GOD, I now ask according to Daniel 7:10 that the Heavenly Court would be seated to hear my case. I ask You to call heavenly angels under your authority and jurisdiction to be witnesses, scribes and officers of the Court to protect me, keep the peace of the Court and execute Your righteous decrees and commands, for it is written:

Psalms 103:20 BSB

"Bless the LORD, all His angels mighty in strength who carry out His word, who hearken to the voice of His command."

Prayer of Repentance For Judgments Made On Others

"LORD GOD, I repent, renounce, break agreement and ask for forgiveness for all bitter-root judgments that I and my ancestors made upon others in the area of freemasonry. I repent, and I ask for You to forgive us for those judgments that were made, and I ask You to lift any negative repercussions that came as a result of those judgments made on others. I repent for all the hypocrisy that has been in my family line and in my personal life, in Jesus name."

Repentance And Asking For Personal Forgiveness

"Heavenly Father, I repent and ask for governess for every ritual, initiation, rites and all ungodly and occult activities that my ancestors and II have done. I ask for forgiveness for all the sins, transgressions, and iniquities of my forefathers and foremothers in Jesus name. I ask according to Psalm 146:7 for complete freedom and deliverance from freemasonry and all of its roots as well as its fruits. I reject freemasonry ideologies and everything antichrist, in Jesus name.

Prayer Asking For Justice

Psalm 146:7 KJV

"Which executeth judgment for the oppressed: Which giveth food to the hungry. The LORD looseth the prisoners:"

"Heavenly Father, I renounce all the degrees of freemasonry as well as all of their branches, including but not limited to the following:

Blue Lodge

(Craft Lodge)

1. Entered Apprentice
2. Fellow Craft
3. Master Mason

York Rite

Chapter

(Royal Arch)

4. Mark Master
5. Past Master
6. Most Excellent Master
7. Royal Arch Mason

Council

(Cryptic Masonry)

8. Royal Master
9. Select Master
10. Super Excellent Master

Commandery

(Knights Templar)

11. Order of the Red Cross
12. Order of Knights of Malta

13. Order of the Temple

Scottish Rite

(Southern Jurisdiction)

14. Secret Master
15. Perfect Master
16. Intimate Secretary
17. Provost and Judge
18. Intendant of the Building
19. Master of the Ninth Arch
20. Sublime Master Elected
21. Grand Master Architect
22. Grand Elect Mason
23. Knight of the East
24. Knight of the Sword
25. Knight of the West
26. Prince of Jerusalem
27. Knight of the East and West
28. Knight of the Rose Croix
29. Knight of the Rose Croix of H.R.D.M.
30. Grand Pontiff
31. Master ad Vitam
32. Patriarch Noachite
33. Prince of Libanus

34. Chief of the Tabernacle
35. Prince of the Tabernacle
36. Knight of the Brazen Serpent
37. Prince of Mercy
38. Commander of the Temple
39. Knight of the Sun
40. Knight of St. Andrew
41. Grand Elect Knight
42. Inspector General
43. Grand Inspector Inquisitor Commander
44. Sublime Prince of the Royal Secret
45. Sovereign Grand Inspector General

Additional Bodies
Shriners
(Ancient Arabic Order of the Nobles of the Mystic Shrine)

46. Potentate
47. Chief Rabban
48. Assistant Rabban
49. High Priest and Prophet
50. Recorder
51. Treasurer

Tall Cedars of Lebanon
52. Tall Cedar

53. Junior Cedar

54. Senior Cedar

Order of the Eastern Star

55. Worthy Matron

56. Worthy Patron

57. Associate Matron

58. Secretary

59. Treasurer

Job's Daughters

60. Bethel Guardian

61. Honored Queen

62. Senior Princess

63. Junior Princess

64. Guide

65. Treasurer

66. Secretary

Rainbow Girls

67. Worthy Advisor

68. Charity

69. Hope

70. Faith

DeMolay

71. Master Councilor
72. Senior Councilor
73. Junior Councilor
74. Scribe
75. Treasurer

Affiliated Organizations

— Shriners

— Grotto (Mysterious Order of Nobles of the Mystic Shrine)

— Tall Cedars of Lebanon

— Order of the Eastern Star

— Job's Daughters

— Rainbow Girls

— DeMolay

"Heavenly Father, Lord Jesus Christ, Holy Spirit, I renounce every single degree of freemasonry including its associated societies as well as any not specifically mentioned within this list and prayer LORD GOD. I renounce all secrets, secret handshakes, secret knowledge, secret passcodes, secret passwords, secret words, initiation rites, all sworn in oaths, vows, covenants, contracts, agreements made within the structures of freemasonry and their affiliated societies including covenants made with death, spirits of deception, deception, false baptisms, counterfeit spiritual experiences, demonic out-of-body experiences, astral projection, health curses, spirits of infirmity, infirmity, sickness, disease, unholy alliances and all unrighteous covenants, in Jesus name.

Renouncing The Unrighteous Altars of Freemasonry

"Heavenly Father, I renounce, break agreement, confess, association, ask forgiveness for and cut ties to and with every unrighteous altar associated and identified with freemasonry, along with all of its subsidiaries and affiliated organizations. I renounce the altars of freemasonry and I petition You Heavenly Father in Your wisdom to set me free from all roots and ties to freemasonry including freemasonry's spiritual technologies, altars, spirits and any mind control in Jesus name. I ask You LORD according to 1 Kings 13:1-5:

1 Kings 13:1-5 BSB

"Suddenly, as Jeroboam was standing beside the altar to burn incense, there came a man of God from Judah to Bethel by the word of the Lord. And he cried out against the altar by the word of the Lord, "O altar, O altar, this is what the Lord says: 'A son named Josiah will be born to the house of David, and upon you he will sacrifice the priests of the high places who burn incense upon you, and human bones will be burned upon you.'" That day the man of God gave a sign, saying, "The Lord has spoken this sign: 'Surely the altar will be split apart, and the ashes upon it will be poured out.'" Now when King Jeroboam, who was at the altar in Bethel, heard the word that the man of God had cried out against it, he stretched out his hand and said, "Seize him!" But the hand he stretched out toward him withered, so that he could not pull it back. And the altar was split apart, and the ashes poured out, according to the sign that the man of God had given by the word of the Lord."

"LORD, I ask that You would send Your Word against every altar of freemasonry that has been attached to my bloodline and severe it off of my and my family, as I ask that the Blood of Jesus would be applied to me and my family and cover us from head to toe. May You send your Word and destroy those altars of freemasonry that were attached to my bloodline, and I ask for deliverance and freedom in Jesus name. For where the Spirit of the Lord is, there is freedom!"

END OF PRAYER

CHAPTER 47: PRAYER OF FREEDOM AGAINST THE SPIRIT OF INFIRMITY

Psalms 103:2-6 WEB

"Praise Yahweh, my soul, and don't forget all his benefits; who forgives all your sins; who heals all your diseases; who redeems your life from destruction; who crowns you with loving kindness and tender mercies; who satisfies your desire with good things, so that your youth is renewed like the eagle's. Yahweh executes righteous acts, and justice for all who are oppressed."

Luke 13:12 WEB

"When Jesus saw her, he called her, and said to her, "Woman, you are freed from your infirmity."

Asking The Court To Be In Session

"LORD GOD, I now ask according to Daniel 7:10, that the Heavenly Court would be seated to hear my case, in Jesus name. I ask You to call heavenly angels under your authority and jurisdiction to be witnesses, scribes and officers of the Court to protect me, keep the peace of the Court and execute

Your righteous decrees and commands, in Jesus name."

Repentance For Judgments Made On Others And Asking For Personal Forgiveness

"LORD GOD, I repent, renounce, break agreement and ask for forgiveness for all bitter-root judgments that I and my ancestors made upon others in the area of infirmary and sickness. I repent, and I ask for You to forgive us for those judgments that were made, and I ask You to lift any negative repercussions that came as a result of those judgments made on others. I repent for all the hypocrisy that has been in my family line and in my personal life, in Jesus name."

"I request now Lord Jesus for my complete deliverance according to Luke 13:12 when You spoke to the woman with the infirmity, but Your word also states that You are no respecter of persons and regardless of her gender You are willing and able to heal me. I ask You to render null and void every agreement and every Covenant made with spirits of infirmity, and choose to forgive everybody who has hurt me. This is not me saying what they did was right, this is me saying that I'm forgiving because it is the right thing to do for my own freedom:

Mark 1:40-42 WEB

"A leper came to him, begging him, kneeling down to him, and saying to him, "If you want to, you can make me clean." Being moved with compassion, he stretched out his hand, and touched him, and said to him, "I want to. Be made clean." When he had said this, immediately the leprosy departed from him, and he was made clean."

"I renounce every unholy altar of infirmity and its master spirit. I ask that my name and the name of my family be removed from every demonic altar connected to infirmity and every other demonic altar of various purposes. Lord Jesus, I receive Your healing in full, and I receive Your deliverance, in Jesus name, thank you. Amen!"

END OF PRAYER

CHAPTER 48: PRAYER FOR HEALING OF NEGATIVE BODY IMAGE

Psalms 139:13-18 BSB

"For You formed my inmost being; You knit me together in my mother's womb. I praise You, for I am fearfully and wonderfully made. Marvelous are Your works, and I know this very well. My frame was not hidden from You when I was made in secret, when I was woven together in the depths of the earth. Your eyes saw my unformed body; all my days were written in Your book and ordained for me before one of them came to be. How precious to me are Your thoughts, O God, how vast is their sum! If I were to count them, they would outnumber the grains of sand; and when I awake, I am still with You."

"Heavenly Father, I come before You in prayer today to lift the way that I see myself. I ask that You would help me see myself the way that You do, starting today and going forward. I repent for any time that I neglected my body through purging, not eating, eating out of comfort rather and other various means of neglect rather than coming to You. I also repent for all agreements I have made with negative body image and its associated spirits, as well as those agreements made by my ancestors. I declare anorexia is not my friend and neither is negative body image, and I command it to go in Jesus Name! Today, according to Your Word, I come before You to petition You to execute judgment against any unclean spiritual involvement and unclean spirits that have affected my body image, my eating habits. They are lying to me about the way my body looks. And spirits that have distorted the way I see my body in the mirror and through cameras, in Jesus name, for it is written:

Psalms 149:5-9 BSB

"Let the saints exult in glory; let them shout for joy upon their beds. May the high praises of God be in their mouths, and a double-edged sword in their hands, to inflict vengeance on the nations and punishment on the peoples, to bind their kings with chains and their nobles with shackles of iron, to execute the judgment written against them. This honor is for all His saints. Hallelujah!"

"Heavenly Father, according to Your Word, I now ask that You would send a decree of deliverance for me in Jesus name and that You would issue a permanent order of protection against these unclean spirits. I ask You to seal me from spirit, soul, and body head to toe in Your Blood Lord Jesus and with Your Holy Spirit. I declare that I am Yours and I also declare that I want nothing to do with anorexia, bulimia and any unclean spirits that have caused negative body image, in Jesus name.

"I declare that I am fearfully and wonderfully made, and that I will recover stronger and better than I have ever been in Jesus name. I decree and declare that I am Your beloved son (or daughter) and that I will live out all of my ordained days and then some in Jesus name. I thank you for deliverance and freedom LORD, I lean on You Abba, set me free. I receive Your freedom today, in Jesus name, amen!

END OF PRAYER

CHAPTER 49: PRAYER AGAINST DEPRESSION AND OPPRESSION

I pray that you receive a miraculous breakthrough, freedom, healing, and deliverance from depression and oppression, in Jesus name.

Asking The Court To Be In Session

"LORD GOD, I ask that the Heavenly Court would be seated in judgment to hear my case and righteous plea before You, in Jesus name. I petition You as the Judge of all, to call heavenly angels to be witnesses, scribes, officers of the Court to keep the peace, protect and execute Your Righteous decrees, commands, verdicts, sentences, and judgments in my favor and in favor of Your plans and purposes, in Jesus name."

Opening Prayer

"Heavenly Father, I come before You this day to receive freedom and deliverance from the spirits of oppression, heaviness, depression and the associated spirits, in Jesus name."

Repentance For Judgments Made On Others

"LORD GOD, I repent for every time that I and my ancestors judged and said verbally or internally any bitter root judgments against people who were targets for demons that attack the area of the mind. I renounce all bitter root judgments that were made by myself and my ancestors all the way back to Adam and Eve and every ancestor in between, in Jesus name."

Breaking Agreement With Doctor's Diagnosis And Familial History of Depression | Oppression | And Mental Health

"Heavenly Father, I break agreement with all affiliations in connection to my family history of any and all depression, oppression, mental fog, lack of clarity, confusion, mental attacks and lack of mental and spiritual clarity. Heavenly Father, I repent for all my ancestors on both my earthly father and earthly mother's side who partook of rebellion and disobedience to You, Your Prophetic Word and Your Written Word, the Holy Bible, in Jesus name."

Prayer of Repentance

"Heavenly Father, I repent for all sins, transgressions, iniquities, rebellion, disobedience that I and my forefathers, ancestors, and my bloodline walked in, in Jesus name." I make a formal appeal to the Lord Jesus as my Heavenly High Priest, Intercessor, and my Atoning Sacrifice to apply His Blood to the Mercy Seat of Heaven and that all the aforementioned sins, transgression, iniquities, disobedience, rebellion would be "paid in full by the Blood of the Lamb of God, in Jesus name."

"Heavenly Father, I now repent for any other legitimate and legally binding accusations as well as unrepented of sins, transgressions, and iniquities that the accuser of the brethren has been using to oppress me with oppression, depression, sadness, mental fog, mental and emotional breakdowns, lack of mental clarity, self-hate, self-criticism, being hard on myself, seasonal depression, doctors word curses and diagnosis that were pronounced over me, I break agreement with all negative doctor's diagnosis in Jesus name."

"Heavenly Father, I now appeal to the Atoning Sacrifice of the Body and Blood of my Lord Jesus Christ to be applied as "full payment" to all curses that have resided and or have been assigned to my ancestral bloodline due to various reasons such as, innocent bloodshed, bloodshed from war, manipulation, participation of sorcery, witchcraft, covens, secret societies, black magic, white magic, gray magic, and all other forms of magic, voodoo, shamanism, physically and spiritually occultic activity, judgements, criticisms, back-biting tongues and back-biting speech, unforgiveness, hatred, pride, superiority, racial superiority, infatuation with ungodly movies, substance abuse, mind games that my ancestors played on other people, in Jesus name."

Prayer of Petition For The Court To Issue A Divine Reversal of Familial Curses

"Heavenly Father, I now petition You for a Verdict from the Courts of Heaven concerning any looming effects and all curses that have been on the family from sins as well as *any and all* transgressions of Your Law, iniquities, disobedience, rebellion, bitterness, unforgiveness, hatred, murder, strife, innocent bloodshed, as well as violence. That they would be, by the Authority of Your Court, reversed, and uplifted off of me and my family according to Galatians 3:13-14, in Jesus name."

"LORD GOD, for it is written,

Galatians 3:13-14 BSB

"Christ redeemed us from the curse of the law by becoming a curse for us. For it is written: "Cursed is everyone who is hung on a tree." He redeemed us in order that the blessing promised to Abraham would come to the Gentiles in Christ Jesus, so that by faith we might receive the promise of the Spirit."

Asking For A Verdict Of Mercy

"Heavenly Father, I now repent for any time that I myself and my family failed to show mercy on others, and I now choose to stand in the gap and forgive every single person, people group, ethnic group that harmed and sinned against us in any and every way shape or form. I now request mercy for myself and my family according to Job 13:18 and James 2:13, in Jesus name."

"For it is written,

Job 13:18 BSB

"Behold, now that I have prepared my case,
I know that I will be vindicated."

Asking For Justice

Psalms 103:6 BSB

"The LORD executes righteousness and
justice for all the oppressed."

"Heavenly Father, I now ask You to execute and enforce a Divine verdict of release, freedom, breakthrough, and deliverance from oppression, depression, sadness, mental fog, mental attacks, warfare, mental and emotional breakdowns, lack of mental clarity, self-hate, self-criticism, seasonal depression, doctors word curses and diagnosis that were pronounced over me and all demonic, satanic, familiar, and familiar spirits attached to my family's bloodline that have taken root, advantage, and operated in any area of my life, especially in the area of mental health, in Jesus name."

"Heavenly Father, I now recall before the Court the amount of pain, torment, mental anguish, and mind games that the demonic has caused me and my family and I ask for a verdict of swift judgment for every time a demon afflicted, tormented, played mind games with, spirits of legalism, mind binding spirits, mind taskmasters, and I ask that every drop of affliction that was caused by demons and Arabic forces against me and my family would be remembered before Your Court, and just penalties be swiftly enforced by Your holy angels, in Jesus name."

Prayer of Petition For Divine Protective Order Against Depression, Oppression

Job 5:11 BSB

"He sets the lowly on high, so that mourners are lifted to safety."

"Heavenly Father, I now petition Your Court to issue a *permanent order of protection*, in Jesus name. I ask that You LORD would give Your angels charge over me and to enforce Your *order of protection*, and render null the effect that all demonic forces, satanic forces, seasonal depression, mind binding spirits, seasonal mood swings, irregular mood swings, demonically engineered mental strongholds and belief systems, and all other forms of mood swings especially those connected to witchcraft and divination that have had a hold on me to be rendered useless, unfruitful, and ineffective, in Jesus name."

"Heavenly Father, I also ask for a Sentence for a warrant of arrest from the Courts of Heaven against all unclean spirits that have attacked my soundness of mind. I also ask for a permanent divine order of protection against these unclean spirits that would have the assignment to mess with my mind and my family's minds, in Jesus name."

"LORD GOD, I ask that You would permanently dispose of these unclean spirits, and may I never encounter them ever again as a familiar spirit, according to Exodus 14:13-14:

Exodus 14:13-14 BSB

But Moses told the people, "Do not be afraid. Stand firm and you will see the LORD's salvation, which He will accomplish for you today; for the Egyptians you see today, you will never see again. The LORD will fight for you; you need only to be still."

"LORD GOD, I now like David of Old say,

Psalms 17:2 WEB

"Let my sentence come out of your presence. Let your eyes look on equity."

…in Jesus Name I receive Your freedom, for where the Spirit of the Lord is there is freedom, amen!"

Note

I want to invite you to read Isaiah 61 out loud over yourself, because the One who created us with power in our tongues, regardless of what others have said. Most importantly, it matters what the LORD says about you, and it's also important what you say about yourself, in Jesus name.

Proverbs 18:21 KJV

"Death and life are in the power of the tongue: And they that love it shall eat the fruit thereof."

Isaiah 61:1-11 BSB

"The Spirit of the Lord GOD is on Me, because the LORD has anointed Me to preach good news to the poor. He has sent Me to bind up the brokenhearted, to proclaim liberty to the captives and freedom to the prisoners, to proclaim the year of the LORD's favor and the day of our God's vengeance, to comfort all who mourn, to console the mourners in Zion— to give them a crown of beauty for ashes, the oil of joy for mourning, and a garment of praise for a spirit of despair. So they will be called oaks of righteousness, the planting of the LORD, that He may be glorified. They will rebuild the ancient ruins; they will restore the places long devastated; they will renew the ruined cities, the desolations of many generations. Strangers will stand and feed your flocks, and foreigners will be your plowmen and vinedressers. But you will be called the priests of the LORD; they will speak of you as ministers of our God; you will feed on the wealth of nations, and you will boast in their riches. Instead of shame, My people will have a double portion, and instead of humiliation, they will rejoice in their share; and so they will inherit a double portion in their land, and everlasting joy will be theirs. For I, the LORD, love justice; I hate robbery and iniquity; in My faithfulness I will give them their recompense and make an everlasting covenant with them. Their descendants will be known among the nations, and their offspring among the peoples. All who see them will acknowledge that they are a people the LORD has blessed. I will rejoice greatly in the LORD, my soul will exult in my God; for He has clothed me with garments of salvation and wrapped me in a robe of righteousness, as a bridegroom wears a priestly headdress, as a bride adorns herself with her jewels. For as the earth brings forth its growth, and as a garden enables seed to spring up, so the Lord GOD will cause righteousness and praise to spring up before all the nations."

Nehemiah 8:10-11 BSB

"Then Nehemiah told them, "Go and eat what is rich, drink what is sweet, and send out portions to those who have nothing prepared, since today is holy to our Lord. Do not grieve, for the joy of the LORD is your strength." And the Levites calmed all the people, saying, "Be still, since today is holy. Do not grieve."

Nehemiah 12:43 BSB

"On that day they offered great sacrifices, rejoicing because

God had given them great joy. The women and children also rejoiced, so that the joy of Jerusalem was heard from afar."

"Heavenly Father, I ask for the fulfillment of Isaiah 61, the Joy of the LORD mentioned in Nehemiah 8:10 and the joy of the people mentioned in Nehemiah 12:43 over my life. And may the Joy of the LORD be my Strength forever and for all time, in Jesus Name, amen!"

END OF PRAYER

CHAPTER 50: PRAYER BREAKING SOUL TIES TO UNGODLY POLITICAL MOVEMENTS

Acts 9:17-18 BSB

"So Ananias went to the house, and when he arrived, he placed his hands on Saul. "Brother Saul," he said, "the Lord Jesus, who appeared to you on the road as you were coming here, has sent me so that you may see again and be filled with the Holy Spirit." At that instant, something like scales fell from Saul's eyes, and his sight was restored. He got up and was baptized,"

Hebrews 4:12 ASV

"For the word of God is living, and active, and sharper than any two-edged sword, and piercing even to the dividing of soul and spirit, of both joints and marrow, and quick to discern the thoughts and intents of the heart."

1 John 1:9 BSB

"If we confess our sins, He is faithful and just to forgive us our sins and to cleanse us from all unrighteousness."

"Heavenly Father, Lord Jesus, Holy Spirit, I come before you and ask for forgiveness, according to 1 John 1:9 for tying my soul with political and social justice movements that carried a demonic agenda whether known or unknown to the participants of these movements and I break agreement and I ask You to send Your Word to sever all demonic spirit, soul, and body ties made with political spirits, unclean spirits, the spirit of python, divination, incantation, and all other unclean and unclean spirits behind movements such as Black Lives Matter, women's abortion rights, transgender acceptance movements, LGBTQIA+, the *woke* movement, and every other political, social, racial, governmental movement that has demonic doctrines and unclean spirits operating under their titles, in Jesus name."

Matthew 11:28-30 BSB

"Come to Me, all you who are weary and burdened, and I will give you rest. Take My yoke upon you and learn from Me; for I am gentle and humble in heart, and you will find rest for your souls. For My yoke is easy and My burden is light."

1 Thessalonians 5:23 KJV

"And the very God of peace sanctify you wholly; and I pray God your whole spirit and soul and body be preserved blameless unto the coming of our Lord Jesus Christ."

"Lord Jesus, I now declare I want to be tied to You as You said Your yoke is easy, and Your burden is light. I ask You to sanctify me completely spirit, soul, and body, in Jesus Name, amen!"

END OF PRAYER

CHAPTER 51: PRAYER TO BREAK YOKES

Matthew 11:28-30 BSB

"Come to Me, all you who are weary and burdened, and I will give you rest. Take My yoke upon you and learn from Me; for I am gentle and humble in heart, and you will find rest for your souls. For My yoke is easy and My burden is light."

"Heavenly Father, I come before You today to petition You for the breaking of demonic yokes off of me and my family's lineage, according to Matthew 11:28-30. Lord, I renounce the works of darkness and every spirit associated with it as well as any Aztec whistles, Mayan deities, and everything to do with the Inca tribes as well. Heavenly Father, I ask according to Psalm 103:6 for a judgment to be rendered against all demonic yokes to be broken off against me according to Isaiah 10:27, and I declare that today is that day, in Jesus name.

Isaiah 10:27 BSB

"On that day the burden will be lifted from your shoulders, and the yoke from your neck. The yoke will be broken because your neck will be too large."

1 John 2:27 BSB

"And as for you, the anointing you received from Him

remains in you, and you do not need anyone to teach you. But just as His true and genuine anointing teaches you about all things, so remain in Him as you have been taught."

"Lord Jesus, I receive your light and easy yoke and I ask for deliverance from false burdens as well. I receive your freedom and deliverance in Jesus name, amen!"

END OF PRAYER

CHAPTER 52: PRAYER TO COMBAT INSOMNIA, POOR SLEEP, IDOLATRY, AND MOON DEITY WORSHIP

If you have had trouble sleeping or getting a quality good night's rest, this prayer is for you. I pray this prayer helps break the poor quality of sleep you may have experienced in times past. You will need a pen and paper or an electronic note on your phone for this prayer, and you will know why here as you continue reading on...

Asking The Heavenly Court To Be Seated

"Heavenly Father, I come before You and I ask for the Court of Heaven to be made available to me and seated in judgment as I come before You to ask for deliverance, breakthrough, and freedom from insomnia and any demonic interferences to normal healthy sleep, in Jesus name."

Prayer of Repentance

"Heavenly Father, I ask for Your forgiveness for any time I watched movies that involved vampires, werewolves, moon worship, moon goddess worship, moon idols, Dracula, the movie Twilight, and any and all obsession with the sun, moon, stars, constellations, Ishtar, vampires, werewolves, Islam, and things of the like, in Jesus' name.."

Exodus 20:3 BSB

"You shall have no other gods before Me."

!!!VERY IMPORTANT NOTE, DO NOT SKIP!!!

This is a very important notice, Holy Spirit is NOT going to tell you to write the Names of the LORD down in this prayer, **DO NOT WRITE THE LORD's Names In The Prayer Below**, I will give you a proper list of the Names of God, and the names of the idols, if you hear the following Biblical names of God while you are writing, **do not write** the Names of God listed directly below:

God's Biblical Names

ADONAI, Adonai El-Roy, El-Shaddai, LORD, LORD, Any "Jehovah" Name, Yahweh, Yahuwah, I AM, I AM THAT I AM, Ruach HaKodesh, Jesus Hamashiach, Iesous Christos, Jesus Christ, Elohim, Elohim.

Very Important Notice

I also want to be clear about something, the LORD GOD made something very clear when He said something recorded in Exodus 23:13:

Exodus 23:13 KJV

"And in all things that I have said unto you be

circumspect: and make no mention of the name of other gods, neither let it be heard out of thy mouth."

Out of obedience to the Holy Spirit's conviction, and His prompting, I am going to ask you *not* to say these names listed below, but rather to write them down like you would in a contract. No need to worry, a template you can use to write down the prayer will be provided for you below. I ask you not to copy and paste this on your kindle if that's where you are reading this book. Please write it down on a piece of paper, and leave some room for your signature, or you can do it on an electronic note on your electronic device. As long as the electronic file has the feature of an e-signature. Below is a list of some lunar deities, we are going to use these names in a written prayer of renouncement.

Instructions

Please copy the prayer below onto your sheet of paper or your electronic note. And in the signature part, you're going to sign your name as a written declaration of you renouncing these false deities and revoking any legal claims they have had on you and your sleep.

Targeted Written Prayer Renouncing Lunar Deities

"LORD GOD, Heavenly Father, I renounce all covenants, oaths, vows, agreements, demonic mandates, assignments, false mantles, false baptisms, false awakenings, false enlightenment, false promises, sacrifices, curses, health curses, sleep curses, curses that cause lack of rest, spiritual and physical exchanges, spiritual trades, trades done with books of destiny, dedications, dedications of future descendants of the family line, and family bloodline, as well as offerings made and offered to these idols under the aliases of:

(Write the names listed below within the boxes, and any other ones that Holy Spirit highlights or speak to you to write, now please know the Holy Spirit is not going to tell you to write the Names of God in this prayer, but if you hear the names of idols you may write those down, just use discernment) and I renounce all affiliation with all idols,

Your Signature Here: _____

in Jesus name!"

Short Alphabetical List of Lunar Deities
African
abuk
amesemi
ayyur
ela-opitan
gleti
iah
inyanga
khonsu
mawu
thoth
American
abaangui
alignak
arasy

awilix
chía
coniraya
coyolxauhqui
hanwi
huitaca
igaluk
jaci
jive cla or "jive ucla"
ka-ata-killa
kalfu
mama killa
maya
menily
metztli
muuya
pah
tarqiup inua
tecciztecatl
xbalanque
Asian
apsara

dakinis
guanyin
taras
tagalog goddesses
Tagalog gods
sinhalese buddhist deities
leima
ningthou
European
arianrhod
artemis
artume
ataegina
bendis
bil
diana
elatha
hecate
hjúki
hors
ilargi
kuu

losna
luna
máni
mano
meness
myesyats
phoebe
selene
sen
triple goddess
Oceania
andriambahomanana
avatea
bahloo
fati
hina
kidili
mahina
marama
ngalindi

Pray This Part Underneath Out Loud

"LORD GOD, I declare today (insert the date you are making this declaration), that I want *nothing* to do with these demonic entities. I permanently renounce, give up, and give back all demonic inheritances, demonic gifts, demonic mantles, demonic mandates, demonic assignments, demonic powers and abilities that my ancestors and I have personally gained and inherited including powers to levitate, astral project, psychic powers and abilities, demonic intelligence and everything else, in Jesus name."

"I pledge my sole and complete allegiance to You LORD GOD, Lord Jesus, Holy Spirit. And I declare that as for me and my house, LORD, we chose to serve the LORD, in Jesus name."

"LORD, I ask You to keep a heavenly record of my renouncement of these idols, and my loyalty to You, in Jesus Name, amen!"

Joshua 24:14-15 BSB

> Now, therefore, fear the LORD and serve Him in sincerity and truth; cast aside the gods your fathers served beyond the Euphrates and in Egypt, and serve the LORD. But if it is unpleasing in your sight to serve the LORD, then choose for yourselves this day whom you will serve, whether the gods your fathers served beyond the Euphrates, or the gods of the Amorites in whose land you are living. As for me and my house, we will serve the LORD!"

END OF PRAYER

Conclusion

Now that you have gone through this prayer and have asked the LORD to keep a heavenly record of it, if you are able to burn it, feel free to do so. If you can't burn it at the moment, then just wait until a friend has a bonfire, or where you can do it safely. If you have a burn barrel outside, and your city ordinance allows it, and if you're a minor when you have adult supervision, find some way to burn the paper safely. Even in a fireplace if you have one would be ideal. Try not to keep the paper for long after writing it down. If you did an electronic note with an e-signature on it, you're all good. And please comply with your local burn laws. I'm all for the fire of God, but I'm *not* for wildfires!

CHAPTER 53: PRAYER RENOUNCING IDOLS AND IDOLATRY

Asking The Heavenly Court To Be Seated

"Heavenly Father, I come before You and I ask for the Court of Heaven to be made available to me and seated in judgment as I come before You to ask for deliverance, breakthrough, freedom from idols and idolatry, and the unclean spirits associated and attached to these names, in Jesus name."

Exodus 20:3 BSB

"You shall have no other gods before Me."

Prayer of Repentance

"Heavenly Father, I ask for Your forgiveness for any time I and my ancestors partook of idolatry, all false deities, including the Islamic god, and every idol of the like, in Jesus name."

Isaiah 43:25-26 BSB

"I, yes I, am He who blots out your transgressions for My own sake and remembers your sins no more. Remind Me, let us argue the matter together. State your case, so that you may be vindicated."

!!!VERY IMPORTANT NOTE, DO NOT SKIP!!!

Holy Spirit is NOT going to tell you to write the Names of the LORD down in this prayer, **DO NOT WRITE THE LORD'S NAMES IN THE PRAYER BELOW,** I will give you a proper list of the Names of God, and the names of the idols, if you hear the following Biblical names of God while you are writing, **do not write** the Names of God listed directly below:

God's Biblical Names

ADONAI, Adonai El-Roy, El-Shaddai, LORD, LORD, Any "Jehovah" Name, Yahweh, Yahuwah, I AM, I AM THAT I AM, Ruach HaKodesh, Jesus Hamashiach, Iesous Christos, Jesus Christ, Elohiym, Elohim.

Important Note

I want to be clear about something, the LORD GOD made something very clear when He said something recorded in Exodus 23:13:

Exodus 23:13 KJV

"And in all things that I have said unto you be circumspect: and make no mention of the name of other gods, neither let it be heard out of thy mouth."

Out of obedience to the Holy Spirit's conviction, and His prompting, I am going to ask you *not* to verbally say these names listed below, but rather to write them down like you would in a contract. No need to worry, a template you can use to write down the prayer will be provided for you below. I ask you not to copy and paste this on your kindle if that's where you are reading this book. Please write it down on a piece of paper, and leave some room for your signature, or you can do it on an electronic note on your electronic device. As long as the electronic file has the feature of an e-signature. Below is a list of some lunar deities, we are going to use these names in a written prayer of renouncement.

Instructions

Please copy the prayer below onto your sheet of paper or your electronic note. And in the signature part, you're going to sign your name as a written declaration of you renouncing these false deities and revoking any legal claims they have had on you and your sleep.

Targeted Written Prayer Renouncing False Deities

"LORD GOD, Heavenly Father, I renounce all covenants, oaths, vows, agreements, demonic mandates, assignments, false mantles, false baptisms, false awakenings, false enlightenment, false promises, sacrifices, curses, health curses, spiritual and physical exchanges, spiritual trades, trades done with books of destiny, dedications, dedications of future descendants of the family line, and family bloodline, as well as offerings made and offered to these idols under the aliases of:

(Write the names listed below within the boxes, and any other ones that Holy Spirit highlights or speak to you to write, now please know the Holy Spirit is not going to tell you to write the Names of God in this prayer, but if you hear the names of idols you may write those down, just use discernment) and I renounce all affiliation with all the idols listed below, and those unknown as well,

Your Signature Here: _____

in Jesus name, amen!"

Biblical List of Idol Names			
amon	chemosh	hammanim	baal
asheroth	apollyon	diana	nimrod

aven	'elil	'emah	
			tamuz
satyr	serpent	sin	
			Queen of heaven
stars	sun	malcom	
			dagon
miphletzeth	bosheth	gillulim	
			molech
shikkuts	tselem	temunah	
nisroch	noph	rimmon	
'atsab	tsir	maskith	
adonis	calf	ishtar	
adrammelech	golden calf	Malcam, milcom, malkam	
apis	diana	meni	
astarte	hathor	moloch	
baal-berith	hosts of heaven	moon	
baal-peor	image of jealousy	nibhaz	
asherah	dagon	chamman	
psel	masseka	heqet	

	h		
ashtoreth	tammuz	matztzebah	
baal	zeus	asherim	
baal-zebub	hermes	castor and pollux	
bel	artemis	teraphim	
	queen of heaven		

END OF PRAYER

Conclusion

Now that you have gone through this prayer and have asked the LORD to keep a heavenly record of your written prayer, that is, if you wrote this prayer out on paper. If you are able to burn it, please do so. If you can't burn it at the moment, then just wait until a friend has a bonfire, or where you can do it safely and in compliance with your local burning laws. If you have a burn barrel outside, or have adult supervision, some way to burn the paper afterward preferably outside or in a fireplace if you have one, that would be ideal. Try not to keep the paper inside your house after writing it down, if you did an electronic note with e-signature on it, then you're all good, no need to worry.

CHAPTER 54: PRAYER OF DELIVERANCE CONNECTED TO DEMONIC DREAMS

Sleep is crucial for good mental health and spiritual health believe it or not, so it's not surprising that sleep is usually one of those things that gets attacked in a spiritual attack. The good news is that we are more than conquerors through Christ and your sleep can be restored.

Beginning of Prayer

"Heavenly Father, I come before You to petition You for deliverance from demonic dreams. I decree that Your Word says:

Psalms 4:8 BSB

":I will lie down and sleep in peace, for You alone, O LORD, make me dwell in safety."

"I request for an order of protection against the kingdom of darkness and all of its spiritual and human agents, forbidding them from affecting my sleep or even coming anywhere near me while I'm asleep or awake. I repent for every sin, transgression, iniquity committed by me and my ancestors, along with every covenant, agreement, and contract made with the enemy and the kingdom of darkness at various and all levels. I repent for any time someone in my family attended an unholy altar that might have left a door open for the enemy. But You Lord Jesus are the One who is able to shut and open doors that no one can open and close doors that no one else can shut:

Revelation 3:7 BSB

"To the angel of the church in Philadelphia write: These are the words of the One who is holy and true, who holds the key of David. What He opens no one can shut, and what He shuts no one can open."

"I ask You to shut every demonic door and seal with Your Blood Lord Jesus just like how the Israelites covered their doorposts and lintel with the Blood of the Lamb, and they were safe, I ask that You would shut those demonic doors and open the doors of God the Father's will. Lord Jesus, I receive Your freedom and soundness of mind along with sound sleep, in Jesus name, amen!"

END OF PRAYER

CHAPTER 55: PRAYER FOR SNAKES, SNAKE ENCOUNTERS, AND SNAKE ATTACKS IN DREAMS.

Genesis 3:14-15 BSB

"So the LORD God said to the serpent: "Because you have done this, cursed are you above all livestock and every beast of the field! On your belly will you go, and dust you will eat, all the days of your life. And I will put enmity between you and the woman, and between your seed and her seed. He will crush your head, and you will strike his heel."

Beginning of Prayer

"LORD GOD, I come before You as the Judge of all, according to Hebrews 12. I ask that the Court be seated as it is written in Daniel 7:10, and the books of my destiny that were given to me by you, be opened, read, understood and prophesied over my life by the Lord Jesus Christ Himself over me. Lord God, as I stand before You, I ask that you would cleanse my hands and purify my heart. I accept and receive the payment

He made on my behalf to appear before You as covered and cleansed by His Precious Blood, thank You, Lord Jesus for Your eternal sacrifice for me and humanity, in Jesus Name, amen!"

Repentance For Anything Connected To Snakes

"LORD GOD, I renounce, repent, break agreement, and ask for forgiveness for every ancestor of mine that participated and had any connection with the obsession of reptiles, snakes, lizards, Pokémon card games, demonic video games, demonic movies, and television shows that included reptilian-like creatures, snakes and those of like manner. I also repent, renounce, break agreement, and ask for Your forgives for all oaths, vows, partnerships, covenants, contracts, sacrifices, sacrificial offerings, rituals, chants, dance circles, chanting circles, idolatry, and idol worship of snakes, ancestors that created idols of snakes, kept them as pets, all prayers, and worship offered to leviathan, python, cobras, garden snakes, snake like and reptilian idols. I myself renounce all snakes and reptilian obsessions that I and my ancestors have ever had or that of my ancestors, in Jesus name."

"I ask for all the above-mentioned sacrifices, covenants, oaths, vows, sacrifices and sacrificial offerings to be nullified and revoked by the authority of Your Supreme Court, and I ask according to 1 John 1:9 and Isiah 43:25-26 for a court verdict of pardon to be issued for me and my family. I ask for deliverance and healing to take place in my life and for my family members and I to live in freedom according to Your Word which states where the Spirit of the Lord is there is freedom, in Jesus name, amen!"

2 Corinthians 3:17 BSB

"Now the Lord is the Spirit, and where the
Spirit of the Lord is, there is freedom."

END OF PRAYER

CHAPTER 56: PRAYER AGAINST FALSE PROPHECIES

Beginning of Prayer

"Heavenly Father, I come before You today on the premise of Daniel 7:10 and request that the Heavenly Court would be seated and ready to listen to my case. I present to the Court the following Scripture as my foundation for this prayer because false prophecy can be considered a weapon of the enemy:

Isaiah 54:17 BSB

"No weapon formed against you shall prosper, and you will refute every tongue that accuses you. This is the heritage of the servants of the LORD, and their vindication is from Me," declares the LORD."

"Heavenly Father, I now request that every negative word that has been spoken against me through words of false prophecy be nullified and revoked by the Court, in Jesus name. I decree and declare that I come out of the agreement with every false prophecy that has been spoken about me and to me through various sources. And I receive the genuine God ordained prophecy that You have released though Your true prophets Lord Jesus. I decree and declare today that I want freedom and I break agreement with those false prophetic words and I cast those false words down in Jesus name. I ask according to Psalm 63:11 that the mouths of *prophaliars* would be shut and that the word of the LORD through *prophesiers* would be established:

Psalms 63:11 BSB

> "But the king will rejoice in God; all who swear by Him will exult, for the mouths of liars will be shut."

"Heavenly Father, I bless those who have spoken genuine prophetic words to me and I thank You for their service to the Kingdom through that in Jesus name. I ask that You would issue a *heavenly order of protection* against all false prophets and *propheliars* to keep them away from me, and I ask that You would assign angels to enforce it as well. I ask that You would put genuine prophets of the LORD around me to edify, encourage, strengthen and equip me in my time of need and I receive Your protection according to the promises found within Psalms 91, in Jesus name, amen!"

END OF PRAYER

CHAPTER 57: DISMANTLING PITFALLS AND TRAPS THROUGH SCRIPTURE

Beginning of Prayer

"Heavenly Father, I come before You to day to request You to assign heavenly angels to uproot and remove any future pitfalls and traps that the enemy has or might try to set up through whatever means he would try to do it, whether it be a person, a job opportunity, a ministry opportunity etc. I repent for any time that I set a trap for others, whether it was a verbal trap or a physical trap to confound somebody. I ask for Your forgiveness, and I ask that You would help me live in a manner that I would be blameless before You.

Proverbs 26:27 BSB

"He who digs a pit will fall into it, and he who rolls a stone will have it roll back on him."

Isaiah 54:17 BSB

"No weapon formed against you shall prosper, and you will refute every tongue that accuses you. This is the heritage of the servants of the LORD, and their vindication is from Me," declares the LORD."

"I ask according to Proverbs 26:27 and Isaiah 54:17 that every spiritual trap that might be attempted to be set up for me would be dismantled before it can be completed. I decree and declare that every weapon cannot prevail against me because You have said so. Ask You to dispatch angels to dismantle those traps throughout the timeline, and may I see success in the call that You have placed upon this life of mine that You have graciously bestowed upon me. Thank You, Lord, that I have received what I have asked for, in Jesus name, amen!"

1 John 5:14-15 BSB

"And this is the confidence that we have before Him: If we ask anything according to His will, He hears us. And if we know that He hears us in whatever we ask, we know that we already possess what we have asked of Him."

END OF PRAYER

CHAPTER 58: PRAYER AGAINST DEMONIC HARVESTERS

If you've ever felt like your harvest was being eaten up or taken from you before you could really enjoy it, it may be because of a spiritual reason rather than a physical one. If you've found yourself in that situation, then I hope this prayer helps alleviate that for you.

Malachi 3:10-11 BSB

"Bring the full tithe into the storehouse, so that there may be food in My house. Test Me in this," says the LORD of Hosts. "See if I will not open the windows of heaven and pour out for you blessing without measure. I will rebuke the devourer for you, so that it will not destroy the fruits of your land, and the vine in your field will not fail to produce fruit," says the LORD of Hosts."

Beginning of Prayer

"Heavenly Father, I come before You today to ask You to rebuke the devourer for my sake, as Your Word declares in Malachi. I repent for any time that I didn't pay the tithe in full, and I ask You to forgive me. I ask that You would show me the prosperity that comes with tithing to You. And through that I ask for a heart that waits in expectation to give because of an act of obedience and for the rewards that You have said come along with it. I ask that You would rebuke the devourer for my sake, and I ask that You would arrest all demonic harvesters, unholy reapers that have assignments to try to steal seed and rob Your people of their harvests. And I ask that You would bless both my harvests along with my family's harvests and Your people's harvests abundantly just like You did for Isaac but in even greater measure:

Genesis 26:12-13 BSB

"Now Isaac sowed seed in the land, and that very year he reaped a hundredfold. And the LORD blessed him, and he became richer and richer, until he was exceedingly wealthy."

"Heavenly Father, I receive Your blessings and I seal this petition in the Blood of Jesus, and I leave my case in Your hands. I ask for a breakthrough. Thank You for taking the time to listen to my petition, I receive breakthrough Lord, in Jesus name, amen!"

END OF PRAYER

CHAPTER 59.1: PRAYER OF DELIVERANCE FROM RACISM

Racism is not something that benefits anybody. It all boils down to the content of people's character, not the color of their skin. I do believe that culture has played a part in festering racism amongst communities and different races, but just because someone has lighter skin or darker skin doesn't mean anything about their character. Culture plays a part in how people act, but so do parents. We all came from Adam and Eve. Racism has no room for the child of God. Remember that there is no condemnation for those in Christ Jesus who walk in the Spirit and not the flesh. Racism is a fleshy thing, and if you're desiring freedom from its grip, this prayer is for you.

Galatians 3:28 BSB

"There is neither Jew nor Greek, slave nor free, male nor female, for you are all one in Christ Jesus."

Beginning of Prayer

"Heavenly Father, I come before You today to seek freedom from racism and its tendencies. I acknowledge that racism is a form of hate, and it stands against Who You are. Lord, I repent for the ancestors that I had who walked in racist groups such as the Ku Klux Klan and those who have held similar ideologies regardless of whom they discriminated against. I ask that you remove any trauma from my DNA from racism. I repent for every racist comment, word, and thought that I personally had, as well as those of my ancestors. I ask according to 1 John 1:9 that the Blood of Jesus would cover all of my sins, transgressions, and iniquities. And I ask the that the Blood of Jesus would speak a better word, according to Hebrews 12:24:

Hebrews 12:24 BSB

"to Jesus the mediator of a new covenant,
and to the sprinkled blood that speaks a
better word than the blood of Abel."

"Heavenly Father, I ask that the legalities of the Cross would be applied to my bloodline. I ask that the Blood of Jesus would permanently sever every unclean spirit that has afflicted and includes my bloodline, thinking and family, especially those connected to racism. I ask for a heavenly decree of destruction to be issued against every altar of racism, and all of their associated unclean spirits, according to 1 Kings 13:

1 Kings 13:2-5 BSB

"And he cried out against the altar by the word of the LORD, "O altar, O altar, this is what the LORD says: 'A son named Josiah will be born to the house of David, and upon you he will sacrifice the priests of the high places who burn incense upon you, and human bones will be burned upon you.'"
That day the man of God gave a sign, saying, "The LORD has spoken this sign: 'Surely the altar will be split apart, and the ashes upon it will be poured out.'" Now when King Jeroboam, who was at the altar in Bethel, heard the word that the man of God had cried out against it, he stretched out his hand and said, "Seize him!" But the hand he stretched out toward him withered, so that he could not pull it back. And the altar was split apart, and the ashes poured out, according to the sign

that the man of God had given by the word of the LORD."

"I receive deliverance and freedom according to the Word of the Lord, in Jesus name, amen!"

———————————

END OF PRAYER

———————————

CHAPTER 59.2: PRAYER OF DELIVERANCE FROM FEMINISM

The LORD created Adam and then Eve came after, which means that Eve was created to complement Adam. Adam was not created for Eve, but Eve was created for Adam. The LORD did not create men and women to be rivals, but He created them to be a team to work together to spread the beauty of His creation. Modern day feminism has turned into women wanting to be men and trying to prove themselves as if they were stronger and that they can do everything a man can. At surface this might look like a positive thing, but the fact of the matter is, is that the Lord did not create Eve to fill Adam's role, and God did not create Adam to fill Eve's role. Modern day ideologies have tried to create weak men and strong women, and thereby trying to flip the roles of men and women upside down. Women are not supposed to be alpha males! God created the man to be the protector, provider, the strength, and head of the home:

Ephesians 5:22-24 BSB

"Wives, submit to your husbands as to the Lord. For the husband is the head of the wife as Christ is the head of the church, His body, of which He is the Savior.

> Now as the church submits to Christ, so also wives should submit to their husbands in everything."

Now please don't hear what I'm not saying in this because society today likes to perceive and hear things through the lens of offense. Wives are called to submit to their husbands (this does not mean that wives aren't supposed to have an opinion or absolutely agree with everything their husbands say or do) but it means that in order to have a successful marriage, both parties need to love Jesus more than they love each other. Marriage is not fifty-fifty, it takes a hundred percent from both to have a happy marriage. Through that love for Jesus, they both submit to one another and love each other as Christ loves His bride-the church:

Ephesians 5:25 BSB

> "Husbands, love your wives, just as Christ loved the church and gave Himself up for her"

Husbands are called to love their wives like Jesus loved His church–He died for her. The Greek word used for *gave* in that verse is the Greek word παραδίδωμι (*paradidōmi*) and it means to *surrender or yield up*. So you can read it as, *"Husbands, love your wives, just as Christ loved the church, surrendering and yielded Himself up for her."*

When a woman knows that her husband genuinely loves and respects her and has her best interests in mind, she has a much easier time submitting to his leadership because she knows that what he is doing is with her well-being in mind. Now, of course both parties have a part to play in their character and morals, but the point I'm getting at here is that man and woman are a team, not enemies and competitors. Being a strong-willed woman isn't a bad thing, it might be an indicator that you have been called to minister or administration on some level, and learning to tame that will in obedience to God and His word is the balance you should aim for. God didn't put a lioness inside of you for no reason, but letting the lioness out on people that God has called you to nurture and protect is not the answer. You'll end up hurting and hindering them rather than nurturing and helping them. The lioness is a warrior, and it's to be used under the Holy Spirit's leadership. And likewise men, God put the lion heart in you to defend your family, and raise up young men who are warriors, but know how to love others with the tenderness of a lamb. Jesus knows when to be the Lion, and He knows when to be the Lamb, and as men being restored to His image, we should too.

Beginning of Prayer

"Heavenly Father, I come before You to ask for Your help having the right heart and mind towards men. Heavenly Father, I ask You to heal my heart, mind, spirit, and soul from all wounds caused by men and women that have contributed to any hate towards men or women. Please show me that I don't have to be like a man, but that I can be exactly who you created me to be and that it's not considered a weakness to be meek. Lord, show me how to be the woman, mother, and friend to those You've placed around me to show them the beauty of who You've made me to be. Lord, I now come before You and I renounce all spirits, altars, ideologies, and ungodly influences that have exploited feminism, its ideals, and its principles. I renounce feminism and its associated spirits, including pride, hate, and any possible craving for rebellious independence. I ask for deliverance from those things, and I ask for forgiveness for all sins, transgressions, and iniquities that have empowered those unclean spirits and unholy altars that were committed by my bloodline and those committed by me. I thank You for freedom, and I ask for a divine order of protection against all unclean spirits and people who would try to influence me to rebel to Your will and Your Word. I receive Your freedom and deliverance. Thank You, Lord Jesus, that those who the Son sets free are free indeed, in Jesus name, amen!"

John 8:36 BSB

"So if the Son sets you free, you will be free indeed."

END OF PRAYER

CHAPTER 60: PRAYER OF DELIVERANCE FROM LEGALISM

If you've struggled with legalism, I want you to take a look at these Scriptures below and choose to believe the truth of God's Word rather than what your feelings may say, or if you agree with it or not. I can promise you that legalism doesn't produce fruits of righteousness and the legalists were one of the few people that Jesus constantly was rebuking and even called them a brood of vipers. Jesus called them snakes! [63]

Matthew 23:23-24 BSB

"Woe to you, scribes and Pharisees, you hypocrites! You pay tithes of mint, dill, and cumin. But you have disregarded the weightier matters of the law: justice, mercy, and faithfulness. You should have practiced the latter, without neglecting the former. You blind guides! You strain out a gnat but swallow a camel."

Galatians 3:5-9 BSB

"Does God lavish His Spirit on you and work miracles among you because you practice the law, or because you hear and believe? So also, "Abraham believed God, and it was credited to him as righteousness." Understand, then, that those who have faith are sons of Abraham. The Scripture foresaw that God would justify the Gentiles by faith, and foretold the gospel to Abraham: "All nations will be blessed through you." So those who have faith are blessed along with Abraham, the man of faith."

Hebrews 8:10-13 BSB

"For this is the covenant I will make with the house of Israel after those days, declares the Lord. I will put My laws in their minds and inscribe them on their hearts. And I will be their God, and they will be My people. No longer will each one teach his neighbor or his brother, saying, 'Know the Lord,' because they will all know Me, from the least of them to the greatest. For I will forgive their iniquities and will remember their sins no more." By speaking of a new covenant, He has made the first one obsolete; and what is obsolete and aging will soon disappear." [1]

Tattoos

Galatians 5:1 BSB

"It is for freedom that Christ has set us free. Stand firm, then, and do not be encumbered once more by a yoke of slavery."

I want to briefly address this topic because I know some believers have gotten tattoos and I don't want anyone living with regret or even feeling agonized in conscious because of some ink on their skin. Does the Old Testament condemn tattoos? Yes. But in the above Scripture that we can see in the book of Hebrews the Old Law is obsolete and has already passed away because it's been fulfilled by Jesus. We are under the New Covenant fixed on better promises that are not based on our performance for salvation. We are saved by Jesus' finished work. However, we are rewarded in Heaven based on our performance, there's a difference between salvation, anointing, crowns, and rewards. Salvation's a gift, the rest is earned separately. If the tattoo was clearly ungodly then ask God for forgiveness, repent and pay for laser removal on that tattoo and move forward soldier! It's nothing to regret over because there is redemption in Jesus!

Beginning of Prayer

"Heavenly Father, I come before You today seeking freedom from legalism and every spirit associated with legalism, in Jesus name. As I bring these requests before You I ask that You would violently remove these spirits from my life and my family's lives forever so that I never see those unclean spirits again, as Your word states:

Exodus 14:13 BSB

"But Moses told the people, "Do not be afraid. Stand firm and you will see the LORD's salvation, which He will accomplish for you today; for the Egyptians you see today, you will never see again."

"Heavenly Father, I ask that You would destroy every altar of legalism that has any ties to my bloodline and I ask that You would remove my name and that of my family's off of those unholy altars as I dedicate myself and my entire family lineage to You and Your calling and purposes on their lives, including mine. I ask according to Psalm 103:6 that You would execute judgment against these unclean spirits of legalism that have affected my thinking, heart and soul as well, in Jesus name. I ask that You would free me from any grasp of these unholy spirits and the mindset that they try to reproduce in people. I renounce religious pride, pride of knowledge and even prideful knowledge of the Scriptures. Help me to be an intimate lover of God while being a scholar of Your Word. Help me to not neglect intimacy for head knowledge of who You are and what Your Word says. I receive Your freedom Lord Jesus and I thank you that I have what I have asked for, in Jesus name, amen!" [64]

END OF PRAYER

CHAPTER 60.1: RENOUNCING CONTROL & MICROMANAGEMENT

Some people will really resonate with this. If you grew up with a parent that micromanaged your every move. For example, what time you were supposed to be back, what color your bedsheets were. They made sure to inspect your bedsheets for wrinkles, made sure that you strived for perfection and punished you if you did not attain their standard of perfection. I'm sorry you had to experience that in life, but there's good news, the LORD isn't like that towards His kids! And if you're someone who experienced that, you may or may not have noticed that you have done the same to your kids. Generational cycles start and continue, but you can be the one that breaks that cycle off your family today. You don't have to put up with that, and just hope for the best outcome. You change the outcome, and shift the storm!

Romans 8:37 BSB

"No, in all these things we are more than conquerors through Him who loved us."

Philippians 4:13 BSB

"I can do all things through Christ who gives me strength."

I hope through this prayer, you'll find more enjoyment in life by experiencing the freedom that comes with living in Christ, and out of legalism, micromanaging, and the strive for perfection. Shalom, and blessings to you, it gets better!

Beginning of Prayer

"Heavenly Father, I come before You today to ask for deliverance from micromanaging others, myself, and my household. I ask that You according to Your Scriptures would set me free, as Your Word states:

John 8:36 BSB

"So if the Son sets you free, you will be free indeed."

"I ask for deliverance from these things in Jesus name, and I ask according to Your Word for love, joy, peace, patience, kindness, goodness, faithfulness, meekness, gentleness, boldness, and self-control to be my portion from now on. I renounce legalism and the striving for perfection, and I ask that You would set my kids free from any residue of those negative things in Jesus name as well, I receive your freedom, in Jesus name, amen!"

END OF PRAYER

CHAPTER 61: PRAYER TO REQUEST ORDERS OF PROTECTION AGAINST DESTINY DERAILERS

Psalms 91:9-11 BSB

"Because you have made the LORD your dwelling— my refuge, the Most High— no evil will befall you, no plague will approach your tent. For He will command His angels concerning you to guard you in all your ways."

Beginning of Prayer

"Heavenly Father, I come before You today to request indefinite and permanent orders of protection against every man, woman, and spirit that would try to derail me from the destiny You have assigned for me to accomplish, including men and women who would pursue an intimate relationship outside Your will, as well as those who would try to use sexual temptations to derail me from what You're calling me to do, in Jesus name.

"Lord, I ask that You keep them far away from me and

restrain them from making any form of contact with me. I ask for those people who would be agents of the enemy to have technical difficulties if they tried to reach me through in person conversation, text messages, emails, social media and the internet, in Jesus name.

"Heavenly Father, I ask for the sake of the call of God upon this life of mine that You have given me and for my conscience's sake, I receive these orders of protection. I ask according to Psalm 91 that You would assign angels to guard and protect me in real life and even through the internet and social media. I receive Your orders of protection and I thank You that I have received what I have prayed for in Jesus name, amen!"

END OF PRAYER

CHAPTER 62: PRAYER OF REPENTANCE FOR HALLOWEEN

A lot of people don't know this, but Halloween has a very weird, occultic and dark Celtic origin, and it's really unfortunate that so many Americans and even Christians alike partake in it. If you want to know more about it, you can read my book: *Prayers of The Saints: A Collection of Prayers To Help You Sharpen The Sword of Your Prayer Life*. But it's dark in its origin and even from the imagery used in Halloween is very symbolic of death and the dark side of paranormal activity. It's not something that Christians should be embracing, because it's an open celebration of death and demons. If you'd like to repent for partaking in Halloween, the prayer is available below for you.

1 Thessalonians 5:22 KJV

"Abstain from all appearance of evil."

Beginning of Prayer

"Heavenly Father, I come before You to renounce and repent for any time I celebrated Halloween and openly celebrated death, demons, and the kingdom of darkness. I ask You to forgive me and my family bloodline for this pagan unholy holiday. I renounce every form of evil, and I also ask for forgiveness for any time I let my kids partake in it. I ask that Your Blood, Lord Jesus, would cover us, the doorposts and lintels of our homes and my families homes, in Jesus name."

"Heavenly Father, I renounce the altars, spirits, witchcraft, sacrifices and the dark practices of Halloween and every evil thing practiced on that day and I ask that Your Blood would speak a better word on my behalf and that of my family's behalf as well. I receive Your freedom and I thank you for granting my petition in Jesus name, amen!"

END OF PRAYER

CHAPTER 63: PRAYER OF PROTECTION AGAINST RETALIATION

Joel 3:4 BSB

"Now what do you have against Me, O Tyre, Sidon, and all the regions of Philistia? Are you rendering against Me a recompense? If you retaliate against Me, I will swiftly and speedily return your recompense upon your heads."

Beginning of Prayer

"Heavenly Father, I come before You today to request for an order of protection against specific people, spirits, and events that would be considered acts of retaliation. Heavenly Father, Your word declares that You will give your angels charge over me and that no evil shall befall me:

Psalms 91:9-11 BSB

"Because you have made the LORD your dwelling— my refuge, the Most High— no evil will befall you, no plague will approach your tent. For He will command His angels concerning you to guard you in all your ways."

"Heavenly Father, I come to You to request the fulfillment of these promises found in Psalm 91 and beyond. Lord, I ask that You would issue spiritual angelic officers to enforce orders of protection that list me and my family as the one who are to be protected. I receive Your protection and Your promises, Lord. I ask that You would preserve me and aid me in accomplishing Your will on this earth before I come home to You, Father God. Help me have courage, faith, and confidence in You and in Your abilities as well as those You have gifted and bless me with. May I make You fond of me as a Father, and may the kingdom of darkness suffer because of my existence on this earth. May people be saved, healed, and delivered because of me and my family being on this earth. May the enemy not be able to do anything about it because You are our shield and bucklers, our Mighty God in whom we trust. I receive Your protection, in Jesus name, amen!"

END OF PRAYER

CHAPTER 64: PRAYER RENOUNCING ANCIENT HOSTILITY

It's no secret that there has been past hostility between certain people and ethnic groups. If you've found yourself as a believer having feelings of unprovoked animosity for no reason against a group, it may be rooted in something much older than you, and this prayer is meant to address that. For example, if someone used to be a former Muslim, after they got saved and became a Christian, they might struggle or harbor resentment in their hearts towards the Jewish people. This could possibly be connected to something that the Lord called *ancient hostility*. If you've found yourself inherently having a negative predisposition towards a certain group of people that they no longer want to harbor anymore because they desire to be free. They want to love people with the Heart of Jesus. If that's you, this prayer is for you.

Ezekiel 25:15-17 BSB

"This is what the Lord GOD says: 'Because the Philistines acted in vengeance, taking vengeance with malice of soul to destroy Judah with ancient hostility, therefore this is what the Lord GOD says: Behold, I will stretch out My hand against the Philistines, and I will cut off the Cherethites and destroy the remnant along the coast. I will execute great vengeance against them with furious reproof. Then they will know that I am the LORD, when I lay My vengeance upon them.'"

Beginning of Prayer

"Heavenly Father, I come before You today to clear my DNA of ancient hostility towards [name the people group you or your ethnicity has had conflicts with and animosity towards]. I repent Lord for harboring any and all hate, anger, racism, and murder in my heart because even though I may have not acted out anything physical Lord Jesus You said that to be angry with someone in your heart is to be guilty of murder."

Matthew 5:21-22 BSB

"You have heard that it was said to the ancients, 'Do not murder' and 'Anyone who murders will be subject to judgment.' But I tell you that anyone who is angry with his brother will be subject to judgment. Again, anyone who says to his brother, 'Raca,' will be subject to the Sanhedrin. But anyone who says, 'You fool!' will be subject to the fire of hell."

"Heavenly Father, I forgive those who have wronged me and the people that I physically descended from according to the flesh, and I ask that You would forgive me and the ethnicity that I physically descended from for all the anger, hatred, murder, and violence committed against others, and I ask that You would change the hearts of both sides to love one another instead of hating one another. I ask that Your love would pour into my heart in a greater measure, and I ask that You would help me overcome evil with good. I now petition You Heavenly Father for my complete deliverance, spirit, soul, and body from any spirits of anger, revenge, murder-violence, and unclean spirits that have exploited those emotions. Furthermore, I break agreement and I break covenant with those unclean spirits and I repent for all bloodshed on their unholy altars in the name of jihad, ethnic cleansing, murder and through war casualties, in Jesus name."

John 8:36 BSB

"So if the Son sets you free, you will be free indeed."

"Lord Jesus, I receive Your freedom and I ask You to set me free today in Jesus name, amen!"

END OF PRAYER

CHAPTER 65: DEALING WITH FERTILITY ISSUES AND IDOLATRY

So, if you are reading this, and you are a Christian sister, and you have been trying to have a baby or have had resistance to your fertility, especially if it has seemed to try following the family line. I would like to bring something to light through this chapter, as the Holy Spirit has allowed me to connect the dots. So, I would like to state that as of the current time of writing this book, I am not a professional medical doctor nor am I a certified physician as of now. But I do have some knowledge and understanding about what is about to be communicated as Spirit expands my knowledge.

The Womb, A Place of Nurture

But I want to briefly mention as to why in the world the enemy would come after pregnancies. Well we know that women are the ones that carry and birth the next generation of apostles, prophets, pastors, teachers, evangelists, Kingdom financiers, boys, and girls that could be the possible solution to major problems in the earth. It's not a surprise that the womb, in times past, has been a war zone. Even if you look at modern society, it seems like there has been a demonically fueled hatred of babies in the womb.

It's no wonder why the enemy would try to resist godly men and women who are going to discipline and "train up a child in the way he should go and even when he is old he will not depart from it," from having a successful full term birthing. It's not only a good thing for the world, but also a threat to the enemy's agenda.

Matthew 2:16 BSB

> "When Herod saw that he had been outwitted by the Magi, he was filled with rage. Sending orders, he put to death all the boys in Bethlehem and its vicinity who were two years old and under, according to the time he had learned from the Magi."

Proverbs 22:6 BSB

> "Train up a child in the way he should go, and when he is old he will not depart from it."

Proverbs 22:6 ASV

> "Train up a child in the way he should go, And even when he is old, he will not depart from it."

And remember, don't succumb to the temptation of being angry with God because of the current or previous circumstances. The Lord Jesus was pretty clear when He said:

John 10:10 BSB

> "The thief comes only to steal and kill and destroy. I have come that they may have life, and have it in all its fullness."

The Woman's Cycle

So when it comes to a woman's monthly cycle, the typical time according to what we know medically is around 28 days, with some women varying. Why in the world did I just mention this? We'll start with a couple of Scriptures and I'll explain:

Genesis 1:14-19 KJV

> "And God said, Let there be lights in the firmament of the heaven to divide the day from the night; and let them be for signs, and for seasons, and for days, and years: and let them be for lights in the firmament of the heaven to give light upon the earth: and it was so. And God made two great lights; the greater light to rule the day, and the lesser light to rule the night: he made the stars also. And God set them in the firmament of the heaven to give light upon the earth, and to rule over the day and over the night, and to divide the light from the darkness: and God saw that it was good. And the evening and the morning were the fourth day."

We can see the original intent of the LORD according to Genesis 1 is for the sun, moon, and stars to serve the purposes of dividing the day from the night; to be for signs and seasons, for days and years and to give light upon the face of the earth. Let's proceed to Deuteronomy next.

Deuteronomy 4:19 KJV

> "and lest thou lift up thine eyes unto heaven, and when thou seest the sun, and the moon, and the stars, even all the host of heaven, shouldest be driven to worship them, and serve them, which the LORD thy God hath divided unto all nations under the whole heaven."

we see in Deuteronomy 4:19, the Word of the Lord was clear to the Israelites to be careful not to worship the sun, moon, and stars. Why bring up the sun, moon, and stars? Let me ask you a question, and as you read it, I encourage you to pause before considering the answer. How many days are in a month? It's anywhere from twenty-eight to thirty-one days, depending on the calendar you use as a reference. Why the difference? Because there are two calendars: a solar (Gregorian) and a lunar calendar. The typical cycle of the moon lasts anywhere from twenty-eight to twenty-nine and a half days. Why is this relevant? If you've been struggling with a difficult pregnancy, it might be connected to idolatry somewhere in your bloodline, from ancestors who worshiped the sun, especially the moon, fertility idols, stars, or constellations. This is particularly true if your ancestors were involved in ancient or modern moon worship, or even Islam. Moon goddesses and moon deities were worshiped by past generations, and many of us haven't fully realized to what extent some of these idols influenced our forebears' practices. With that said, I want to share some Scripture that I hope will encourage you as you make your petition to the Lord. He is not a respecter of persons, and God does not show favoritism. What Hannah did in her prayer, you are about to do as well. She cried out to the Lord, and He answered her. The key was in her words, and here's a paraphrase: "If You give me a son, I'll dedicate him back to You for all the days of his life, and no razor will touch his head." Now, you don't have to make a Nazarite vow for your child, but her heart was clear: "If You give him to me, he's Yours." The Lord listened to her, honored her prayerful vow, and did exactly as she asked. That moved the heart of God, and the prophet Samuel was born! I remember a man of God, Michael Koulianos, saying something like, "If you move His heart, He'll move His hand"

1 Samuel 1:7-20 BSB

"And this went on year after year. Whenever Hannah went up to the house of the LORD, her rival taunted her until she wept and would not eat. "Hannah, why are you crying?" her husband Elkanah asked. "Why won't you eat? Why is your heart so grieved? Am I not better to you than ten sons?" So after they had finished eating and drinking in Shiloh, Hannah stood up. Now Eli the priest was sitting on a chair by the doorpost of the temple of the LORD. In her bitter distress, Hannah prayed to the LORD and wept with many tears. And she made a vow, pleading, "O LORD of Hosts, if only You will look upon the affliction of Your maidservant and remember me, not forgetting Your maidservant but giving her a son, then I will dedicate him to the LORD all the days of his life, and no razor shall ever come over his head." As Hannah kept on praying before the LORD, Eli watched her mouth. Hannah was praying in her heart, and though her lips were moving, her voice could not be heard. So Eli thought she was drunk and said to her, "How long will you be drunk? Put away your wine!" "No, my lord," Hannah replied. "I am a woman oppressed in spirit. I have not had any wine or strong drink, but I have poured out my soul before the LORD. Do not take your servant for a wicked woman; for all this time I have been praying out of the depth of my anguish and grief." "Go in peace," Eli replied, "and may the God of Israel grant the petition you have asked of Him." "May your maidservant find favor with you," said Hannah. Then she went on her way, and she began eating again, and her face was no longer downcast. The next morning Elkanah and Hannah got up early to bow in worship before the LORD, and then returned home to Ramah. And Elkanah had relations with his wife Hannah, and the LORD remembered her. So in the course of time, Hannah conceived and gave birth to a son. She named him Samuel, saying, "Because I have asked for him from the LORD."

If you've been desiring to have children and have been asking the Lord for kids, whether for a short time or a long time, I hope that this prayer helps you present your case and brings a breakthrough for successful pregnancies, in Jesus' name. [65]

Opening Prayer

"LORD God, I come before You as the Heavenly Father, and I now request and petition for access to You and Your Heavenly Courtroom of Fertility and Idolatry, in Jesus name.

LORD God, Heavenly Father, I come before You and I stand in the gap on behalf of myself and my ancestors connected to my bloodline and those who have been grafted into the family tree through covenants and marriage covenant. Heavenly Father, I now request access and legal standing in Heaven's Court of Fertility and Idolatry to be made available and opened to me. I further request for You to summon angels to be witnesses, scribe angels, angelic officers of the Court to keep my safety and order in the spirit realm and in the physical natural realm in my current place of prayer. Holy Spirit, I ask You to help me by bringing to my remembrance anything I specially need to repent of that I and my ancestors did, said, or did not do. This is connected to anything that would negatively affect my fertility and chance to have a successful pregnancy. And I, (say your full name), forgive everyone who has sinned against me and wronged me in any way. I now ask You, Lord Jesus, to forgive them and forgive me for any grudges I've healed against (try to specifically name the people that you are forgiving. Remember that forgiveness is more about our personal freedom than it is about those who have wronged us. Trust me, it's not worth holding on to), in Jesus name."

"LORD God, I now come before You on the Scriptural foundation of Isaiah 43:25-26, 1 John 1:9 and the Finished work of the Lord Jesus on the Cross. As I begin to confess and repent and ask for forgiveness, breakthrough, healing, and deliverance from anything and any legal right that the devil has had to deny me successful pregnancies. LORD, I remind You of Your Word, which states:

> Psalms 127:3 BSB
>
> "Children are indeed a heritage from the LORD, and the fruit of the womb is His reward."

Prayer of Repentance

"LORD, I begin by confessing and repenting and asking for

the Blood of Jesus to cleanse me and my ancestral bloodline for the following; every sacrificial offering and sacrifice made to the gods of Islam, Hinduism, Roman fertility idols, idols of abortion, the idols behind planned parenthood, the queen of heaven, African, Native American, Asians, European, Oceanian, Australian, Hittite, and American gods of fertility, Jezebel, the worship of spiritual spouses and intimate acts with unclean spirits, lucid dreaming, self gratification, Bestiality, homosexual relations, blood sacrifice, sacrifices of children to demons, dedications of future descendants and their wombs by previous ancestors, sexual sacrifices and fertility sacrifices, dedications of newborn babies to the purposes and plans of the devil and his kingdom, sacrifices to organizations with unholy roots and unclean spirits operating behind them, male seed sacrifice to demons, sacrifices to organizations with unholy roots and unclean spirits operating behind them, the worship of the sun, moon, stars, constellations, horoscopes, palm readings, tea leave readings, false prophecies spoken by mediums, necromancers, the involvement of necromancers, all sacrifice made to *pharmakia* and the spirits associated with them, and anything else that would have given the enemy legal rights to resist a successful healthy, full term pregnancy, in Jesus name."

Deuteronomy 4:15-19 BSB

"So since you saw no form of any kind on the day the LORD spoke to you out of the fire at Horeb, be careful that you do not act corruptly and make an idol for yourselves of any form or shape, whether in the likeness of a male or female, of any beast that is on the earth or bird that flies in the air, or of any creature that crawls on the ground or fish that is in the waters below. When you look to the heavens and see the sun and moon and stars—all the host of heaven—do not be enticed to bow down and worship what the LORD your God has apportioned to all the nations under heaven."

"LORD God, Your Word is clear to take heed not to worship creation, sun, moon, stars, fish, birds, LORD I repent for every male and female in my ancestry and connected to my bloodline of the sins of idolatry, participation of the new age movement, all of its subsidiaries, for chakra meditation, new age meditation, and all other things associated with those movements. I ask for forgiveness on behalf of my ancestors and myself for anyone who was guilty of worshiping, sacrificing and praying to the sun, moon, stars, worshiping the host of heaven, the earth and calling earth mother earth. The fish of the sea, the birds of the air, angels, saints, and all prayers made to them and the unclean spirits that were behind them. I also repent for any ancestor of mine who worshiped apostles, prophets, pastors, evangelists, and teachers. I furthermore repent and ask for pardon for the sins, transgressions, and iniquities of my ancestors and I, everything listed and the sins I'm not even aware of that my ancestors did, in Jesus name."

Addressing Enemy Altars

Exodus 23:24-26 BSB

"You must not bow down to their gods or serve them or follow their practices. Instead, you are to demolish them and smash their sacred stones to pieces. So you shall serve the Lord your God, and He will bless your bread and your water. And I will take away sickness from among you. No woman in your land will miscarry or be barren; I will fulfill the number of your days."

Deuteronomy 16:21-22 BSB

"Do not set up any wooden Asherah pole next to the altar you will build for the Lord your God, and do not set up for yourselves a sacred pillar, which the Lord your God hates."

"LORD God, I renounce and repent and ask for forgives or everyone who partook of, became human attendants to, supervised, had a soul tie with, and or were connected to unholy altars, along with the associated idols and supervision spirits associated with them, especially those connected to fertility and fertility idols, in Jesus name."

Breaking Agreement With Demonic Covenants

"LORD God, I break agreement with every covenant made and entered into with unholy and satanic altars and all of their associated sacrifice and sacrificial offerings, in Jesus name."

Repentance For Sexual Immorality

"LORD God, I repent for anyone who committed sexual immorality at all wicked altars, including fornication, incest, adultery, orgies, and everything of the like. I declare that is wickedness. And I declare I want nothing to do with it has no more effect on me, in Jesus name!"

Asking For Legal Rights Be Revoked

"LORD God, Lord Jesus, Holy Spirit, I ask that every legal right the enemy has had on my female and male side of my family lineage and family tree and ancestral bloodline, and any genetic and generational curses that would have or have had any adverse effects on me and especially my fertility and ability to get pregnant and conceive a child. You have declared children as blessing, and they are the fruit of the womb:"

Psalms 127:3-5 BSB

"Children are indeed a heritage from the LORD, and the fruit of the womb is His reward. Like arrows in the hand of a warrior, so are children born in one's youth. Blessed is the man whose quiver is full of them. He will not be put to shame when he confronts the enemies at the gate."

Declarations of Faith

"I now declare and decree the Word of the LORD over me that Christ has redeemed (say your full name, out loud, including your middle if you have one, and the last names of your mother's side of the family and the last name of your father's side of the family. If you don't know your father's and mother's last name the LORD understands just say my father's bloodline and my mother's bloodlines) from the curse of the law, being made a curse for me: for it is written:

Galatians 3:13-14 KJV

"Christ hath redeemed us from the curse of the law, being made a curse for us: for it is written, Cursed is every one that hangeth on a tree: that the blessing of Abraham might come on the Gentiles through Jesus Christ; that we might receive the promise of the Spirit through faith."

Psalms 82:1 KJV

"God standeth in the congregation of the mighty; He judgeth among the gods."

"LORD God, Your Word says in Psalm 103:6 that you: "Execute righteousness and justice for all that are oppressed.'

"As it is written,

Psalms 103:6 BSB

"The LORD executes righteousness and justice for all the oppressed."

"LORD God, Heavenly Father, I ask You to bring an end to the oppression of the enemy against my fertility and ability to successfully become pregnant and bear healthy offspring."

Isaiah 54:17 KJV

"No weapon that is formed against thee shall prosper; and every tongue that shall rise against thee in judgment thou shalt condemn. This is the heritage of the servants of the LORD, and their righteousness is of me, saith the LORD."

Breaking Agreement With Negative Words

"LORD God I break agreement with every negative word spoken over me by myself, medical physicians, those within the medical field such as nurses, doctors, physicians, chiropractors, doctors, medical health professionals and medical health specialists including those that specialize in pregnancies, in Jesus name."

Note

Ask the Holy Spirit to remind you of specific words you said out of frustration, hurt, anger, and negative emotions that may be working against your ability to bear children. Take some time and try not to rush, but make sure to say the following:

Prayer Continued...

"LORD God, I repent for any time I have spoken out against myself and my ability to get pregnant, I break agreement with what I said concerning," (*fill in here what you remember speaking that you spoke against yourself and if it's something someone else spoke over you, just be sure to say and mean*), "... and I break agreement with what (say the person's names, if you know it. If not that's okay just label them as he, she, the doctor, etc.) said, concerning my ability that was negative concerning my ability to get successfully pregnant, and carry a healthy baby to full-term. I decree and declare, according to Isaiah 54:17, 'No weapon formed against me shall prosper, and I will condemn every tongue that rises up against me in judgment, because this is my heritage as a servant of the LORD, and my Righteousness comes from You LORD' and You Lord Jesus, in Jesus name."

"LORD God, I now ask You for a *Righteous Verdict of Judgment* to be rendered against every unholy and satanic spirit, unholy and satanic assignment, and weapon that has been assigned to my family line as well as my bloodline with the assignment of affecting my fertility and every other unholy assignment, and I ask from this present moment forward may I be fully capable of bearing healthy children to full term and giving birth naturally, in Jesus name."

"LORD God, I now ask that the legal implications of the Cross of the Lord Jesus would be applied into effect according to Galatians 3:13-14 and 1 John 1:9 to break all genetic curses and abnormalities, demonically inspired DNA mutations, generational curses and things of the like, in Jesus name."

"LORD God, I receive Your Righteous Verdict and I ask You for a Divine Judgment enforcing my permanent release, breakthrough, deliverance, freedom, refreshment, restoration, and the Blessing of the LORD to be upon my physical womb and my spiritual womb, and may the LORD's blessings be over me, upon me and my entire household, in Jesus name. I receive the written promise of Your Word in the book of Psalms that states:

Psalm 113:9 KJV

"He maketh the barren woman to keep house, And to be a joyful mother of children. Praise ye the LORD."

Asking For A Permanent Order Of Protection

"LORD God, I further request and go on record to ask You for a permanent Order of Protection that forbids the enemy and the kingdom of darkness from coming near me and my household by a set distance of Your choosing. I also ask for holy heavenly angels to be assigned to ensure the *Divine*

Order of Protection does not get violated. And if it does, I ask You to charge your heavenly angels to enforce the heavenly verdict and to take rapid actions of binding, punishing, and casting into the abyss any demonic entities. They would try violating the Order of Protection established in place by You and Your Heavenly Court. I ask that the verdict would be enforced by Your holy angels. LORD God, Lord Jesus, Holy Spirit, I surrender all areas of this life you've given to me under Your Protection, Lordship, and Priesthood Lord Jesus, in Jesus Name, amen!"

END OF PRAYER

CHAPTER 66: PRAYER OF REPENTANCE AND DELIVERANCE FROM NEW AGE MOVEMENT AND THE OCCULT

Beginning of Prayer

"Heavenly Father, I repent for every time I and my ancestors chose to worship the universe and partnered with spirit guides rather than Your Holy Spirit. I verbally break agreement with every spirit guide and false holy spirit from the New Age and other various religions that are not centered on the deity of Jesus Christ as the Son of the Living God. I renounce false religions, including Mormonism. I renounce every sacrifice and prayer I and my ancestors prayed to spirits connected to the New Age and the occult. I renounce every New Age theology, doctrine, altar, and demons behind that belief. And I petition You from my heart for freedom and deliverance:

John 6:37 BSB

"Everyone the Father gives Me will come to Me, and the one who comes to Me I will never drive away."

John 8:36 BSB

"So if the Son sets you free, you will be free indeed."

"Jesus, today I declare You as Lord. I declare You as the Lord of my life and that I belong to You. I ask that the full price of freedom that You paid for with Your Blood would be enforced on my behalf, and I ask You to deliver me. You won't turn me away because You said so. I perceive Your healing, freedom, and deliverance in full. Thank You for starting to set me free and seeing it through until it's one-hundred percent complete, in Jesus name, amen!"

END OF PRAYER

CHAPTER 67: REPENTANCE PRAYER FOR ANCESTORS WHO PARTOOK IN ASTRAL PROJECTION

1 Corinthians 6:20 BSB

"You were bought at a price. Therefore glorify God with your body."

Beginning of Prayer

"Heavenly Father, I repent for every time I and my ancestors chose to astral project and willingly lucid dream. I ask according to 1 John 1:9 that You would forgive me and my ancestors for astral projecting, lucid dreaming, and even taking drugs such as mushrooms, and other substances to induce a high and a spiritual experience. I renounce the New Age, witchcraft, and the practice of astral projection. I repent for every time my ancestors and I ever stepped foot onto the astral plane, and for everything done on the astral field. I ask for Your forgiveness and for deliverance for anything connected to astral projection. I ask for peaceful and restful sleep according to Your Word, which states:

Psalms 4:8 BSB

"I will lie down and sleep in peace, for You alone, O LORD, make me dwell in safety."

"Heavenly Father, I ask that You would station angels in my bedroom and around me while I sleep, wherever I may be sleeping or going, to guard me physically and in the spirit. Lord Jesus, I receive Your freedom and deliverance, in Jesus name, amen!" [66]

END OF PRAYER

CHAPTER 68: PRAYER OF DELIVERANCE FROM EATING DISORDERS AND TORMENTING VOICES

Feel free to play worship songs during the prayer, just try to keep the volume at a level where your words can be clearly heard and to where you aren't being distracted as Holy Spirit leads you.

A Personal Prayer For Anyone Dealing With

Beginning of Prayer

"Heavenly Father, I now submit a formal appeal and request for your Heavenly Courtroom to be seated, and for You to take Your rightful seat as the Righteous Judge. I now ask You, Heavenly Father, to call forth your angels to be witnesses to this Righteous Prosecution, in Jesus name."

Isaiah 43:25-26 BSB

"I, yes I, am He who blots out your transgressions for My own sake and remembers your sins no more.

Remind Me, let us argue the matter together. State your case, so that you may be vindicated."

Presenting Your Case

"Heavenly Father, I come before you to present my case according to Isaiah 43:25-26, against abnormal eating habits, food idols, unrighteous altars, and any demons that have oppressed my eating habits, in Jesus name."

Ask The Lord Jesus To Help You Present Your Case And Advocate For You

"Lord Jesus, I, (say your full name), now ask You as my Heavenly Advocate for You to be my Representative within the Courts of Heaven to help me effectively present my case before God the Father, the Heavenly Father, and for you to help me personally present my case before God the Father, in Jesus name."

Confession And Repentance

"Heavenly Father, I confess and repent of any lack of self-control while eating, binge-eating, purging food, unhealthy eating habits, and anything that I've done personally to empower unwholesome eating habits and any unhealthy eating patterns. I further confess and ask for Your forgiveness for (try to be specific and ask Holy Spirit to help you confess of anything specific, it might be a bad attitude or bitterness towards another person who wronged you or mistreated you, trust me it's not worth holding onto a wrong someone else did at the expense of your own personal freedom, please forgive for your own freedom's sake), and any other unconfessed sins that I have been personally guilty of committing against You LORD God, Lord Jesus, Holy Spirit. I repent for violating your Holy Decrees, Statues, Your Written, and Spoken Prophetic Word, I now ask for You to forgive me according to what is written in 1 John 1:9:

1 John 1:9 BSB

"If we confess our sins, He is faithful and just to forgive us our sins and to cleanse us from all unrighteousness."

Prayer Continued

"I have now confessed, and I ask for Your forgiveness according to the work that the Lord Jesus did on the Cross for me at Calvary and 1 John 1:9 in Jesus name."

Scripture Concerning Forgiveness

Matthew 6:12-15 KJV

"And forgive us our debts, as we forgive our debtors. And lead us not into temptation, but deliver us from evil: For thine is the kingdom, and the power, and the glory, for ever. Amen. For if ye forgive men their trespasses, your Heavenly Father will also forgive you: but if ye forgive not men their trespasses, neither will your Father forgive your trespasses."

Prayer Concerning Forgiveness

"Heavenly Father, I now choose to forgive everybody who has wronged me. I release, forgive, and ask You to bless them in alignment with Your Perfect Will and Heart Desire. I release (try to name those who you need to forgive, if you don't know their names just substitute their name with 'them'), from all the debt that they have owed towards me, even if I feel like that it's a simple apology that they owe me. I release (name the people you have decided to forgive), from the debt they have owed me. LORD, may these people who have wronged me become the best of them that you've created them to be, in Jesus name."

Repent For Negative Words And Word Curses You've Spoken Over Yourself

"Heavenly Father, I repent for any negative words that I've spoken over my eating habits that have empowered the enemy to work in that area and every other area of my life. I now officially break agreement with those negative words. Instead, I choose to speak blessing and life into these areas that I and others, in times past, spoke against myself, especially my eating habits, and eating schedule, in Jesus name."

"I, (say your full name), further appeal and submit a formal request to You and Your Court The Righteous Judge to render null, void, ineffective and fruitless every word curse and negative word that has been spoken against me, my eating, and my eating habits by others, even those from my childhood by my parents, friends, family members, co-workers, and strangers, according to what is written in Isaiah 54:17:

Isaiah 54:17 KJV

"No weapon that is formed against thee shall prosper; and every tongue that shall rise against thee in judgment thou shalt condemn. This is the heritage of the servants of the LORD, and their righteousness is of me, saith the LORD."

"I forgive those who have spoken against me. I now judge as unrighteous and condemn as useless all negative words, spiritual and physical weapons that were spoken and fashioned against me. And I now formally request this Court to condemn as legally null, void, fruitless and ineffective all negative words and word curses associated and connected with unhealthy eating habits, anorexia, overeating, and bulimia against me, and my eating habits according to Isaiah 54:17, in Jesus name."

Repenting For Anything In Common With Idols And Evil Altars Associated With Food

"Heavenly Father, I now confess and break agreement with and ask for forgiveness for any of my ancestors who were human attendants to an unrighteous altar connected to food and food consumption. I asked for forgiveness for my ancestors who sacrificed food and meal offerings to idols (demons in disguise). I repent and ask for Your forgiveness on behalf of myself and my ancestry for any partnership with demons and idols associated with food altars and any actions and sacrifices that were made on them, whether they were physical or spiritual sacrifices, including any blood, food, money, yielding physical bodies to these unclean spirits, word covenants, and everything else that might have given legal access to these unclean spirits to operate in my life, as well as my family line, in Jesus name."

Declare You That You Want Nothing To Do With Or Have "In Common" With These Idols And Their Associated Altars

"I declare that I want nothing to do with unclean spirits, evil altars, including spirits that cause eating disorders, binge-eating disorders, anorexia, bulimia, purging (eating food, then willingly vomiting it out later), overeating, including every unclean spirit that has tried to exploit these things as well as cause negative body image. I repent and break agreement with every legal right that these spirits might have to operate in my life. And I ask You Heavenly Father to condemn these demons that carry out an assignment of unhealthy eating and try to cause issues with eating according to what is written in Psalms 103:6 for judgment to be declared against those unclean spirits in Jesus name."

"I now declare that my spirit, soul, and physical body are the temple of the true Holy Spirit of God, in Jesus name. Amen."

Repent For The Sins Of Your Ancestors

"Heavenly Father, I, (say your full name, including middle if applicable), repent and confess for all the sins, transgressions, and generational iniquities that have been empowering all unclean and unclean spirits to afflict my eating habits and cause an unhealthy view and unhealthy relationship with food. Including those that gave legal rights to unclean and unclean spirits to operate and work in any area of my life. And I surrender these areas and all other areas of my life to You, LORD God, Lord Jesus, and Holy Spirit, in Jesus name."

"Heavenly Father, I now agree with all true and legitimate accusations that the accuser of the brethren has filed against me, my ancestors, and my bloodline concerning guilt connected to sins, transgressions, generational iniquities, ungodly agreements, ungodly contracts, and ungodly covenants that the enemy had filed against me. And I make a formal appeal today on (say the date you are praying this prayer). I ask the Lord Jesus to apply His Blood as the legal atonement for all the sins, transgressions, iniquities, ungodly contracts, ungodly word covenants and agreements, and ungodly covenants of myself and my ancestors. I also ask the Heavenly Court to dismiss and silence all the accusations of the enemy against me and my family lineage, in Jesus name."

Ask The Court To Dismiss The Legal Charges Submitted As Evidence Against You And Your Family

"I now submit a plea to this Court to dismiss any and all submitted, written, hidden evidence, accusations, and allegations of the enemy against me based on the Finished Work of the Cross of the Lord Jesus Christ, in Jesus name."

Begin To Prosecute Any Idols And Unholy Altars Connected To Food Consumption And Sacrifice

"Heavenly Father, I now begin my prayer of prosecution of these idols and all wicked and unrighteous altars connected to unhealthy food consumption, unhealthy eating habits in general according to Psalms 103:6, Luke 18:1-8, 1 Corinthians 6:3 which testify:

Psalm 103:6 KJV

> "The LORD executeth righteousness and
> judgment For all that are oppressed."

Luke 18:1-8 BSB

"Then Jesus told them a parable about their need to pray at all times and not lose heart: "In a certain town there was a judge who neither feared God nor respected men. And there was a widow in that town who kept appealing to him, 'Give me justice against my adversary.' For a while he refused, but later he said to himself, 'Though I neither fear God nor respect men, yet because this widow keeps pestering me, I will give her justice. Then she will stop wearing me out with her perpetual requests.'" And the Lord said, "Listen to the words of the unjust judge. Will not God bring about justice for His elect who cry out to Him day and night? Will He continue to defer their help? I tell you, He will promptly carry out justice on their behalf. Nevertheless, when the Son of Man comes, will He find faith on earth?"

1 Corinthians 6:3 BSB

> "Do you not know that we will judge angels?
> How much more the things of this life!"

The Secret To Justification: A Humble And Contrite Heart

Psalm 51:15-17 KJV

"O LORD, open thou my lips; And my mouth shall shew forth thy praise. For thou desirest not sacrifice; else would I give it: Thou delightest not in burnt offering. The sacrifices of God are a broken spirit: A broken and a contrite heart, O God, thou wilt not despise."

Luke 18:10-14 KJV

"Two men went up into the temple to pray; the one a Pharisee, and the other a publican. The Pharisee stood and prayed thus with himself, God, I thank thee, that I am not as other men are, extortioners, unjust, adulterers, or even as this publican. I fast twice in the week, I give tithes of all that I possess. And the publican, standing afar off, would not lift up so much as his eyes unto heaven, but smote upon his breast, saying, God be merciful to me a sinner. I tell you, this man went down to his house justified rather than the other: for every one that exalteth himself shall be abased; and he that humbleth himself shall be exalted."

Time To Make Your Appeal

"Heavenly Father, I now make an appeal for your Court to issue a Divine Decree of judgment against any and all wicked altars connects to irregular eating and unhealthy eating habits and any altars connected and associated with food, specially food altars and every spirit attending and supervising these altars in my life according to 1 Kings 12:2-5, in Jesus name."

1 Kings 13:1-6 KJV

"And, behold, there came a man of God out of Judah by the word of the LORD unto Beth-el: and Jeroboam stood by the altar to burn incense. And he cried against the altar in the word of the LORD, and said, O altar, altar, thus saith the LORD ; Behold, a child shall be born unto the house of David, Josiah by name; and upon thee shall he offer the priests of the high places that burn incense upon thee, and men's bones shall be burnt upon thee. And he gave a sign the same day, saying, This is the sign which the LORD hath spoken; Behold, the altar shall be rent, and the ashes that are upon it shall be poured out. And it came to pass, when king Jeroboam heard the saying of the man of God, which had cried against the altar in Beth-el, that he put forth his hand from the altar, saying, Lay hold on him. And his hand, which he put forth against him, dried up, so that he could not pull it in again to him. The altar also was rent, and the ashes poured out from the altar, according to the sign which the man of God had given by the word of the

LORD. And the king answered and said unto the man of God, Intreat now the face of the LORD thy God, and pray for me, that my hand may be restored to me again. And the man of God besought the LORD, and the king's hand was restored to him again, and became as it was before."

Petition The LORD For The Destruction of unholy altars

"Heavenly Father, I now ask for You to speak Your Prophetic Word of destruction and tear down and the assignment of angels to go permanently dismantle and destroy all unholy altars connected to ungodly and unhealthy food consumption. I now ask for Your Court to assign angels to supervise, prevent, and dismantle any further construction of all unholy altars, especially those connected to food, and false holy spirits, in Jesus name."

"Heavenly Father, I now move upon You and Your Court to issue a Divine Decree of Judgment against these demonic entities that have manipulated and robbed me of blessings, peace, prosperity, soundness of mind, sleep, rest, breakthrough, and that have tormented and played with my mind, and eating habits, in accordance to Psalms 103:6 read prior. I now ask for a divine declaration and decree to be released from Your Heavenly Throne into the spirit realm and the earthly realm. For my release, breakthrough, freedom, deliverance, and an eviction notice to every demonic entity that has oppressed me and or possessed any and all parts of my spirit, soul and or body. I repent forever having given any legal rights to any unclean spirits that have operated within my life and against my life. And I now ask You Heavenly Father, Lord Jesus Christ, and Holy Spirit to remove any demonic entity from my life, soul, and body. I dedicate my spirit, soul, body, and life to Your Holiness, purity, power, heavenly revelations, the destiny of the LORD God upon my life, my Heavenly Father God, the Lord Jesus Christ, and the Holy Spirit of God. I now declare deliverance and freedom now, in Jesus name!"

Commanding The Unclean Spirits To Go

"I now command and charge by the Authority of the Lord Jesus Christ to every unclean spirit to find its exit out of my spirit, soul, and body NOW in the Name of Jesus, and never gain to return as a familiar spirit to me, or my family, or my kids, in Jesus name! Come out now or be forcefully removed, I command you to not harm me on the way out, in Jesus name."

"Heavenly Father, I ask punishable by your Supreme Authority and angelic officers to bind and to remove anything that is not of You LORD on me or in me, and I now ask your holy angels to bind, remove, and cast into the abyss all demonic entities that have possessed me, oppressed me, or both, in Jesus name."

Asking For An Immediate And Permanent Order of Protection

"Heavenly Father, I now ask for this Court hearing to be inscribed and recorded into a Book in the Courts of Heaven and sealed for a written or audio record for future reference. I am Yours LORD, in Jesus Name, amen!"

Scripture To Declare Over Yourself

Psalms 23:1-6 BSB

"A Psalm of David. The LORD is my shepherd; I shall not want. He makes me lie down in green pastures; He leads me beside quiet waters. He restores my soul; He guides me in the paths of righteousness for the sake of His name. Even though I walk through the valley of the shadow of death, I will fear no evil, for You are with me; Your rod and Your staff, they comfort me. You prepare a table before me in the presence of my enemies. You anoint my head with oil; my cup overflows. Surely goodness and mercy will follow me all the days of my life, and I will dwell in the house of the LORD forever."

Note

I would recommend turning on some intimate Christian worship and just spending some time in the LORD's Presence, and letting Him love you, and you love on Him.

―――――――――――

END OF PRAYER

―――――――――――

CHAPTER 69: PRAYER FOR DISMANTLING TRAUMA

Prayer Asking The Court To Be Seated In Session

"LORD GOD, I now ask according to Daniel 7:10 that the Heavenly Court would be seated to hear my case, in Jesus name. I ask You to call heavenly angels under your authority and jurisdiction to be witnesses, scribes, and officers of the Court to protect me, keep the peace of the Court, and execute Your righteous decrees, commands, and judgments, in Jesus name."

Prayer of Repentance For Judgments Made On Others

"LORD GOD, I repent, renounce, break agreement, and ask for forgiveness for every bitter-root judgment that my ancestors and I made upon others in the area of trauma. I repent, and I ask for You to forgive us for those judgments that were made, and I ask You to lift any negative repercussions that came as a result of those judgments made on others. I repent for all the hypocrisy that has been in my family line and in my personal life, in Jesus name."

Asking For Personal Forgiveness

"LORD GOD, I come before You at this present moment in

time to ask for your forgiveness. I choose to humble myself under your mighty hand, so that You may exalt me in due time. I now renounce and ask for your forgiveness for all willful involvement with occultic activities and traumatic activities. I also repent, renounce, and I now ask for your forgiveness according to 1 John 1:9 and 1 John 2:1-2, in Jesus name.

Prayer Asking For Justice

"I now ask for the court according to Matthew 7:7-12, Luke 18:1-8, Job 13:18, Psalms 103:6, and Psalms 146:7 to render a sentencing of judgment against all demonic spiritual oppressors from the kingdom of darkness and for an order to protection be placed immediately against them on my behalf. I also request accordion to 1 John 1:9 for the court to issue a verdict rendering me forgiven and cleansed based upon the blood of Jesus and His finished work on His Cross at Calvary, I ask now that all my sins, transgressions, and iniquities be blotted out of Heaven and hell's records, in Jesus name."

END OF PRAYER

CHAPTER 70: PRAYER AGAINST TASKMASTER SPIRITS

So you might be wondering, "What are some symptoms of a taskmaster spirit?" or "How can I recognize one?" Those are two valid questions that I will attempt to answer here below. First I want to start off by saying that I believe taskmaster spirits, spirits of fear and spirits of false religion work together, and a couple symptoms of a taskmaster spirit can include the following:

   a. A burden to do things perfectly, obsessively, like washing hands a specific number of times, doing things extremely meticulously, and if it's not done in a precise manner, perfectly, a specific number of times, or in a particular order there might be an attack on your peace and possibly hearing voices urging to: *"Do it right!"*

   b. Feeling an uncomfortable spiritual and unexplainable burden on the top back part on the shoulders or the back.

   c. Forceful voices saying and urging you to do things such as: "Go do ___." "Go do ___." "Don't you dare touch that, that's not for you." "If you touch that, you will sin."

    d. Forceful voices that try to urge you to do things, or especially that try to distract you from going into the Secret Place while you're trying to spend time with the LORD. This might include things such as: urges, voices, compulsive pulls and tugs to check the phone, make calls, check texts, scroll through social media, clean the house, anything to try to distract you from the Presence of the LORD.

    e. Lack of Joy in the LORD.

    f. Fear, or fear of punishment.

    g. Harassing or tormenting voices

If the above is a pretty accurate description of what you have been going through or experiencing, then I would like to invite you to pray the following prayer below. Remember this...*the pressure is NOT ON YOU.* Your Heavenly Father, the Lord Jesus, and the Holy Spirit, are the deliverers. My goal in these prayers is to provide a helpful outline to presenting your case before God the Father, the Judge of all. Sometimes the enemy clings to legal rights in the spirit realm to afflict somebody, while the LORD's Heart desire has been to liberate those under demonic oppression. Especially those whose hearts are geared towards Him:[67]

Psalms 34:15-22 BSB

> "The eyes of the LORD are on the righteous, and His ears are inclined to their cry. But the face of the LORD is against those who do evil, to wipe out all memory of them from the earth. The righteous cry out, and the LORD hears; He delivers them from all their troubles. The LORD is near to the brokenhearted; He saves the contrite in spirit. Many are the afflictions of the righteous, but the LORD delivers him from them all. He protects

all his bones; not one of them will be broken. Evil will slay the wicked, and the haters of the righteous will be condemned. The LORD redeems His servants, and none who take refuge in Him will be condemned."

A judge is meant to administer justice, not pervert it. When we learn how to properly present cases before God the Father, our Righteous Judge, we, like the woman in Luke 18:1-8 who cried out for justice from her "adversary," can and will receive verdicts and legal protection from our King and the Righteous Judge. I pray that this prayer below helps bring deliverance, freedom, breakthrough, and the joy of your salvation for you, my precious reader. If you feel afraid to pray this prayer below, it's probably not you, it's probably the spirit afflicting you.

James 2:19 BSB

"You believe that God is one. Good for you! Even the demons believe that—and shudder." [68]

Strong's Definition

Shudder, fear, tremble.

Asking The Court To Be Seated

"Heavenly Father, I ask the Court of Deliverance be opened and seated according to Daniel 7:10, and I ask You to call heavenly angels to be heavenly witnesses to this court hearing along with scribe angels and officers of the Court to keep the order, pace, and safety of myself and those connected to these prayers, in Jesus name."

Beginning of Petition

"Heavenly Father, I now ask You to summon to the Court of the LORD, and command every taskmaster spirit that has been attached to me whether by inheritance, my ancestors, or my family lineage to face prosecution, in Jesus name."

Appealing For The Courts Forgiveness

"Heavenly Father, on the Scriptural foundation of Isaiah 43:25-36, 1 John 1:9 and the Finished Work of the Cross of the Lord Jesus Christ, I begin by confessing and repenting for all the sins, transgressions, and iniquities of my forefathers and foremothers, including participation, blood guilt, as well as guilt of participating in false religion, disobedience, rebellion, stubbornness, deception and deceiving others, lies of anything whether big or small, resisting the Holy Spirit, resistance to the Purposes and or Plans of the LORD God, any time that I myself and my ancestors abused and caused someone to live in a perpetual state of fear, anxiety, or both, and for anyone in my family lineage who became a willful human vessel and attendant for any taskmaster spirits, I renounce, repent, release, and ask for Your forgiveness Father God, in Jesus name."

Breaking Agreement For Every Covenant Created And Made With Taskmasters

"Heavenly Father, I repent for all agreements, contracts, leases, oaths, vows, and covenants created, signed, entered into verbally and with verbal consent, signature on spiritual and physical contracts, blood covenants, animal blood sacrifices that were associated to empower these agreements and covenants, in Jesus name."

Asking For Justice

"I now ask for a divine judgment and order of protection against the works of the enemy, taskmaster spirits, and for You to give Your angels active charge over me according to Psalm 91 and Matthew 11:28-30, for it is written:

Psalms 91:1-16 BSB

"He who dwells in the shelter of the Most High will abide in the shadow of the Almighty. I will say to the LORD, "You are my refuge and my fortress, my God, in whom I trust." Surely He will deliver you from the snare of the fowler, and from the deadly plague. He will cover you with His feathers; under His wings you will find refuge; His faithfulness is a shield and rampart. You will not fear the terror of the night, nor the arrow that flies by day, nor the pestilence that stalks in the darkness, nor the calamity that destroys at noon. Though a thousand may fall at your side, and ten thousand at your right hand, no harm will come near you. You will only see it with your eyes and witness the punishment of the wicked. Because you have made the LORD your dwelling— my refuge, the Most High— no evil will befall you, no plague will approach your tent. For He will command His angels concerning you to guard you in all your ways. They will lift you up in their hands, so that you will not strike your foot against a stone. You will tread on the lion and cobra; you will trample the young lion and serpent. "Because he loves Me, I will deliver him; because he knows My name, I will protect him. When he calls out to Me, I will answer him; I will be with him in trouble. I will deliver him and honor him. With long life I will satisfy him and show him My salvation."

Matthew 11:28-30 BSB

"Come to Me, all you who are weary and burdened, and I will give you rest. Take My yoke upon you and learn from Me; for I am gentle and humble in heart, and you will find rest for your souls. For My yoke is easy and My burden is light."

"In Jesus Name, amen!"

END OF PRAYER

CHAPTER 70.1: ADDRESSING AND OVERCOMING THE HIDDEN SCARS OF COMBAT

A lot of people cannot fully grasp or comprehend without being deeply disturbed at the absolute atrocities that military service members have seen and experienced firsthand and were eyewitnesses of, absolutely no idea. A majority of these things, if you were to tell a child, it would deeply scar that child. Something that I've learned over time as well as others that have exited their childhood and entered into adulthood is that people are capable of great good as well great evil. God created and designed us to reproduce and give life in a holy way as He intended, because He is the Author and Giver of Life. However, there are some people who have chosen harm and destruction over the life that God gives. We've seen that in terrorist organizations such as ISIS, Hezbollah, and Hamas, just to name a few. The unfortunate reality of the world that we live in is that there have been men and women who carry a deep hatred in their hearts towards other people who don't see or believe the way they do, which has been shown through bloodshed and violence. If you were in the military, and you fought to keep others safe from these people, I want you to know that it's not something you need to feel guilty of. As a man or woman who was in uniform or currently is in uniform that has served to protect people from murderous people, then you may have been God's instrument to keep His people safe. Some people may think that the Bible doesn't have warfare mentioned, but it does, both physical and spiritual warfare is mentioned in the Word. King David was a man after God's own Heart, yet he was both a warrior on the battlefield and a poet in his secret place. For some, it may sound like I'm trying to justify violence, and it's because I am, however, in limited circumstances. As Christians, Jesus did tell us to turn the other cheek, but the same Jesus that said to turn your cheek also said to sell your cloak and buy a sword:

Luke 22:36 BSB

"Now, however," He told them, "the one with a purse should take it, and likewise a bag; and the one without a sword should sell his cloak and buy one. For I tell you that this Scripture must be fulfilled in Me: 'And He was numbered with the transgressors.' For what is written about Me is reaching its fulfillment." So they said, "Look, Lord, here are two swords." "That is enough," He answered."

There are two sides of Jesus that are well known in the Bible. Most know Him as the Lamb of God and this is true, however most overlook that He is not just the Lamb of god but also the Lion of Judah:

Revelation 5:5 BSB

"Then one of the elders said to me, "Do not weep! Behold, the Lion of the tribe of Judah, the Root of David, has triumphed to open the scroll and its seven seals."

Revelation 5:8 BSB

"When He had taken the scroll, the four living creatures and the twenty-four elders fell down before the Lamb.

Each one had a harp, and they were holding golden bowls full of incense, which are the prayers of the saints."

Not to mention the part in the Scripture where we see Nehemiah encouraging the men to take up arms and fight for their homes, their sisters, brothers, and households:

> Nehemiah 4:14 BBE

"And after looking, I got up and said to the great ones and to the chiefs and to the rest of the people, Have no fear of them: keep in mind the Lord who is great and greatly to be feared, and take up arms for your brothers, your sons, and your daughters, your wives and your houses."

> Nehemiah 4:18 BSB

"And each of the builders worked with his sword strapped at his side. But the trumpeter stayed beside me."

> Nehemiah 4:23 BSB

"So neither I nor my brothers nor my servants nor the guards with me changed out of our clothes; each carried his weapon, even to go for water."

> Psalms 144:1 BSB

"Of David. Blessed be the LORD, my Rock, who trains my hands for war, my fingers for battle."

And I want to encourage veterans to read the full book of Nehemiah, as well as to check out the life of King David in the Scriptures and the Psalms that he wrote. David was a *worshiping warrior* that God called, a man after His own Heart:

> Acts 13:22 BSB

"After removing Saul, He raised up David as their king and testified about him: 'I have found David son of Jesse a man after My own heart; he will carry out My will in its entirety.'"

If you are or were a military service veteran, and you were given orders to do something that just didn't sit right with you, or you felt guilty about it, you don't have to carry that weight anymore. You can ask God to forgive you, and the Bible says that He is faithful and just to forgive us of our sins *and to cleanse us of all unrighteousness:*

1 John 1:9 BSB

"If we confess our sins, He is faithful and just to forgive us our sins and to cleanse us from all unrighteousness."

You don't have to carry that junk, the weight of sin, guilt, shame, and condemnation anymore, it's time to let it go and give it to God. Sometimes healing comes through tears, and freedom comes through the surrender to God. I hope the prayers in the following chapters are a source of relief for you. God bless!

CHAPTER 70.2: PRAYER FOR PROSECUTING THE SPIRIT OF SUICIDE

In 2020 alone, there were a little over 6,000 reported veteran related suicides. As I've gone through writing this book, I believe the Holy Spirit has dropped this topic into my heart, and there's a reason I believe He did that. In this chapter, my goal is to provide a prayer for prosecuting the spirit of suicide that those who have come across this book can pray. I want to share with you that life is worth living with Jesus, and the thing that you think that you can't get through right now, you can get through this, and it can turn into a beautiful testimony that you look back on and just have a sense of thankfulness to the Lord for saving you from whatever it is that you're going through right now. There are future things in life that you don't want to miss out on, you have more to offer, your life is worth living and valuable, Jesus does love you, there is redemption in Jesus, you're not too far gone, you can make it through this, you are more than a conqueror through Christ Who strengthens you. I remember that I had a past season where there were spiritual attacks and to put it this way, had I succumbed to it, you wouldn't be reading or listening to this book right now. You are not a lone soldier. Your suffering was not in vain. You didn't go through everything you went through just to have it end like that, keep going!

1 John 1:9 BSB

"If we confess our sins, He is faithful and just to forgive us our sins and to cleanse us from all unrighteousness."

Isaiah 41:21 BSB

"Present your case," says the LORD. "Submit your arguments," says the King of Jacob."

Beginning of Prayer

"Heavenly Father, I come before You today to petition You for breakthrough in the state of my heart, mind, spirit, and soul, in Jesus name. I begin by saying I repent for all my sins, transgressions, and iniquities listed within Your Word, and for those that may not be specifically listed within Your Word. I break agreement and recent for every word that I spoke that was a verbal agreement with death, and or suicide, including any thoughts. I break agreement with those unhealthy emotions, thoughts, and negative words for good, in Jesus Name. I repent and ask for Your forgiveness for any time I carried out an order that violated my conscience or caused unnecessary and or innocent casualties. I ask according to 1 John 1:9 for Your forgiveness and the cleansing power of the Blood of Jesus to be applied to my heavenly records as well as any unrecorded, and recorded debts that of myself and my family, and for the records of the enemy to be wiped clean from my name, as the Blood of Jesus pays for all of my spiritual and physical debts. I invoke the power of the Blood of Jesus to be applied to my testimony and my spirit, mind, soul, heart, and body in Jesus name.

1 Corinthians 6:3 BSB

"Do you not know that we will judge angels? How much more the things of this life!"

"Heavenly Father, Your Word says that believers will judge angels. As a step of faith, I present my case to You as Your Word says in Isaiah, and I now ask for judgment to be pronounced against every unclean spirit that has been associated and or caused suicidal thoughts, tendencies, and emotions, in Jesus name. I further ask for a permanent divine *order to protect* against every unclean spirit that has operated on or in the earth at one point or another, as well as spirits of suicide, and those that were operating in the areas of my military deployment(s). I ask for a divine verdict to be rendered against them unclean spirits, and I ask for a divine verdict from Your Throne declaring healing, breakthrough, restoration, soundness of mind, and peace to be restored to me permanently, in Jesus Name. Lord, I thank You for Your freedom, over, life, joy, and peace being restored in this life You've graciously given to me. I forgive those who've hurt me, and I ask that You would pour the same love that caused Jesus to forgive those who crucified Him into me to forgive my adversaries. I declare that Your Word says:

Hebrews 10:30 BSB

"For we know Him who said, "Vengeance is Mine; I will repay," and again, "The Lord will judge His people."

"I renounce all emotions and desires of vengeance and revenge and I relinquish them to You for good, and help me never to pick them back up again. I ask that You would help me love like You love, I ask You to show me my identity in Christ, and I ask You to use me to be a healing instrument to those You want to touch with my story. May others receive and experience breakthroughs as well Lord, and may You show me that there is hope, and I ask that you would show those who have fought suicidal thoughts that there is hope for them as well. I receive Your freedom, healing, forgiveness, deliverance, love, joy, and peace. I choose to forgive myself for what I've held against myself, because since You can forgive me, who would I be to not forgive myself? I give my heart to You as well as every part of me to You Heavenly Father, in Jesus name, amen!"

ADDITIONAL RESOURCES

If you would like or need additional resources, or someone to talk to, I'll leave a hotline number you can dial. I would also recommend praying to the LORD to send you to a church where you'll be surrounded with a godly community who would be willing to pray for you, cover you, and encourage you. It's okay to seek help, it doesn't make you weak for seeking help, it just makes you human. It's okay to call for spiritual backup.

Suicide Hotline (Available 24/7 USA & Canada): 988

U.S. Based Emergency Number (If You Need Medical Attention): 911

U.K. Suicide Hotline: 0800-689-5652 (Available 24/7)

CHAPTER 70.3: EQUIPPING VETERANS FOR SPIRITUAL VICTORY

Many combat vets have gone through training, bootcamp, and CQB. Something the military teaches veterans is how to be ready for a fight. However, there are many combat veterans who have never been taught how to fight spiritually. If I asked you: "H*ow do you fight spiritually*?" How would you respond? What's the first thing that comes to mind? If prayer came to mind, that's right on, prayer is one of the things that is both a spiritual shield and a spiritual weapon. The Bible teaches us that the weapons of our warfare (our talking about Christians) are not carnal, but mighty in God for the pulling down of strongholds:

2 Corinthians 10:4-6 BSB

"The weapons of our warfare are not the weapons of the world. Instead, they have divine power to demolish strongholds. We tear down arguments and every presumption set up against the knowledge of God; and we take captive every thought to make it obedient to Christ. And we will be ready to punish every act of disobedience, as soon as your obedience is complete."

That's a spiritual truth in the Word of God that once we know helps to equip us to overcome the tactics of the enemy. Here is a list of the spiritual tools that we have in our spiritual arsenal to come out victorious:

1. God's Spirit

Holy Spirit is our Comforter, our Helper, our Advocate, our Intercessor, the One who gives us much needed wisdom and guidance. He is not only those things, but Holy Spirit is also our Comrade, our heavenly Battle Buddy, if you will. Holy Spirit is often the One that people reference as *the Presence of the Lord.* Oftentimes, whenever God's presence is felt in a tangible way, it's the Holy Spirit who they are feeling. There was one expecting in the Word of God where the LORD came down Himself, and it was so awesome that the Israelites couldn't take it, and they just told Moses to go talk to God and then Moses to relay what God said to him back to the people, because they couldn't even handle the LORD's Presence. God can manifest Himself in multiple ways, and we see this in the Exodus, the Pillar of Cloud by day and the Pillar of Fire by night. If you're looking for a friend, you don't need to look around anymore, look up to Him.

2. The Truth of God's Word

God's word, the Holy Bible, comes very close to first when it comes to our Spiritual arsenal, right behind Holy Spirit. The reason I decided to put God's Spirit before God's written word was because God's written word is inspired and breathed by His Spirit.

2 Timothy 3:16-17 BSB

"All Scripture is God-breathed and is useful for instruction, for conviction, for correction, and for training in righteousness, so that the man of God may be complete, fully equipped for every good work."

Without God the Father, God the Son, and God the Holy Spirit, there would be no Word of God. God's Spirit is the weight, authority, and power behind His word because He enforces the Word of God. The angels of Heaven also play a part in the enforcement of God's Word.

3. Praying In The Spirit

Ephesians 6:18 BSB

"Pray in the Spirit at all times, with every kind of prayer and petition. To this end, stay alert with all perseverance in your prayers for all the saints."

Romans 8:26-28 BSB

"In the same way, the Spirit helps us in our weakness. For we do not know how we ought to pray, but the Spirit Himself intercedes for us with groans too deep for words. And He who searches our hearts knows the mind of the Spirit, because the Spirit intercedes for the saints according to the will of God. And we know that God works all things together for the good of those who love Him, who are called according to His purpose."

When we pray in the Spirit, we aren't praying with our minds, we pray from our spirit. It's a supernatural gift that gets stronger over time as we use it. For those who are reading this and have no clue about what I'm talking about, just ask the LORD to baptize you with your heavenly language, and for those who are wanting even more of God, ask Him to baptize you in fire and His Spirit. Just be careful, though, you just might become a spiritual freight train that hell fears and heaven rejoices over.

4. Community Prayer

Leviticus 26:7-8 BSB

"You will pursue your enemies, and they will fall by the sword before you. Five of you will pursue a hundred, and a hundred of you will pursue ten thousand, and your enemies will fall by the sword before you."

I want to propose the question that what if a community praying in harmony and unity with the Spirit of God generates more spiritual momentum compared to a single person praying? Not that a single person's prayers aren't powerful, but what if it can be more powerful when we pray together in unity with God's Spirit and each other? While you're on this journey to recovery, finding a church community that isn't afraid to stand in prayer with you is helpful. In the military, you don't want a soldier getting isolated from his or her platoon in enemy territory and that's common sense, but why then do some people find it acceptable in their spiritual walk? Just something to think about.

5. Prayer

James 5:16 BSB

> "Therefore confess your sins to each other and pray for each other so that you may be healed. The prayer of a righteous man has great power to prevail."

What makes prayer powerful is when we pray the will of God out loud. When humans agree with God it's like an airport landing strip opens up in the spiritual realm for God's Word to land on the earth and manifest in a greater measure, and this comes back down to the dominion that God gave to Adam and Eve which you can review in an earlier chapter of this book if you'd like.

Zechariah 5:1-2 BSB

> "Again I lifted up my eyes and saw before me a flying scroll. "What do you see?" asked the angel. "I see a flying scroll," I replied, "twenty cubits long and ten cubits wide."

God was showing Zechariah a spiritual vision of a scroll flying through the air that contained writing on it. I wanted to show us a Biblical example of what I mentioned earlier about when we agree with God's Word on the earth, it's like a spiritual airport landing strip opens for His word to land to take greater effect on the earth. You might be wondering how to pray effectively against the lies of the enemy. I want to share that you can actually take negative and ungodly thoughts captive, and even ungodly emotions as well. I'll provide a sample prayer for you, just to show how you might pray to overcome negative emotions and negative thoughts, including suicidal thoughts. Quickly, before we get into this prayer, I want to share that it's important and helpful to have Scriptural foundation for whatever you're going to pray because it'll give you confidence and faith that what you're praying is in alignment with God's will.

CHAPTER 70.4: PRAYER TAKING THOUGHTS CAPTIVE

There are fewer things less edifying than someone teaching, and then not giving practical examples for people about how to practically apply what they're teaching. It's like the same as a manager telling a brand-new hire to do something they have never done before, and then not showing them how to do it! Faith is a working substance, not a passive substance. It's called faith in action, not faith in passivity!

Hebrews 11:1 KJV

"Now faith is the substance of things hoped for, the evidence of things not seen."

James 2:20 WEB

"But do you want to know, vain man, that faith apart from works is dead?"

"Heavenly Father, I welcome You into this moment of prayer. In the Name of Jesus, I take every negative thought, word, emotion and ungodly spirit that has caused suicidal thoughts and tendencies captive to the obedience of Christ because God is the Author and Giver of life:

Job 33:4 BSB

"The Spirit of God has made me, and the breath of the Almighty gives me life."

"According to 2 Corinthians 10:4-5 I take every thought, word, emotion, and unclean spirit captive to the obedience of Christ that has influenced negative emotions, thoughts, and suicidal tendencies or thoughts, in Jesus Name. I ask, Heavenly Father, that You would assign heavenly angelic officers to bind and take away permanently every unclean spirit that caused affection to me in any way, shape, and form. I thank You for freedom, in Jesus Name, amen!"

END OF PRAYER

Spiritual Armor

On top of prayer, the Bible mentions spiritual armor. Just like in the military, there is protective gear that soldiers wear to protect them in combat. The Bible mentions spiritual armor in Ephesians 6:10-18, let's break down the pieces of armor:

1. <u>Belt of Truth</u>

2. <u>Breastplate of Righteousness</u>

3. <u>Sandals of The Gospel of Peace</u>

4. <u>Shield of Faith</u>

5. <u>Helmet of Salvation</u>

Ephesians 6:10-18 BSB

"Finally, be strong in the Lord and in His mighty power. Put on the full armor of God, so that you can make your stand against the devil's schemes. For our struggle is not against flesh and blood, but against the rulers, against the authorities, against the powers of this world's darkness, and against the spiritual forces of evil in the heavenly realms. Therefore take up the full armor of God, so that when the day of evil comes, you will be able to stand your ground, and having done everything, to stand. Stand firm then, with the belt of truth buckled around your waist, with the breastplate of righteousness arrayed, and with your feet fitted with the readiness of the gospel of peace. In addition to all this, take up the shield of faith, with which you can extinguish all the flaming arrows of the evil one. And take the helmet of salvation and the sword of the Spirit, which is the word of God. Pray in the Spirit at all times, with every kind of prayer and petition. To this end, stay alert with all perseverance in your prayers for all the saints."

When we choose to embrace the truth, freedom ensues. And I'll say it again, if you haven't done so already, **it's time to** *forgive yourself, and* **it's okay to forgive yourself.** *If God can forgive you, who are you not to forgive yourself?*

John 8:32 BSB

"Then you will know the truth, and the truth will set you free."

CHAPTER 70.5: DEAR OFFICER, IT'S NOT YOUR FAULT

Romans 13:1-5 BSB

"Everyone must submit himself to the governing authorities, for there is no authority except that which is from God. The authorities that exist have been appointed by God. Consequently, whoever resists authority is opposing what God has set in place, and those who do so will bring judgment on themselves. For rulers are not a terror to good conduct, but to bad. Do you want to be unafraid of the one in authority? Then do what is right, and you will have his approval. For he is God's servant for your good. But if you do wrong, be afraid, for he does not carry the sword in vain. He is God's servant, an agent of retribution to the wrongdoer. Therefore it is necessary to submit to authority, not only to avoid punishment, but also as a matter of conscience."

Sometimes a police officer may have had to make a tough decision that they didn't want to make because of the cards dealt to them at a particular call or interaction that they find themselves involved in, whether they got called to the scene, or just happened to be in the general vicinity. Whether that be pulling the trigger on someone who was armed and shooting at civilians, the officer, or threatening to shoot others of the officer(s). It's not your fault, officer. I now speak to all guilt, shame, condemnation, and survivors guilt as well as every unclean spirit attached to those things to leave and go to the Abyss never to return again, in Jesus name, amen. It's not your fault officer, sometimes there were people that made unwise decisions and faced the consequences of their actions. Sometimes you have to learn to forgive yourself.

CHAPTER 71: PRAYER FOR MENTAL HEALTH

Before we go into this prayer, if you have been struggling with torment, a valid question to ask yourself is, "Am I holding unforgiveness against someone?" Because of the parable that Jesus spoke of in Matthew 18. If the answer is yes, then I would like to just encourage you to release and forgive the person or multiple people who wronged you. Remember when you forgive you are not saying what this person or people did was right, you are, however, saying that you desire your personal freedom more than holding onto a grudge or unforgiveness.

Beginning of Prayer

"Heavenly Father, Lord Jesus, Holy Spirit, as I am praying and giving my witness before You, I confess and ask for Your forgiveness for everything that my ancestors did that displeased, grieved, hurt, angered and or challenged You. I confess and repent for every sin and transgression of Your Word, the Holy Bible, as well as any generational sin cycles that have empowered the following:

"Abulia, acute stress disorders, adverse effects of medications, age related cognitive decline, Alzheimer's, amnesia, anxiety, autism spectrum disorders, attention deficiency, ADD, ADHD, autophagia, cannibalism, avoidant personality, bereavement, binge-eating, bipolar, emotional instability, manic depression, excessive bereavement, anorexia, fear of weight gain, fear, tormenting fear, phobias of spiders, snakes, phobias of the dark, nocturnal phobias, extreme antisocial behaviors, post-traumatic stress, seizures, epilepsy, schizophrenia, and all other diagnosis that would be negatively impact or affect the definition of a sound mind. And every unclean spirit attached to these listed things, in Jesus name.

"Heavenly Father, I break agreement with every unclean spirit that has been included with these listed diagnoses, and I come out of agreement with every doctor's diagnosis of the list above and every personal diagnosis I received. I declare that sickness, disease, cancer, terminal illness, mental anguish, mental torment *is not my portion. I do not accept them*, I *decree* and *declare* over myself:

Isaiah 53:5 BSB

"But He was pierced for our transgressions, He was crushed for our iniquities; the punishment that brought us peace was upon Him, and by His stripes we are healed."

2 Timothy 1:7 LSV

"for God did not give us a spirit of fear, but of power, and of love, and of a sound mind;"

"Heavenly Father, Your Word says:

Psalms 103:6 BSB

"The LORD executes righteousness and justice for all the oppressed."

"Therefore, I ask You for every legal right the devil has had to afflict, torment, cause spiritual, mental, emotional, soul and heart anguish, hope deferred, I ask that the Blood of Jesus would pay in full and revoke those legalities in the spirit realm, including those connected to and attached to my DNA and Bloodline. I forgive those who have wronged me and hurt me in time past and time present, I release them and I declare that they are released and loosed from the spiritual and physical debt that they have owed towards me. I renounce and repent for the sins, transgressions, and iniquities of my ancestors and I appeal to the Mercy of the LORD God for a Judgment against these unclean spirits, and I ask for a sound mind from here on out according to 2 Timothy 1:7, in Jesus name."

END OF PRAYER

CHAPTER 71.1: UPROOTING PTSD

2 Timothy 1:7 BSB

"For God has not given us a spirit of fear, but of power, love, and self-control."

War and other traumatic experiences are not pretty, not even a little. Regardless if the fight is being waged on unrighteousness and evil, it's still graphic for troops on all sides. Out of the United States military that served in 2021 approximately ten out of every one-hundred men, and about nineteen out of every hundred women were diagnosed with PTSD, which is about ten percent of men and about nineteen percent of women who served overall. To put that into perspective, that amounts to hundreds of thousands of men and women who were diagnosed with PTSD in 2021 alone. Towards the finishing touches of this book I felt impressed on my heart to add this chapter for combat veterans, and PTSD can expand beyond military service such as police officers, or a traumatic event that occurred in someone's life. Whatever the case, maybe I want to share with you that you are not a victim, you have the victory because Jesus' healing goes beyond what you've been through. You may or may not have physical scars, but this prayer is for those with emotional scars that can be healed permanently and for good through the power of God. Jesus knows a thing or two about scars and suffering, He still carries His:

John 20:25-31 BSB

"So the other disciples told him, "We have seen the Lord!" But he replied, "Unless I see the nail marks in His hands, and put my finger where the nails have been, and put my hand into His side, I will never believe." Eight days later, His disciples were once again inside with the doors locked, and Thomas was with them. Jesus came and stood among them and said, "Peace be with you." Then Jesus said to Thomas, "Put your finger here and look at My hands. Reach out your hand and put it into My side. Stop doubting and believe." Thomas replied, "My Lord and my God!" Jesus said to him, "Because you have seen Me, you have believed; blessed are those who have not seen and yet have believed." Jesus performed many other signs in the presence of His disciples, which are not written in this book. But these are written so that you may believe that Jesus is the Christ, the Son of God, and that by believing you may have life in His name."

Matthew 19:26 BSB

"Jesus looked at them and said, "With man this is impossible, but with God all things are possible."

Mark 9:23 BSB

"If You can?" echoed Jesus. "All things are possible to him who believes!"

Regardless of the cause of those symptoms you may have experienced, this prayer is for you. The scars of your past can become a testimony of God's goodness if you give them to Him. There is forgiveness and redemption found in Jesus, you are accepted, love, and valuable to the Lord, and you have a purpose in life. Your life is worth living, and anything or anyone else that says otherwise is lying. I pray that this prayer brings freedom to the lives of those who pray it, in Jesus name, amen.

Beginning of Prayer

"Heavenly Father, I come before You to ask for freedom from any and all PTSD symptoms. I repent and ask for Your forgiveness for anything and everything, including sins, transgressions, and iniquities that I have participated in that grieved Your Heart while in active duty and out of active duty. Father, I ask today that the Blood of Jesus would be applied to all of my actions, words, my mind, my thoughts, heart, spirit, body, and soul, in Jesus name.

Psalms 103:6 BSB

"The LORD executes righteousness and justice for all the oppressed."

"Heavenly Father, I ask according to Psalm 103:6 that You would execute judgment against every spirit that has capitalized, manipulated, caused and or is associated with PTSD and its subsequent symptoms including traumatic brain injuries, memory, loss, sensitivity to light and sound, physical instability, mood swings, anxiety, depression, and things of the like. I renounce night terrors, flashbacks, insomnia, fear, a fear to sleep and close my eyes, avoidance symptoms, irritability, trouble sleeping, guilt, shame, anger, as well as fear, in Jesus name. I repent for any guilt of bloodshed from combat or my personal life. I renounce all of these things, and I ask You to forgive me, and to be my personal Lord and Savior Jesus. I ask You to heal my body, soul, mind, and spirit from all trauma, PTSD, PTSD symptoms, and I ask You to restore peace into my life and heart through Your healing power. I ask that You would renew my mind through Your power, and help give me the grace to do my part in renewing my mind by reading Your Word, the Holy Bible, even if You have to supernaturally rewire my brain to completely heal it Lord I trust You to do that because You wouldn't hurt me, but Your Heart is to help me.

Luke 9:56 LSV

"for the Son of Man did not come to destroy men's lives, but to save"; and they went on to another village."

John 6:39 LSV

"And this is the will of the Father who sent Me, that all that He has given to Me, I may lose none of it, but may raise it up in the last day;"

"Help me to understand Your Word with both my heart and my mind, and help me understand You and Your Heart in the process. Thank You, Jesus, for healing me, and I ask that You would comfort me and be the Rock that I stand on from here on out, in Jesus name, amen."

END OF PRAYER

My Prayer For You

"Lord, I ask You to heal every single person reading this who has experienced PTSD symptoms. I agree for their deliverance Heavenly Father, and I ask that they live in love, joy, peace, patience, kindness, goodness, faithfulness, gentleness, righteousness, and bravery for the rest of their days. I also ask that any relationship strains that were caused by PTSD symptoms would be healed, and I ask that every person reading this, including those who may not read this but are serving or have served in the military and or as a police officer that You would heal every relationship that You want to see healing take place in. Lord, I ask for every service ember who has contemplated suicide that You would heal them swiftly. I ask that You would deliver them from any spirits that have capitalized on their time in service to afflict or torment them. I decree and declare deliverance over them, in Jesus name. I speak life over them and I bless them, in Jesus name, amen."

Speaking Life Over Yourself

I want to encourage you to be more mindful over what you are speaking about yourself and over yourself, including others as well. There is power in our words, and every word spoken is like a seed sown in the spirit, if you want a good harvest, you have to have good seed, and in this case it's your words, thoughts, and actions. I also want to encourage you to take communion at home when you can, and surround yourself with other Godly believers who are walking with the Lord. Surround yourself with Christians who are Bible believing believers and don't mind praying for you. Having a healthy, and godly community around you can help to foster growth and healing. Simultaneously, it would be a good idea to avoid hanging out with old military buddies who are a negative influence in your life that would try to encourage you to drink or do drugs to escape reality for a bit. I mean that in a good way, with no disrespect intended. Sometimes to heal you have to separate yourself from negative environments, this doesn't mean you have to cut off contact with them, but if their negative influence overrides your positive influence on them and sucks you down into a hole of depression and anxiety, it's time to plug in to a healthy community so you can heal, and you can even invite them to church. Once you've experienced more healing you can be a godly influence in their lives and who knows, you might just see that one guy or girl that was very against God who you were doing tours with come to know Jesus as his or her personal Lord and Savior as well, but it starts with you. God bless you and Godspeed!

CHAPTER 72: TEACHING AND PRAYER FOR PROSECUTING DEMONIC VOICES IN THE COURTS OF HEAVEN

Okay, so I want to lay a foundation, and I'm going to add a practical guided prayer for this very subject on prosecuting demonic voices before the LORD, the Righteous Judge. Prepare to confess and repent for any legal rights the enemy has had to torment you with voices on your own behalf and your ancestors' behalf. Sometimes in the family lineage, which you might see as "ancestors, ancestral bloodline, or family line," listed in this prayer, there were legal doorways that could have possibly been opened by previous generations from whom you physically descended. Let's say hypothetically that you had an ancestor or ancestors who lived in a state of poverty and wanted to get rich. This ancestor started exploring ways to get rich quickly, but in their search, they didn't find many ways of doing so. A bit of time went by, and they came across some information on how to "get rich quick," which included a spiritual aspect. They got curious about the things of the enemy and read a book about how to summon spirits, coming into this knowledge and abusing it for personal gain. They ended up summoning a false "spirit guide" that promised help to get rich if they let this spirit use their physical human body to carry out "missions" while controlling their physical body. This ancestor consented, and this spirit guide, a demon or a fallen angel, laid out specific details—basically a contract—and even asked this ancestor to give legal verbal claim of future descendants to this spirit. This spirit, or multiple spirits, might have gone as far as to request this person to write out a consent form, contract, or covenant, and asked that the person write down a spiritual transfer contract for current or future descendants, along with a written or verbal signature, and a drop of blood on the contract or covenant. These ancestors consented because they wanted to benefit from personal gain from these spirits. Now this spirit began speaking to this person, giving them knowledge and insight they wouldn't know under normal circumstances, and became a false "holy spirit," an unclean spirit that mimics the voice of the Holy Spirit. This ancestor became familiar with this spirit, intimately acquainted with it, and it became a "friend" and a familiar spirit. What they did was give the enemy legal claim not only to the ancestor who did it themselves but, if it is not repented of and dealt with, for future generations to come. Take a look at what the Lord Jesus said to His disciples before He was about to be examined by the enemy:

John 14:30 BSB

"I will not speak with you much longer, for the prince of this world is coming, and he has no claim on Me."

The Greek Words Used There For "No

Claim" Are The Following

Greek: οὐδείς[69]

Transliteration: *oudeis*

Greek: ἔχω[70]

Transliteration: *echō*

The Lord Jesus was basically saying, "the ruler of this world is coming" [but he has no hold on me]. A bold statement, but the Lord Jesus never sinned on this Earth. He had nothing in common with the enemy, the enemy had sinned and rebelled against the LORD and the Scriptures testify that he was cast out of heaven. The enemy was an outcast because of his pride, and what went up through pride came down through the LORD's judgment. The Scriptures say about Satan that, "...iniquity was found in you." Had Jesus sinned, he would have had something in common with the enemy, but He didn't and secured the Victory. Thank you, Lord Jesus, may Your Name be lifted and glorified for all generations to come, amen. So, this person made a covenant with an unclean spirit and now it has legal rights to operate within a family line because of a legal claim that was given to it through consent. So the first part of this prayer will be repentance based, so be prepared to forgive. Also be ready to confess, repent, and break agreement with unclean spirits and humble yourself to truly receive breakthrough and freedom once and for all. If you've done so, also ask for the LORD's forgiveness for any blame that was put on Him for the hurt the enemy was responsible for, in Jesus name.

Beginning of Prayer

Job 13:18 BSB

"Behold, now that I have prepared my case,
I know that I will be vindicated."

Beginning of Prayer

"Heavenly Father, I now ask the court to be seated according to Daniel 7:10, in Jesus name. LORD, I ask you to take your rightful seat along with heavenly witnesses of your choosing to witness this prosecution, in Jesus name."

Isaiah 43:25-26 BSB

"I, yes I, am He who blots out your transgressions for My own sake and remembers your sins no more. Remind Me, let us argue the matter together. State your case, so that you may be vindicated."

"LORD God, I now start by confessing and asking for forgiveness for all my personal sins, transgressions, and iniquities that I have personally been guilty of committing. I agree with any legitimate and true accusations of the enemy against me and my bloodline concerning all sinful behavior that I and my forefathers and foremothers were guilty of committing. I now appeal to the Blood of the Lord Jesus according to 1 John 1:9, to cleanse my spirit, soul, and body of any and all defilement of sinful behavior including, (list specific things if you are able), and to atone for all my wrong behavior, negative words and sinful actions and iniquities, in Jesus name."

"I confess, repent, and break agreement with all the sins, transgressions, and iniquities of my ancestors, especially idolatry, rebellion, and disobedience towards you LORD God and your Word The Holy Bible. I now repent for all unholy agreements, contracts, leases, and covenants that were entered into and or created by my ancestors with unclean spirits in exchange for personal gain. Especially any contracts and covenants and blood covenants that stated anything along the lines of 'dedication of future descendants,' I break agreement with all unholy and satanic covenants made with false "spirit guides" and false "holy spirits," in Jesus' Mighty Name."

"I now make a formal appeal before the Courts of Heaven to forgive and dismiss all the legitimate accusations of the enemy against me, my personal sins, transgressions, and iniquities and those of my forefathers and foremothers all the way back to Adam and Eve, according to Isaiah 43:25-26, 1 John 1:9, and James 2:13. I now acknowledge before You, Lord God, that your Word clearly states in James 2:13 that: "For judgment without mercy will be shown to anyone who has not been merciful." But Your Word also says in that very same verse that: "Mercy triumphs over judgment." So, because of this, I repent for any times I failed to show mercy. I also repent for any times I asked for judgment to come on another person because of a sinful action, wrong, and or injustice done to me and or against me. And I forgive those who have wronged me and I ask for You to have mercy towards me and them alike, and I ask for your forgiveness for them as well in Jesus name."

PRAYER PAUSE

There may be some who are reading that need to verbally release, forgive, and repent for asking judgment to come upon a spouse who was unfaithful in marriage if they cheated. Please remember this my dear reader, we forgive for our own sake, you aren't saying what they did was right, but by forgiving you are making a statement that you are *not going to let that keep you bound.* Moving on from someone who wronged you is very liberating for the one who chooses to forgive their oppressor.

Matthew 6:14-15 BSB

"For if you forgive men their trespasses, your Heavenly Father will also forgive you. But if you do not forgive men their trespasses, neither will your Father forgive yours."

Forgiveness grants us personal freedom, trust me you don't want to forgive. The Lord Jesus said you don't get forgiveness until you are willing to forgive and release others from a debt they've owed you, even if you feel like the debt they owe you is a simple apology.

PRAYER CONTINUED

"I now appeal to the court for a divine verdict of mercy to be rendered on the basis of James 2:13 on my behalf, as well as an order of protection against everything unclean and unholy, in Jesus name. I also now repent for any and all times I willingly or unknowingly yielded myself to spirit guides and false holy spirits. I break agreement and permanently come out of agreement with all unholy covenants and claims of ownership connected to me and my bloodline and family line. I declare that I want freedom and the false unholy voices that I'm hearing in my head that try to torment, afflict, and deceive me. I declare I want absolutely *nothing to do with them*. I accept the leading of the Lord, and I repent for every time that I myself partnered with unclean voices, spiritual false shepherds, and the lies they spewed. I ask for forgiveness for any time I was guilty of agreeing and believing those lies, and I break agreement and detach myself with all associated lies I've believed and myself have told in my life up until now. I repent for every time that I and my ancestors participated in manipulation, witchcraft, mind games, ungodly uses of the soul, including lucid dreaming, astral projection, ungodly uses of the mind, will, emotions, perversion of mind, unholy thought patterns, demonic strongholds, mental witchcraft, rebellion, stubbornness, and idolatry."

"Righteous Judge, I now formally appeal and move upon your

Court to silence all the false deceiving spiritual voices that have been speaking to me and that have been speaking in my head, and wreaking havoc on my mind, in Jesus name according to these four Scriptures:

Psalms 63:11 BSB

"But the king will rejoice in God; all who swear by Him will exult, for the mouths of liars will be shut."

John 10:4-5 BSB

"When he has brought out all his own, he goes on ahead of them, and his sheep follow him because they know his voice. But they will never follow a stranger; in fact, they will flee from him because they do not recognize his voice."

2 Timothy 1:7 LSV

"for God did not give us a spirit of fear, but of power, and of love, and of a sound mind;"

Psalm 103:6 KJV

"The LORD executeth righteousness and judgment for all that are oppressed."

"Heavenly Father, I now petition you to issue a divine and righteous verdict, as well as a protective order that states that under Divine punishment by your heavenly hosts that these unclean spirits, false "spirit guides," and false "holy spirits," are forbidden by Your court's authority to speak to me. Heavenly Father, I surrender my soul, mind, will, heart, emotions, spirit, and my body to being an instrument of righteousness according to Romans 6 for your Holy Spirit. Lord Jesus, I am Yours."

Requesting A Verdict of Release And Breakthrough

"Heavenly Father, I now appeal for a divine verdict of release, deliverance, breakthrough, and permanent freedom from tormenting voices, demonic voices, and anything of the like from speaking and or influencing my thought life, my mind, will, emotions, craving and desires, in Jesus name."

"Heavenly Father, I now appeal to You to help me with renewing and sanctifying and making holy the desires of my heart, and may they be in alignment with your heart in Jesus name."

Romans 6:7-9 BSB

"For anyone who has died has been freed from sin. Now if we died with Christ, we believe that we will also live with Him. For we know that since Christ was raised from the dead, He cannot die again; death no longer has dominion over Him."

PRAYER PAUSED

In the Old Testament, the only true way a marriage covenant was legally broken in God's eyes was the death of either the initiator or the recipient of the Covenant Promise. The Scriptures bear witness to us, that we have been buried with Christ in baptism, and we have been raised up with Him into new life. And that we are seated in heavenly places with Him. He tasted death for all of us, and took our place in death, and through His death the covenants that were made were rendered void because the length of covenants is life long. One example we see of this is in the Old Testament Law concerning a wife:

1 Corinthians 7:39 KJV

"The wife is bound by the law as long as her husband liveth; but if her husband be dead, she is at liberty to be married to whom she will; only in the LORD."

PRAYER CONTINUED

Asking Lord Jesus' Sacrifice To Be Established

"Heavenly Father, I now proclaim and ask You to establish the full legal implications of the death, burial, and resurrection of the Lord Jesus Christ of Nazareth over the life you've given to me. I accept the full endowment that the Lord Jesus paid for me to receive, carry, and steward, and I receive and accept the forgiveness of my sins, and I choose to forgive myself as You have decided to forgive me, and I ask that these ungodly entities would never afflict, harass, torment, and mess with me ever again, teach me how to live a lifestyle of humility and being quick to repent and walk in Pure Love in Jesus name."

"Heavenly Father, I repent and break agreement with any and all legal footing that the enemy has had or currently does have over me and I now petition these footholds to be revoked and for the Blood of Jesus to be applied over me and for it to be written in the records of Heaven that the Lord Jesus' Sacrifice has *Paid In Full* and that all my records of spiritual debt and physical debt owed along with all of my shortcomings, sins, transgressions, iniquities, idolatry, generational iniquities along with those of my ancestors that affected me or afflicted me in any way shape or form known or unknown to me. I petition You to dismantle the weapons of the enemy against me and to bind and cast into the abyss permanently to await Judgment Day the demons and satanic forces that have tormented me, my mind, my will, my emotions, my spirit man, and every other part of me and I now request the total deliverance and freedom from this oppression and I ask for a Divine Protective Order against the kingdom of darkness and all of its spiritual and physical accomplices in accordance to Your will, Heavenly Father, and I ask this in Jesus name."

"I further request that everything stolen from me, including sleep, peace, finances, soundness of mind, self-control be restored to me completely, and I receive Your verdict of release, freedom, deliverance, and breakthrough. I now, like King David of old, say:

> Psalms 17:2 WEB
>
> "Let my sentence come out of your presence. Let your eyes look on equity."

Prayer Renouncing Ungodly Covenants

> Job 5:23 BSB
>
> "For you will have a covenant with the stones of the field, and the wild animals will be at peace with you."

"Heavenly Father, I renounce every covenant made with creation, the sun, moon, stars, angelic beings, angelic hosts, fallen angels, demons, principalities, powers, rulers, and all the forces of wickedness in the heavenly places and in the underworld below, especially those covenants, contracts, agreements, dedications, oaths made through Native American tribes of my ancestors that directly or indirectly impacted me, Heavenly Father I repent of and renounce any and all personal gain that cam from these legally binding agreements and I permanently renounce the devil, the sun idols, moon idols, the queen of heaven, the Old Testament idols mentioned in the Hebrew Old Testament Bible, the Greek, and Roman idols of the New Testament churches day and I ask that these covenants would be annulled and rendered void by Your Court and I pledge my sole allegiance to You Heavenly Father, Lord Jesus Christ of Nazareth, and the Holy Spirit of the LORD God. Thank you LORD for hearing me and I now rest my case and appeal to the mercy of You LORD God and Your Mercy, in Jesus Name, amen!"

END OF PRAYER

CHAPTER 73: PRAYER TO BREAK DOWN STRONGHOLDS AND MENTAL PRISONS

Prisons are not only physical, but they can be mental as well. And if you've found yourself in that situation, then you can honestly ask yourself which is worse, someone being stuck in a cell or being stuck in their own head?

Isaiah 61:1-5 BSB

"The Spirit of the Lord GOD is on Me, because the LORD has anointed Me to preach good news to the poor. He has sent Me to bind up the brokenhearted, to proclaim liberty to the captives and freedom to the prisoners, to proclaim the year of the LORD's favor and the day of our God's vengeance, to comfort all who mourn, to console the mourners in Zion—to give them a crown of beauty for ashes, the oil of joy for mourning, and a garment of praise for a spirit of despair. So they will be called oaks of righteousness, the planting of the LORD, that He may be glorified. They will rebuild the ancient ruins; they will restore the places long devastated; they will renew the ruined cities, the desolations of many generations. Strangers will stand and feed your flocks, and foreigners will be your plowmen and vinedressers."

Jesus came to set the prisoners free. There is hope. And if you're one who has ever felt like you were a prisoner stuck in your own mind, through Jesus every believer walking in faith can have a sound mind. This is exactly as the Scriptures state that God has not given us a spirit of fear but rather that of power, love, and soundness of mind in 2 Timothy 2 Timothy. 1:7. God desires His people's minds to be clear and sound, not foggy. And there may be some people that think that's easier said than done. What you may not know is that oftentimes the things that God commissions others to do, are the very things that God has taught them to overcome themselves. How do you think this book came about? I promise there is freedom in Jesus. So if you can relate to what I just said, then this prayer is specifically made for you.

Beginning of Prayer

"LORD GOD, I repent, renounce, break agreement, and ask for forgiveness for every bitter-root judgment that my ancestors and I made upon others in the area of mental health. I repent, and I ask for You to forgive us for those judgments that were made, and I ask You to lift any negative repercussions that came as a result of those judgments made on others. I repent for all the hypocrisy that has been in my family line and in my personal life, in Jesus name. Heavenly Father, I come before you today to ask for freedom in my mind. Your word declares in 2 Timothy 1:7:

2 Timothy 1:7 BSB

"For God has not given us a spirit of fear, but of power, love, and self-control."

"I ask for complete freedom from every spirit that has negatively affected my mental health and tried to construct a mental prison. I forgive everybody who has hurt me and I come to You asking for forgiveness for every I hurt You and others, Heavenly Father. I take a stand today and say enough is enough, I want soundness of mind again Lord both now and forever. I renounce all oaths, covenants, vows, and agreements made with the enemy by my ancestors and even those I made with or without realizing it by my words, actions and or thoughts. I renounce every unholy altar as well, and I request my name and my family's name be forever removed from unholy altars and for my record and my family's record be removed from the enemy's records permanently in Jesus name. I ask according to Psalm 103:6 that you would execute judgment against the enemy for oppressing my mind in the past and I ask for a permanent order of protection to be enforced against the kingdom of darkness, so they can never touch me or my family again. Today I chose life, I chose love, righteousness, soundness of mind and I choose to be Yours Jesus.

Romans 5:5 BSB

"And hope does not disappoint us, because God has poured out His love into our hearts through the Holy Spirit, whom He has given us."

2 Corinthians 3:17 BSB

"Now the Lord is the Spirit, and where the Spirit of the Lord is, there is freedom."

Set me free, Lord, You are my only hope. I receive Your freedom, Lord, and I cry out in my heart to You in hope, and hope does not disappoint. I receive Your freedom and liberty, in Jesus name, amen!"

END OF PRAYER AND BEGINNING OF NOTE

After you've gone through that prayer, there is a part that you can play in this process, and it's renewing your mind with the Word of God. As you read the Bible, you may come across Scriptural truths that conflict the things you've heard all of your life or believed. I want to encourage you to start reading Matthew and go through all the way to Revelation. Do this two or three times and go back to Genesis and read through all the way to Revelation. Your theology will adapt along the way as you read the whole Bible, not just segments. So, with that being said, reading God's Word will help you not only renew your mind but also strengthen your faith.

Romans 10:17 KJV

"So then faith cometh by hearing, and hearing by the word of God."

Ephesians 4:21-24 WEB

"if indeed you heard him, and were taught in him, even as truth is in Jesus: that you put away, as concerning your former way of life, the old man, that grows corrupt after the lusts of deceit; and that you be renewed in the spirit of your mind, and put on the new man, who in the likeness of God has been created in righteousness and holiness of truth."

END OF PRAYER

CHAPTER 74: PRAYER DEALING WITH OBSTACLES IN MINISTRY

1 Thessalonians 2:18 KJV

"Wherefore we would have come unto you, even I Paul, once and again; but Satan hindered us."

If you've been in ministry for however many amount of years, you may have experienced frustration because you've known and felt that the ministry that you've been entrusted with or that God has called you to has so much more potential than what it's currently operating in. Almost like there's a greater *metron* that you're supposed to be operating in.

2 Corinthians 10:13-15 BSB

"We, however, will not boast beyond our limits, but only within the field of influence that God has assigned to us— a field that reaches even to you. We are not overstepping our bounds, as if we had not come to you. Indeed, we were the first to reach you with the gospel of Christ. Neither do we boast beyond our limits in the labors of others. But we hope that as your faith increases, our area of influence among you will greatly increase as well,"

The word here influence is the Greek word *metron* and it literally means *measure*. Some translations might say *sphere of influence*. But it was basically their allotted circle that the Lord grants them authority over. It's like a state governor, the entire state is under their authority however, not other states. But the President has authority over all fifty states, while they also simultaneously maintain their autonomy. They have differing *metrons.* In this chapter I want to give you a prayer that helps address any hindrances and or spiritual roadblocks to help get them out of the way, so that you can do ministry His Way because Jesus is The Way! I also want to let you know that this prayer is probably going to be more effective if you and Holy Spirit take some time to pray about specific instances, and to repent through these things with Him. These prayers are meant to be a helpful guide, however, could you imagine how much typing would be involved if I listed every single thing known to man for every person? It would be quite lengthy. Nonetheless, I have provided a guide here, but let Holy Spirit be your ultimate guide! He is the Helper!

Beginning of Prayer

"Heavenly Father, I come before You today to lay the ministry that You've entrusted and given to me on Your Altar, like Abraham placed His promised Isaac on the altar. I likewise place the ministry You've given or promised me on Your Altar of Sacrifice.

"I repent for every time that anyone in our ministry staff, our church(s), connected churches, other members of different churches that are associated with this church body, their spouses including mine, and myself for every action committed or things not done that would have enabled any spiritual blockades or hindrances.

"I ask now for You to commission angels to go and break down any demonically inspired barriers, hindrances, and spiritual blockades. I ask that You would work in the foreground and background to accomplish Your purposes, not mine, Lord, but Yours in ministry. Help my heart be right and in alignment with You at all times, and I ask for you to protect me, and that which You have entrusted me and my family with, in Jesus name, I receive, amen!"

END OF PRAYER

CHAPTER 75: PRAYER OF REPENTANCE FOR YOUR BUSINESS

I want to be *very clear* on something here. You *cannot* and *absolutely should not* try to use God to get things for personal gain or benefit—that's called manipulation. If you are a Christian business owner, and you are actively seeking to honor the LORD with the finances. And you are sowing into God's Kingdom work and truly have a heart desire to be blessed in order to be a blessing. Then I would encourage you to pray this prayer. If you are a Christian business owner that has had attacks, seemingly unexplainable business losses and unexplainable things happen with money, you know it's not physical. I hope this prayer helps provide a prayer template to alleviate and bring a breakthrough. I would strongly suggest checking your motives before praying this prayer, though. **Right motives are everything**!

Prayer Asking The Court To Be Seated In Session

"LORD GOD, I now ask according to Daniel 7:10 that the Heavenly Court would be seated to hear my case, in Jesus name. I ask You to call heavenly angels under your authority and jurisdiction to be witnesses, scribes, and officers of the Court to protect me, keep the peace of the Court, and execute

Your righteous decrees and commands, in Jesus name."

Prayer of Repentance For Judgments Made On Others

"LORD GOD, I repent, renounce, break agreement, and ask for forgiveness for all bitter-root judgments that I and my ancestors made upon others in the area of business and finances. I repent, and I ask for You to forgive us for those judgments that were made, and I ask You to lift any negative repercussions that came as a result of those judgments made on others. I repent for all the hypocrisy that has been in my family line and in my personal life, in Jesus name."

Scriptures For Asking For Personal Forgiveness

Proverbs 11:1 AMP

"A false balance and dishonest business
practices are extremely offensive to the LORD,
But an accurate scale is His delight."

"Heavenly Father, I begin by confessing and asking for forgiveness for every time that I used a false balance, dishonest business practices, offended You, neglected tithes and offerings, used unethical, dishonest, manipulative business practices, ungodly loan sharking, unjustly taxing others, evasion of taxes, dishonest tax filing, hidden income, unreported income, theft of physical, mental, emotional, and intellectual property, as well as unjust treatment of employees, withholding wages earned by employees and I repent for any corrupt business practices, as James states:

James 5:4 BSB

"Look, the wages you withheld from the workmen who
mowed your fields are crying out against you. The cries of
the harvesters have reached the ears of the Lord of Hosts." [71]

Repentance And Asking For Personal Forgiveness

"LORD forgive me I ask You, You are not a man that you should lie, I repent for doing any unethical and unjust business practices and I ask for Your help to stop doing those things, and to start doing the right thing through the grace and enablement of Your Holy Spirit, help keep my motives pure and upright before You, in Jesus name."

Prayer of Consecration For Business

"LORD GOD, I now choose to consecrate the business that I've been entrusted with. I now declare You to be the CEO and Head of the business, may Your blessings rest upon this business and may You be the One building it. May this business be sources with blessings from above, and a source of blessings, a source of financing for the Kingdom of God, in Jesus name."

Proverbs 13:22 KJV

"A good man leaveth an inheritance to his children's children: And the wealth of the sinner is laid up for the just."

Prayer Asking For Justice

"I now ask for the court according to Matthew 7:7-12, Luke 18:1-8, Job 13:18, Psalms 103:6, and Psalms 146:7 to render a sentencing of judgment against all demonic spiritual oppressors from the kingdom of darkness and for an order to protection be placed immediately against them on my behalf. I also request accordion to 1 John 1:9 for the court to issue a verdict rendering me forgiven and cleansed based upon the blood of Jesus and His finished work on His Cross at Calvary, I ask now that all my sins, transgressions, and iniquities be blotted out of Heaven and hell's records, in Jesus name."

Proverbs 11:18 KJV

"The wicked worketh a deceitful work: But to him that soweth righteousness shall be a sure reward."

Proverbs 11:31 KJV

"Behold, the righteous shall be recompensed in the

earth: Much more the wicked and the sinner."

Psalms 17:2 BSB

"May my vindication come from Your presence; may Your eyes see what is right."

END OF PRAYER

End Notes

So, after you've gone through these prayers, you will more than likely feel a burden or weight come off of you or being lifted off of you. You also might experience feeling lighter due to the fact that sin carries a burden or weight to it. Please see Hebrews 12:1 for reference. When the Blood of Jesus is applied to transgressions the record gets blotted out according to the Word of God in Isaiah 43:25-26, and 1 John 1:9. I also want to make mention that you can follow the template that has been laid out in this book to bring before God the Righteous Judge a number of things. You can bring your marriage before the courts. Just be sure to present Scripture and come before the LORD's Courts with an attitude of humility, repentance, a willingness to forgive, and a desire to cleanse your record through the Lord Jesus' Atoning Sacrifice for all humanity. And to see the Purposes of God manifest through the life as the LORD has entrusted to you as a stewardship. I also want to make mention that it is not pure motives to try to come to the LORD's Court to try to make an appeal to justify habitual sin or impure motives. The Court is a place to receive verdicts of freedom, release, breakthrough, security of Destiny. To see mountains that have been firmly planted moved by the power of God, and to experience greater levels of freedom and deliverance from demonic oppression. We come before God as our Father to encounter intimacy with Him, we come before God as Friend to have fellowship and intercede for others. We come before God as the Righteous Judge when there is a serious legal issue, demonic oppression, and as the Holy Spirit leads on various topics concerning the will of God. I think for myself included that it would be a good and wise thing to maintain all three aspects of who God is in our prayer lives. Not neglecting His Father Heart on the basis of His status as the Righteous Judge.

Prayer

> "LORD God, help us not neglect your Father Heart, and the fellowship of Your Friendship, in Jesus Name, amen."

I believe that bloodline cleansing is just one of the entry levels when it comes to functioning in the heavenly courts. How far do you think an earthly army will get if it exhibits passivity? I say it's time for an end of passive Christianity, and time for Kingdom advancement, in Jesus name!

Exodus 15:3 BSB

> "The LORD is a warrior, the LORD is His name."

"LORD God, Lord Jesus, Holy Spirit, may you raise up a generation of Lion-hearted warriors and tender-hearted lovers. May your church rise up and may principalities, ungodly authorities, ungodly powers, and rulers of wickedness be dethroned, and the Kingdom of God established here on earth. May passivity within the Christian walk come to an end, and may the time of accepting defeat and the devil harassment come to a complete end. Your people learn to walk in true and pure obedience to You, and operate within the Courts of Heaven to see victory, breakthrough, and judgments rendered in favor of Your church, and the Kingdom of God, in Jesus name. May You burn passivity off Your people, may fear be sent back to the Pit where it belongs. And may the roar of the Lion of Judah come forth from your people. May You raise up, and establish a people that don't take defeat or no as a valid answer when it comes to beholding, and seeing Your Kingdom and Will accomplished here on the earth. LORD release the roar of the Lion of Judah from Heaven, and shake kingdoms, in Jesus name!

Amos 3:8 BSB

> "The lion has roared— who will not fear? The Lord GOD has spoken— who will not prophesy?"

THIS CONCLUDES PART II OF THE BOOK

Author's Conclusion

And just like that, you've come to the part of the book where we wrap it up. Congratulations on getting through to the end of this book, and I hope that You will be able to come back to it more than once to learn and refresh your memory on the teachings shared, and the prayers provided. I hope that the prayers in this book are used in deliverance sessions and that the Lord uses this book as a tool to help set others free. It's a cool thing to have your labor in the Lord have a positive effect on others, and I do believe that it's one of the highest forms of payment. This book has been a multiyear journey of writing, learning, editing, and even the season that the Lord brought me through prior to this book being published. Even though I did not see it at the moment when I was going through it, it served a higher purpose. What I went through prior to this book, had I yielded, you wouldn't be holding this book in your hands, reading this book on your screen, or listening to it. My dear reader, continually remind yourself of the Lord's goodness, faithfulness, and His Heart for you and all of His people. Never focus on the negative more than God's goodness. Pursue Him for Who He is, rather than what He can do for you. Enjoy the moment you are currently in, cherish the life you've been given, and glorify God in this life through the way you live and obey, and *never underestimate your potential and capability in Christ*. Nothing is small and insignificant when it's an act of obedience to the Lord. Your simple act of kindness and hospitality could be the reason Jesus is made known to someone who desperately needs Him. Acts of kindness can easily become doors of opportunity to share Jesus with others. And for the mothers out there, your role is important. Because you are going to be raising the next generation of apostles, prophets, pastors, evangelists, and teachers that will carry the Good News of Salvation for the coming generations, never think that your role isn't somehow significant. You can propel your children years ahead of others by the way you choose to raise them. And by the way, you walk with Jesus and live the Christian life in front of them in a way that they witness Christ in and through you. Sometimes you could be the only Bible others read, depending on how much time they have left. So stay at home moms, don't discredit yourself or the importance of your role. There will be heavenly rewards for acts of obedience done here on Earth, but the reason should always be a love for Jesus, rewards are just a bonus. God bless you and may the Lamb receive the full reward of His suffering.

A Prayer For You

"Lord, I ask that you would enlighten the eyes of every reader's understanding. I ask for the people who read this that you have given a scribal anointing to write books authored by You, that you would upload the content to them, that they would record and then publish it in your timing. May prophetic books be published under Your Authorship in the appropriate time and may souls be saved and may revelation be built upon through these messages shared. May you set everyone who is reading this free from everything they have been crying out to You for, and may You set them ablaze for You in power and love, Lord. And may you meet them wherever they are in life to strengthen them, in Jesus Name. May they become stronger and stronger week by week and grow in their faith and walk with you, in Jesus Name. Amen! Blessings and Shalom to you!"

Psalms 119:45 BSB

"And I will walk in freedom, for I have sought Your precepts."

Endorsements

If you're interested on the topic of the Courts of Heaven, I would like to personally recommend some books from a few authors:

Robert Henderson

Operating In The Courts of Heaven Series

Dr. Francis Myles

Issuing Divine Restraining Orders From The Courts of Heaven

Dangerous Prayers From The Courts of Heaven That Destroy Evil Altars

Dr. Bruce Cook

Cleansing Ancestral Bloodlines From The Courts of Heaven

Contact

I would like to encourage you to share with me any testimonies of breakthroughs, healings, and deliverances from ungodly oppression broken off of your life, or the lives of those you have prayed for with this book after the prayers. That is a blessing and personal encouragement for me, and possibly for others as well. I ask that you also would please leave a note somewhere within the testimony email whether you would permit me to share your testimony. I really do believe, based on the magnitude of the testimony, it could be a huge blessing, encouragement and faith builder to others who might be going through the same or similar things. So please leave a note in the email whether you'd like me to:

1. Share it, including personal details such as name, location based information.

2. Share the testimony but anonymize the names, location based details and personal information.

3. Keep the testimony private between you and me.

Testimonials

If you are emailing me I would like to ask if you could properly title the *subject* heading on top of the email, for example if you have a Testimony of healing please title the email *Testimony of Healing*. And please do not shy away from sending me a good long testimony of freedom, healing, breakthrough, deliverance, and the redemptive Power of our God that you've experienced. I would love to be encouraged and blessed by your blessings, breakthroughs, testimonies, freedom, personal deliverance etc.

Testimony Template To Use For Email

Date:

Subject:

Permission To Use And Share Testimony:

Testimony:

Author's Contact Information

Website: *Pending*

Email: contactscribedd@gmail.com

Instagram: @ddjordjic_official

About The Author

Djordje was saved back in 2018 when the reality of the Lord's Love was revealed to him when the Spirit of God encountered him in his bedroom. Since then, Brother Djordje has been walking with the Lord. Above all the titles, accolades, or status a person may receive, Brother Djordje is first and foremost the Lord's. All other titles given to men and women here on earth are temporary, but we will remain His forever.

Books By This Author

Unveiling The Prophetic Counsel of God: Peeling Back The Curtain of God's Prophetic Counsel In The Last Days

In today's day and age there are many things that people have questions to and seek for answers whether from Google or those with doctorate degrees, but how many people with questions look for answers from God? After all, God is the absolute best resource to seek answers from because He cannot lie. (Hebrews 6:18) This book serves as an answer to some of these questions, as well as giving readers and listeners insight right from the Lord Himself through what He has spoken to me. I give the credit and glory to Yeshua Jesus. And I hope this book blesses you, as it's a compilation of what the Lord has spoken to me over the years. This book is a call to action in a sense. The last thing I want or what the Lord wants is for people to read what He has said and sit idly and do nothing in response. As you read this book, listen to the Lord's Voice & the Voice of His Holy Spirit and engage in conversation with Jesus if you need to while reading. But I want to encourage you to let what He has spoken really permeate in your heart and meditate on what He is saying. His Word is alive and every Word spoken from Him rings true, not only in this age but in the ages to come also, amen. Shalom, shalom.

A Call For Reformation: A Modern Day Call For A Reformation Out Of Religious Church Structure And Into Unity And Freedom With The Spirit of God

The Lord always has a remnant. In the days of Elijah, almost the entire nation of Israel went into apostasy. The prophet of the LORD, namely Elijah, thought he was the only one left that didn't turn from the LORD, but what did the LORD say to Elijah? "I have reserved for Myself seven thousand who have not bowed the knee to baal..." (1 Kings 19:18). You're not alone if you've seen some things in the church and pondered about what happened. This book serves as A Call For Reformation. If you desire to grow in your walk with the LORD, I welcome you to embark on this journey that will challenge you to walk stronger, better and with integrity. This is a generation that is craving to see the Light in a world full of darkness. The darker the world, the brighter the Light will become. Are you ready to be challenged and grow in your faith? If so, I welcome you to A Call For Reformation.

Unveiling The Secret Of Bloodline Cleansing: Breaking Bondages And Receiving The Full Victory Jesus Paid For

Do you know anybody that seems to be stuck in a vicious cycle they are trying to overcome? What if I told you that it might be due to a legal right the enemy is holding onto in their bloodline to keep them bound to the very thing they are desiring freedom from? They might have cried out to the LORD over and over again to set them free, but they think their prayers haven't been answered. The LORD desires to set everyone free, but there is also a process that the LORD has established where certain legalities in the spiritual realm need to be addressed and dealt with before the breakthrough is released. Fifty percent of the spiritual battle takes place in the courts, just as much as the spiritual battle takes place on the battlefield that we call Earth. If there's a legal right that hasn't been dealt with in the Courts of the LORD, then the battlefield victory cannot be fully sealed until those legal issues are dealt with. That's a part of the reason that some people who have prayed in alignment with God's will didn't see the breakthrough and created a theology for it called: If it's God's will: "Well maybe it wasn't the LORD's will brother, we did everything we could, it's in God's Hands now." God's Word is clear on what He wants and what He doesn't want and like. There is a reason that the the the Holy Spirit and the

Lord Jesus are called our Advocates:

John 14:26 LSV

"And the Comforter, the Holy Spirit, whom the Father will send in My Name, He will teach you all things, and remind you of all things that I said to you."

1 John 2:1 LSV

"My little children, these things I write to you that you may not sin: and if anyone may sin, we have an Advocate with the Father, Jesus Christ, the Righteous One,"

The same Greek word *parakletos* used in John 14 to describe the Holy Spirit is the exact same word used to describe Jesus as our Advocate. *Parakletos* means: Intercessor, Advocate, Consoler, Comforter. You see, the victory is won in the courts and the victory is enforced on the battlefield. But so many Christians due to a lack of knowledge have treated spiritual warfare as a battlefield and not a courtroom. That's why they haven't seen sweeping victories but have constantly struggled, always in a spiritual battle. Don't get me wrong, if someone is in a spiritual battle they are either called, made unfortunate choices or they're deeply pursuing the Lord. We win through God's Gavel and His Sword. The gavel precedes the Sword and once the Sword comes backed by the Court's Ruling look out, because Heaven is enforcing it and God doesn't lose in battle. Hallelujah! It's no secret that Jesus came to set us free, but what many don't know is that a part of Who Jesus is, in Heaven, is our Defense Lawyer. Advocate is another word for it. It's clear in the Scriptures that Jesus came to deliver the oppressed, and we see that clearly in the Scriptures. Every believer that desires the deeper things of God and is surrendering their will goes through a process that I would call the Process of Sanctification:

---

1. Moment of Salvation

2. Honeymoon

3. Hardship

4. Spiritual Warfare

5. Conqueror

6. Victory

7. Continuous Honeymoon

8. Joy of The Lord

And once a believer walks through these phases they become stronger in their faith, know how to fight spiritually, and they don't take defeat as an option because they know God's will is victory. So what do you say, do you want to sharpen your sword? Then let's embark on this journey together!

Philippians 4:13 KJV

"I can do all things through Christ which strengtheneth me."

The End

ONLINE STORE

INSTAGRAM

[1] 2 Samuel 5:30

[2] The New Testament was primarily written in Koine Greek, and the Old Testament was primarily written in Hebrew and some in Aramaic. Since we are currently looking at the New Testament, these are Greek words being used. So, with that stated, let's break this Scripture down:

[3] Angels.

[4] When we present court cases before the LORD, we are to present them for the sake of either our or another person's destiny, safety, God's purposes or God's will on the earth. You are not to present a court case asking for judgment to be rendered against somebody that cut you off in traffic, hurt, or offended you. If that's you, repent. Get your heart right before reading further if your motive to present a court case is to try to hurt somebody.

[5] What a glorious day for the saints and what a dreadful day for those who refused to repent.

[6] Although the number of souls saved will more than likely be called into account in Heaven.

[7] Romans 2:1-11

[8] See 1 Corinthians 13:1-13

[9] G3875 παράκλητος (paraklētos) Occurrences in Bible: 5 Occurrences in Verses: 5 KJV usage: comforter, advocate.

[10] Transliteration: katēgoreō Pronunciation: kat-ay-gor-eh'-o

[11] KJV Usage: adversary. Occurrences in Bible: 5 Occurrences in verses: 4 Transliteration: antidikos Pronunciation: an-tid'-ee-kos

[12] H4941 Part of Speech: Noun Masculine Root Word (Etymology): From שָׁפַט H8199 Pronunciation: mish-pawt'

[13] https://en.wiktionary.org/wiki/acquittal

[14] https://en.wiktionary.org/wiki/vindicate

[15] H3722 Part of Speech: Verb Pronunciation: kaw-far'

[16] KJV Usage: desire. Occurrences in Bible: 1 Occurrences in verses: 1 Pronunciation: ex-ahee-teh'-om-ahee

[17] G4617 Pronunciation: sin-ee-ad'-zo Part of Speech: Verb Root Word Etymology: From sinion (a sieve)

[18] Transliteration: σινιάζω

[19] https://en.wiktionary.org/wiki/sift

[20] Reading the full chapter is recommended.

[21] H5771 Part of Speech: Noun Masculine Root Word (Etymology): From עָוָה H5753

[22] Also known as *standard of procedure*

[23] Melchizedek means King of Righteousness

[24] If you want to learn more about this, please refer to Robert Henderson's book

[25] https://www.heartmath.org/assets/uploads/2023/04/modulation-of-dna-conformation-by-heart-focused-intention.pdf

[26] The KJV says: "The serpent was more subtle."

[27] Enmity means hatred.

[28] https://arep.med.harvard.edu/pdf/Church_Science_12.pdf

[29] https://www.extremetech.com/extreme/134672-harvard-cracks-dna-storage-crams-700-terabytes-of-data-into-a-single-gram

[30] Koine Greek: *laleo* meaning to *talk* or *utter words*.

[31] Noah's name in Hebrew means *rest*.

[32] https://en.wiktionary.org/wiki/sabotage

[33] Psalms 25:14 BSB "The LORD confides in those who fear Him, and reveals His covenant to them."

[34] Some translations say: "Perfecter of our faith."

[35] https://en.m.wiktionary.org/wiki/disannul#English

[36] https://en.m.wiktionary.org/wiki/annul

[37] Whet: to sharpen.

[38] Keys are symbolic of authority.

[39] Authority and power flow from submission to God.

[40] Ekklēsía is the Greek word translated as *church* in most of our English Bibles. Also, sometimes translated as *assembly*.

[41] https://www.history.com/topics/ancient-greece/ancient-greece-democracy

[42] https://en.wiktionary.org/wiki/dominion

[43] https://en.wiktionary.org/wiki/authority

[44] https://en.wiktionary.org/wiki/power

[45] The full prophetic word can be found in my book *Unveiling The Prophetic Counsel of God*. It's available on Amazon.

[46] https://petermatthews.com.au/the-bassanos-jewish-guardians-of-the-ancient-arts/

[47] Genesis 2:20-25.

[48] https://en.m.wiktionary.org/wiki/surety

[49] https://www.merriam-webster.com/dictionary/surety

[50] Please see Galatians 3:7-29 for a more complete reference.

[51] Did anyone else discover the prophetic foreshadow about the three days of darkness that the LORD talked about in Exodus 10:22 in connection to the three days after His crucifixion?

[52] God's word is God's law.

[53] Please see James 3:6-12 for greater detail.

[54] H4397 Pronunciation: mal-awk' Part of Speech: Noun Masculine.

[55] If you read further in the Bible, you can actually see that the one who refused to forgive was delivered up to the tormentors until he paid his own debt in full. This is Jesus speaking, and it would be a very wise thing to forgive those who have hurt you right about now.

[56] Try to be specific in this prayer if you can.

[57] If you want to see the full Word it's in my book *Unveiling The Prophetic Counsel of God* which can be found on Amazon.

[58] And you would just continue like so throughout the Scriptures.

[59] 1 Corinthians 7:15, Matthew 5:32.

[60] Make sure to read them out loud.

[61] John 1:1-5, 9-14

[62] The Scriptures don't say Jesus healed *most*, but that He healed *all* who were oppressed...

[63] I'm bringing this up not because that's what Jesus thinks of people struggling with legalism, but to show the fact that legalism does not produce good fruit. You're in the right place if you've been looking for freedom and deliverance from legalism. Jesus loves you and there is freedom in Him!

[64] Jeremiah 2:8

[65] Samuel in Hebrew means *heard of God*.

[66] If you've experienced something that happened to you that was not covered in this prayer but is related to the topic, but you'd like to see it added. Feel free to reach out through email to me found towards the end of the book.

[67] 2 Chronicles 16:9

[68] G5425 Greek: φρίσσω Pronounced: fris'-so

[69] Pronunciation: oo-dice' Definition: *not even one*

[70] Pronunciation: ekh'-o Definition: *to hold*

[71] The AMP says fraudulently withheld.

[1] James 1:19 BSB: "My beloved brothers, understand this: Everyone should be quick to listen, slow to speak, and slow to anger,"

---

[1] If you've struggled with legalism just remember this verse.